To Christine and Bruce,
I hope you enjoy my adventures
Down Under,

Barry

A Hitch Down Under

Hitchhiking around Australia

Barry Humphrey

GW00707549

Sunsplat! Publishing
East Sussex

A Hitch Down Under: published in Great Britain by
Sunsplat! Publishing
PO Box 154
Tunbridge Wells
Kent, England TN2 9AX
SunsplatPublish@aol.com

Copyright © Barry Humphrey 2005
The moral right of the author has been asserted

This book is sold subject to the condition that it shall not, by way of
trade or otherwise, be lent, resold, hired out or otherwise circulated
without the publisher's prior written consent in any form of binding
or cover other than that in which it is published and without a similar
condition including this condition being imposed upon the subsequent
purchaser.

A catalogue record of this book is available from the British Library

ISBN 0 9551205 0 0
978 0 9551205 0 3

Typesetting and printing: David Brown Maynards Green 01435 812506

Contents

To

Sheila and Graham, her husband, and Mary, his sister, who offered to let me stay under their thatched roof, when I researched this book originally, and found the peace to concentrate. I'd just like to say thank you.

Acknowledgements

A Hitch Down Under was written in the 1980s shortly after I arrived home from Hong Kong, and decided to continue my travels in America the following year. Once started, I felt it was important to finish the original idea, before moving on in life. These were my early-mid twenties and primetime for such an adventure, with a good education and work experience behind me. I have tried to be accurate in all instances and also kind! It's to be hoped that those mentioned will enjoy their input, whereby everybody comes out in a natural light. What is left is a wholesome traveller's tale that has been linked together on a daily basis and where possible a historical reference added in helping to understand the environment and its development. Some of my passages are comparatively short and have been kept as such in an effort to avoid duplication or have been used as a stepping-stone to the next anecdote.

The guidebook used, or should that be my bible, was the *Lonely Planets* version, which I have used for my statistics and reference here because that is how we experienced it at the time. During the intervening years a mass of information has also become available. In this revised edition only those books relevant to the time have been used.

On the whole I have stayed tight to the original journals and only deleted a couple of finer points that might be best left alone, or seemed somewhat naive.

In a way all journals become a period piece and a more mature approach with wisdom, would be inappropriate here. What I have tried to maintain is the rawness of being young without the responsibilities that tend to overtake people. A year here really felt like a year with few adult years to draw experience from.

Anybody who has ever studied the Beatles music, will have noticed how their ideas developed from a four piece band playing guitars, and drum, to the more sophisticated sounds that evolved on the *Sergeant Pepper* album five years after their break through in 1962, or from their early to mid twenties and something worth protecting here, by a young man with no writing experience to date.

The names mentioned are as I knew them, and will only be known to a very few people from the outset. Most have been lost in the passage of time, or their likeness is only a blur to the mind now. Naturally one of the problems is keeping within certain parameters, namely how much to give; too little and there is no soul, too much and a trust is betrayed. It's rather like putting your reputation on the line, every other page, and hoping you haven't stepped on a minefield. So I must give a great big thank you to all those concerned; without you this book would not have been possible!

My gratitude is immense, but at a pinch there are five travelling companions who should be acknowledged, as this in part is their book also. Firstly Martin, from Devon, who had the vision to set out originally and gave me the initial confidence to pursue my objectives. Talk is one thing, but he had the desire to do it: Tony from Canberra for his quick thinking when he saw a Brown Tiger snake between my feet in Victoria: Jarv, a Brit cast adrift in Tasmania: Amy, from California, without whom hitchhiking to Ayers Rock would not have been the same and finally Stewart, a young New Zealander, for helping to make my second pear picking season all the more bearable!

It was great to have had you all onboard.

I would also like to acknowledge the following for their help, and faith, in piecing this book together and hope the wait has been worthwhile. Inevitably mistakes occur and will continue to do so; my typing has also improved with the computer course.

Firstly I would like to say thank you to Maggie, who typed the original copy that stayed on my bookshelf for over ten years, cast back in days of the typewriter!

Secondly to Mary who typed my initial efforts, this time around, and showed great patience on the 'rewrites' and proof reading, together with Caroline for the constructive criticism.

Paul may not have made the trip, but it was his idea to place a hiker upside down on a globe, and to Jarv for illustrating the cover with his artistic talents. It is here I should also mention Sid the car cleaner, last seen heading towards Asia, for his "original" imprint contribution; some people liked it, and others did not, but at least it might bring a smile.

My thanks to all for their enthusiasm, the lifts and those that offered me shelter for the night, I'm eternally grateful.

Barry Humphrey
Sussex, England
July 2005.

When my distant cousin Marion was nearing her graduation, as a doctor, she planned a trip to India, but unfortunately a friend let her down almost at the last moment, and so wrecked her dream of experiencing such an adventure.

Years later I spoke to her mother, Sheila, who mentioned the trip in passing, and so I became intrigued. She was about fifty at the time and looking forward to a more peaceful life of answering the phone and taking an interest in her three children's lives away from the family home.

"Marion seemed quite disappointed having planned everything a year in advance, only to find she had nobody to travel with, and of course could not go alone. I thought about this for a moment and said: Never mind we can buy the rucksacks in town and I will come with you!"

They in turn had a great time hopping on and off buses and sleeping in cheap ransacked accommodation, of which she said: "I would not have missed it for the world."

A Hitch Down Under is dedicated to the spirit of adventure.

Introduction

My good friend, who I once schooled with, appeared partly interested in our scheme, but that is about where his enthusiasm ceased. I could sense Paul's heart was not really into spending a year of our young lives cast adrift in Australia. I guess it seemed like an escape route from his mundane office job rather than the deep-rooted desire to experience new horizons, similar to my own hibernation in a bank, before belatedly throwing off the shackles to become a student in London for the past three years.

I was admittedly surprised when he volunteered after he had thrown the towel in at work, and decided to join us on our trip down under. I could hardly say much though, having done the same with Martin, who I phoned and asked if it was all right that I tag along. His was a solo effort and the company would do him good to my advantage.

The difference was Paul's sheltered background and Martin's boarding school existence of ten years. He then spent six months on a farm in New Zealand, which had all encompassed a world of experience in broadening his outlook. Paul though, did not have this to draw upon. In a way it all came down to confidence and vision that one had more of than the other. Fortune invariably favours the brave, when something *has* to happen, and in his case that is certainly true.

We now found ourselves cast back in time when school matters had been taken care of. I also had a car to drive us around for the summer with my mind in a need to recuperate itself, after the pressures of the academic year.

"I wonder if Chris is back, it would be nice to see him again?" Paul remarked, one afternoon.

The time was soon approaching to find a job; anything part time or full, it didn't matter. Martin had given me until December to find the finance, which obviously was not enough with only pin money to my name. Company and a hand to hold was also important when another year would see this opportunity gone 'forever.' It really had to be now or never, I just had to be on that plane!

Our friend was back from university and about to branch out into the teaching profession, in the like father like son tradition, and no longer needed to do the hop harvest.

"I'll give you the number and you can phone them," he said.

We live in Sussex and probably hope to remain so in the long term. But there is more to life than this, and for that Paul can at least say he managed to get over the county line to Kent, and Paddock Wood, where we arrived at the allotted time and found ourselves with the pick of the jobs; the only one that meant we were inside for the duration of the harvest.

Somebody had to hang the vines up, which simply put, meant the tractor drivers drove into a covered way. We then jumped up onto the trailer and fixed the vines individually to hooks above our head. These would drag the vines into the thrashing machine together with our entangled legs on numerous occasions, had it not been for the safety switch within an arms reach. Once caught, and gripped, there is always a time when you have to be freed by others around you, or simply throw a spanner into the works!

Our only other problem had been the vines scratching our wrists that after day one were scratched red raw. However old socks with the ends cut off, and in turn worn over our wrists, coupled with leather gloves soon solved the blood stained scarring.

We arrived at dawn and left at 5.30pm, which also gave us the chance to further our social life, as Paul had also volunteered to move in with me. He left home for five days a week, due to the jobs proximity, and him not having the transport or any ties as such. This was fine by me and saved over an hour each day in chauffer services. I write this all with relevance at a later date and record that our job finally came to an end, and with it our income.

Not to fear though, we still had time and advertised our services around the district. This time we received a phone call from a farmer, who had second thoughts, that perhaps we could pick some apples and then after this help to dismantle a hop field of its wooden structures, before being ploughed in.

"Phasing some out, the common market is changing things, even the trees are being propagated and replanted with ones you only have to walk around," the foreman said one day, as we stood on our ladders.

Jim was in his early fifties, and rented one of the farm cottages. Once married with two daughters now left home, he lived alone and would appreciate a bit of company after work, and perhaps the chance to do some training runs in the evenings.

"Sure why not, we are going to Australia, the fitness will do us good," I replied.

This just about summed up our social life from here on with a man whose idea of a good time was to run marathons and encouraged us to follow suit, albeit at the shorter distance.

By now though things were changing, and it was evident that one persons enthusiasm was not necessary another's delight. To this point I had to finally meet a mute point head on, rather than when the wheels had finally begun to turn on the tarmac. One night, on the way home, I tried to make an effort to find out what Paul really thought.

"We want you to come, but it's not going to be easy, you

never seem to show any interest, make any suggestions or even project enthusiasm," I remarked.

"I don't know," he replied.

"Let me know at the weekend, Martin is going to buy the tickets on Monday," I said.

It was now clear that Paul would not be with us. He had some pension money that he spent on a car, Jim found for him, together with another job close by with some accommodation to match. This would be an experiment in agriculture that did not prove as fruitful as he may have liked. It did though lead him to a niece of Jim's, who he met three weeks after I left at Christmas.

1. Australia

History is as ever evolving while I write. Political elections invariably change a ruling party or its Prime Minister and thus a country's foreign policy. Nobody can be entirely sure where progress is likely to take us. Modern communications have proved the most recent example of this, and who could really have thought regular air flight around the world might become a routine matter a hundred years ago. Then we are all products of our own time, and development.

Today most of us take for granted the English speaking nations of Australia, and New Zealand. But it might have all been so different, if the Aboriginal population had been more organised or less naive of world affairs. Similar to those in mainland Asia, who remained as a whole self-regulated. History might even have developed into another North American Indian saga, and certainly the white man is responsible for pushing those here first to one side.

It's an interesting thought of how the world might have shaped up had the Orientals decided to spread their passage, rather than the Europeans. For example, Australia was first sighted in 1606 by Portuguese navigators of the Brazilian initiative. Perhaps the language might then have been Spanish when Torres sailed through his 'own named strait' between Cape York and New Guinea. It was also the Dutch who charted the North and West coasts around the Great Australian Bight, only to find the arid under-nourished landscape in a stark contrast to their own homeland, and so they made for the Dutch East Indies.

In turn Abel Tasman left Batavia, or Jakarta now, in Indonesia to sail around these shores and discovered Van Dieman's Land

(Tasmania), named after his governor general in 1642. The pirate William Damper though, is credited as being the first Englishman to step ashore here and to bring back the reports of a hot inhospitable land with its alien wildlife to those at home.

It was this account a hundred or so years later that encouraged the legendary mariner Captain James Cook to lead a scientific voyage, sponsored by King George III, at the initiative of the Royal Society. Cook's original Whitby Cat was the Endeavour (1768-71), which initially set out to observe the passing of Venus on January 3rd 1769.

They then continued their search for the mystic southern continent that still compounded their global knowledge. Cook arrived on the fertile east coast from Tahiti in 1770, and established the first temporary settlement. This is where Cooktown now remains, in reminding us that the Barrier Reef can be a hazardous place to navigate, even for such a talented sailor as Cook had proved himself to be.

He eventually wrote on crossing the Antarctic Circle on January 17th 1773 aboard the Resolution (1772-75): "I whose ambition leads me not only further than any other man has been before, but as far as I think it is possible for me to go."

By the time of his premature death on his third expedition, at the hands of the natives of the Sandwich Islands or Hawaii now, with both the Discovery and Resolution in tow, Cook had roughly mapped out the entire continent, with such an eye for detail that he helped to shape the world we know today. But it was the American Revolution that finally led Britain to search out another outlet to take care of her excessive criminal population that finally changed things for good.

The first Australian colony was finally set up in Sydney in 1788, which in turn led to a period of colonialisation. Initially these colonies were solely dependent upon European supplies, until efficient farming methods were developed to such an extent that it became increasingly possible to become self-sufficient, and to further welcome settlers from 'The Albion.'

Some of the convicts, who having served their sentence, felt their prospects were better enhanced in these open spaces, with land for the 'taking' and something they could only dream of back home; now with much milder winters. They might have compared Januarys similarly to an Australian girl I once met in England and harmlessly said: "So are you staying here again this winter?"

"Oh, no way!" she exclaimed.

In 1803 the seeds of Hobart were sown, not just for colonial expansion, but because it was feared that the French could lay claim to these new lands. In turn it might have set up the same kind of situation that had led to the American War of Independence and their defence against British aggression.

This was a conflict in which neither side seemed to be strong enough to dominate the entire continent, added to that of the Spanish influence. The British would have to be content with the eastern dividing line being placed along the 49th Parallel in 1814, (It was extended west in 1846, to take in Vancouver Island) and in turn the creation of an independent Canada in 1867. They had also defended their rights in the conflicts, which eventually ended in 1814, together with a large French civilian population in and around Quebec City.

In Australia, the Port Philip Bay region was considered an appropriate settlement to rival Sydney, and to dispel the expected French interest that never actually materialised. The 'Tasmanians' arrived somewhat belatedly in 1835 to establish Melbourne's present site and then began their colonialisation further inland, similar to the exploration, which had breached the Blue Mountain's and a route towards the Western Plains in 1813.

Self-preservation served its similar purposes, when in 1829 Perth received its first influx of settlers to avert a divided island, had another European power decided to follow suit in claiming these fresh lands for their own outwardly mobile populations.

In turn Brisbane was founded when Sydney decided to distance itself from their resident criminal fraternity, in the hope that they might remain in Queensland upon their release. The penal colony was likewise abandoned in 1839 due to the numbers of fresh settlers arriving to begin the thriving environment that has continued to develop ever since.

Adelaide was set up in 1837 as a free enterprise experiment, which soon stuttered and stalled into bankruptcy without the management skills available to establish its initial independence. It was something the British Government was keen to encourage from the outset and in turn guided it through these initial setbacks with the needed financial influx and organisational skills.

The Distance Chart varies from reference to reference and depends upon the trig point or route taken; the following acts as an overall guide in kilometres, but should not be taken in the literal sense, as they can vary considerably from various guidebooks to signposts.

1. Perth - Sydney	3972 km
2. Perth - Adelaide	2713 km
3. Adelaide - Melbourne	732 km
4. Melbourne - Sydney	873 km
5. Melbourne - Canberra	656 km
6. Canberra - Sydney	292 km
7. Sydney - Brisbane	984 km
8. Brisbane - Cairns	1699 km

9. Brisbane - Alice Springs   2997 km
10. Alice Springs - Adelaide   1544 km
11. Darwin - Alice Springs   1509 km
12. Adelaide - Sydney   1416 km

2. Western Australia

In many respects Perth remains one of the most isolated cities in the world, situated on the west coast, and the edge of 2.56 million square kilometres or a million square miles. It has a population of 1.2 million people in an area larger than Western Europe, South Africa, and even India to add perspective to the surrounding environment.

Captain James Stirling founded the city on August 12th 1829. He had led a group of settlers to this spot and realised almost immediately that the area contained a vast potential for their hopes and future ambitions. Their choice was to be 19 km inland from the mouth of the Swan River at a point where it narrows and then widens again.

Early history was slow to progress, even though Britain had finally claimed it in 1826, but seemed uninterested in its development while the Aboriginals persisted in defending their homelands against the invaders. It was not until 1848 that the New South Wales (NSW) Government was requested to send 9,700 convicts to Perth, that things began to move forward; the crown also sent a further 5,000 of its subjects out to redress an imbalance of two to one against the free settlers.

December 1983

I looked out of the window of our cramped surrounds at what had been the longest twenty-four hours of my life it seemed, with the odd twelve minutes thrown in for good measure. There was no grass or nourishment to be seen, or even houses, and a sign that we had arrived anywhere of significance, in a plane that was

NORTHERN TERRITORY

WESTERN AUSTRALIA

SOUTH AUSTRALIA

Nullarbor Plain

Kalgoorlie
Coolgardie
Perth   *Great Australian Bight*
                                        Renmark
Albany   Adelaide

0 kilometres 400

now fortunately half empty and gave us space to stretch our legs.

I shall return to this flight later on though and concentrate here on our arrival in Australia. I could also now forget about the recent headlines of 'air crash kills one hundred passengers' and 'two planes collide on runway in Spain' for instance. Western Australia is nine hours ahead of England including the one-hour summer time; we had touched down at 7.02am.

Two customs officials soon enquired if either of us have had any connections with farms during the past six months and to declare any illegal animal food we might be carrying. As my passport clearly has the word farm written into my address, there was not much point in denying the obvious, which produced an uninterested glance at my photographic likeness and we proceeded to make our way beyond the officialdom.

The Australians seemed quite laid back in their approach, and neither made us felt guilty of something we have not done, or that 'you are' a welcome guest; rather they were efficient, processed the passports and left us to find our way through the 'have you got anything to declare,' area.

Then we are out into a sparsely populated terminal of Perth International Airport, without the sheer hassle of Bombay, which only left us glad to re-board, the wealth of Singapore, and the crowded domain of our Heathrow starting point. We had certainly been about and seen more airports in this short time than I had seen in a lifetime; for this apart, from a return trip to Poland five years before, was only my third trip in the sky and one I was certainly pleased to see the back of.

The return flight was a long way into the future when I could think about it then. If we had gone by boat we might still be floating along nicely in six weeks time, with even more time to think, but whoever would consider such a thing in 1983!

Martin and myself have known each other since our coming together in the student hall of residence three years ago and even shared a house once in the darkness of Haringey, North London, or a little bit of an ethnic community. We were more the ones out of place with a Greek landlord, a white geography student from Bedford and four Indian students from Southall.

I liked it, strangely cast adrift in a domain, where a girl from Brighton once remarked she was the only white student in her accounts class and felt "a bit lonely." For both of us this was just what we needed in broadening our horizons. Academics are one thing, but the experience it had brought with it was arguably even more important, having both grown up in the country and sheltered backgrounds. Martin is from Devon and a small village that only the few who live, or visit, might know from memory.

We didn't really say anything on the flight, even at the airport, as nothing much had happened of late in his life. He has spent the past year working in a shop selling athletics gear in Exeter, where he has had time to prepare and enjoy his friends in the evenings. I had even done my thesis on his shop as a short cut in cutting corners. It was not my best work, we had three months to prepare for something I did in a weekend pit stop in Devon, and then two nights to write it up, but 'it will do,' and fortunately the lecturers agreed, on the nod. Another tick gave me twelve credits in all and my freedom! Martin you see has been a variable of my life during this time.

We soon found our luggage and proceeded to find the exit, which was not difficult, and very easy that is with a backpacker asleep in the corner; all a bit different to cardboard city under Waterloo Bridge, as the rich blue sunshine hit me in the early morning haze.

"What a difference a day makes," I remarked.

Nothing really stirred in numbers, our fellow passengers have invariably faded themselves into the surrounding area and beyond in taxis, or by family friends to wherever. We would have to take a bus to the centre and then find our bearings from there.

It duly arrived when we sat with the seats facing each other and was much more sociable than looking at the back of somebody's head.

Opposite an old age pensioner sat, and talkative in nature, who once lived in Cranbrook and close in proximity to our hop picking jobs still fresh in the mind. He had emigrated here some forty years ago, with the chance of the fresh opportunities that came his way. This was during a time when workers' rights were still a thing of the future and the chance of earning 'real' money remained out of the reach of all but a few at the time; things have changed since, and at least we can now come here with the chance of seeing for ourselves.

"I grew up there," he remarked.

"That's a coincidence, I'm from near Tunbridge Wells, East Sussex and not Kent," I said.

There are a number of English place names out here designed to help the early settlers feel more at home.

"Did you visit White Hart Lane when you lived in London? Tottenham were my boyhood team," he said.

"I certainly did. Brighton beat them one-nil with Michael Robinson scoring from close range!" I replied.

"Brighton did you say, there is one in every state of Australia."

"Sounds all so familiar, I nearly forgot I have something for you, now where is it, oh here we are," Martin said, looking through his baggage and handing me a good luck card from a mutual friend: 'May God protect you and bring you back safely. Love from Jean,' a friend of his parents wrote.

"Well I never, Jeanie's new address, look at that," I remarked.

"Cranbrook, Kent, England!"

My first day in Australia will always linger in the memory, as the 'four' of us walked through Perth's radiant sunshine at 11am. By which time life had begun to float around in a light-headed haze, and note with interest my new surroundings. The girls had been here for a month already and obtained waitress jobs to supplement their gap year travels; and have had their natural good looks enhanced by dedicated rich suntans and a bubbly enthusiasm you couldn't help but like on our first meeting. Martin knew them from his Devon roots, and had enthused about Clare for some time, with her blonde hair and personality to match. She now has a bronzed tan to enhance her reputation in his eyes; both Sarah, and her, seemed to possess that innocent charm and laughter that appears to take all before them.

For our initial stay here, the two of us soon began to find our way, with myself slowly becoming groggy in the mid-morning sun. The heat was soon making the pavements unbearable to walk on in bare feet, which led to the outlay of ninety-nine cents on some flip flop's my immediate concern.

However I would have to bow out soon and return to the girls' flat, where we were due to sleep on their floor for a night or two, until we could get our bearings together. Martin seemed fine, but he appears more hardened in the mind to such sudden changes of pace that we have put ourselves through.

Clare gave me her key and said: "To make a tea, or there's food in the fridge, you can't really get lost around here."

I certainly had no problem in finding the flat, and noted the backpacks on the floor, as a sign of not having been opened with my head spinning light-headed along the pavement, and out of control of its legs. They just wanted to collapse themselves in a heap and suggested that any kind of long distance walk might be beyond me. The girls had been busy collecting travel agent posters and had covered a wall with an outline collage of Australia and the places they intend to visit, or the islands off Queensland, judging by their enthusiasm.

Saturday 10 December

I now laid on the double bed, and shut my eyes for an hour, waiting for the others to reappear for some chat, and how are things going here. What is the work situation like and how about the beaches? I want to try surfing. But no, that's not quite how it turned out upon waking up on my first morning in Australia, and perhaps one of my most treasured at that, fully clothed and wearing shorts Australian style; Martin was asleep next to me.

On the floor the two pleasant looking girls slept in contentment that they had received some communications from home.

I then crept about the flat, shaved and let myself out now naturally fully awake and ready for the sun to raise itself for another day or my very first in paradise. I now walked outside and breathed the fresh air, somewhat still, and noted the palm trees dotted along the open spaces, where baseball is played and people congregate in the evenings for a beer, or wallow away another hot day with friends and family. But this was the morning before six, and nothing stirred, not a car, not a person, no nothing really, just myself in the stillness of the early morning walking across Terrace Road. It runs parallel with the Swan, from which I picked out a hilltop war memorial, as it turned out, to aim for, past the Western Australian Yachting Club, and then across a freeway complex of roads. The giant green verge, a football pitch's width, was now left to its own devices.

The land is fairly scorched in parts; there is also evidence of constant watering by park wardens intent on trying to enhance my new surroundings. These moments are so peacefully quiet now with an almost entire city in a state of insomnia. High above the trees, the sun strangely reminded me of England and its scraggy looking woodland, that now seems a distant memory of my life 'left' behind.

A footpath then led me up through a pine covered hill face and finally into King's Park. Nothing moved, even the wind remained still, and frightened almost to harm any frail looking wild flowers spread about in various shaded corners, the statues, and car parks with restaurants.

Everything appears to have its rightful place in the 400 hectares of parkland. This is the result of much thought and dedication of which Australians can be proud. Littering the lawns seems to be a sin, which nobody dares do.

Generally Australians have been prone to financing sculptors' livelihoods over the years. Queen Victoria, in Perth, has found her haven among the summer flowers with her head held high, while a small crown balances above; her sceptre is clasped with both hands shielding a buxom cleavage. Below a rather dour, elegantly made period dress ensures that Victoria's 'we are not amused' image will live on in this once crown colony's history.

Staring out across the Perth skyline one can easily recognize that town planners have gone to great lengths to ensure the 20th Century high-rise blocks have been blended in with nature, and thus avoiding a congested mass of rubble, making this an ideal baptism into Australian life; a place where everything remains so calm and at ease with itself.

I'm unsure about how this adventure might turn out. Martin seems pretty much self-assured about our prospects, which gives me great 'confidence.' I'm just grateful that my time has arrived to experience a new environment, and spread my horizons, similar to the multi-ethnic environment that had once seemed so alien to this country boy, whose roots lie amongst the woods and fields of a lush Sussex Weald.

This was a rather naive setting to shield me from the realities of other people's lives. But also wholesome in shaping one's development for the challenges ahead that may or may not all be positive. That's the problem, nothing is certain in life's choppy waters. The test of survival, or success that is, will be when the two of clubs is dealt, rather than an ace of diamonds, which inevitably will come our way from time to time, on this the uncertain road back towards our roots.

It was now time to meet my new friends.

Sunday 11 December

We caught a bus this morning to the beach at North Cothesloe, where we did as you might expect two anaemic looking people from the northern hemisphere to do, and that is strip off and dive into the swimming pool. At first with an abundance of enthusiasm, and then with great ease of our situation in the hot sun, which is the operative word here, hot and very hot, but I didn't care myself, well not right then.

Martin soon found this "all too much" for his mind to concentrate on and took over a nice spot to lie on his towel, with his back to the sun and its strong rays. My ignorance though stopped me from noting the red scorch marks that slowly began to appear, and particularly on his right shoulder blade. While I swam around the pool for about two hours and threw the ball with the local kids, who appreciated an adult joining in with such enthusiasm, and was likewise determined to catch it first!

This was all great fun, and worth recording for one little factor known to anybody who has ever been caught out by the sun and the damage that it can do. Even when you are constantly moving, and swimming half submerged by water, the rays seem to reflect on the white and slowly turn you red on a spit. Then when you have played your last trick and swam the length to get out, the realization becomes clear, just how powerful the rays can be and that all is not well with you and not well at all.

"Martin wake up, you're burning away!" I remarked, who then rolled over and began to inspect his skin.

At first he wondered what the fuss was all about, until he felt the damage that had been done, in such a comparatively short stretch of time.

"Just look at you," he replied.

"Never mind me, it's your back, throw a towel over it otherwise it will be even worse soon," I said, as we curtailed our days sunbathing in the most unexpected of fashions, to us anyway.

Our next mission would be for more suntan lotion and to buy some hats to keep us in the shade.

I didn't feel too good on the bus it has to be admitted, and once more found my head at odds with our surroundings. The girls it has to be said were full of sympathy, in saying that they should have warned us this might happen; that they had some cream to sooth the rawness, which soon began to harden and become tight, with a sweaty kind of film across the surface and something I was not enjoying one little iota.

We were now 'gone' for the day and only fit for the sleeping bags on the floor. Both girls did offer to let the walking wounded sleep in comfort. But the floor seemed a better place to be right then and more comfortable in staying glued to one position, especially for my arms, which had taken a particular bashing from the elements. To such an extent, I could hardly move without a sudden spasm of pain erupting through my body at times of movement.

How Martin felt I cannot say, but "bloody awful" was all he seemed to echo, when at one stage I tried to get to the bathroom; opted for the all fours, and then clasped one arm on the side of the bath to prop myself up and to drop down on the seat.

'Blimey this is agony!' I thought, and soon managed to stand up for the return journey; met with knees on the floor first, and then somehow managed the manoeuvring of my body so that it could rest itself on the floor without so much pain.

"This is all too much for me," I muttered.

"What's that?" Martin said.

"Knackered!" I relied, "Simply knackered."

We have certainly found out the hard way the importance of using a good brand of suntan oil. Our skin was about to shed its outer layer over the next ten days in dusty shades of dried 'dandruff,' at every such interval, as we invariably brushed each other's back to give the fresh skin a chance to feel the sunlight and recover its complexion.

Wednesday 14 December

It is a fair assessment; on the other side of the world and more or less flat broke, that we did not really have a plan of action. Indeed research here and discussion only came about once we had begun to recover from our swimming pool exertions, which had left us the next day rather worse for wear and without the strength to do anything constructive to our advantage.

We were also in desperate need of accommodation; neither of the girls minded us being there. But with one bed between four, night times were something of a jigsaw being put into place and amusing for a little while until we could get on our feet. In effect this was to go on for five nights, until Martin mentioned to the storekeeper, in the next block, if he knew of any accommodation going and explained our situation.

"Sure I have just the thing," he replied, which prompted him to go and see for himself and make the decision that we would put down a deposit; then fetch me to see if I approved or not.

We therefore moved two blocks away, and three stories up along an open corridor. Our home is now complete, with a bathroom, bedroom, and a spacious living room.

I decided to let Martin have the bed, as the settee would do me fine. It was one of those long soft efforts whereby the contours of your body nestle nicely into the grooves and guarantee a long night's sleep, protected from the sun by the overpowering skyscrapers outside our balcony. This made the temperatures almost perfect and led to the most wonderful of mornings as I slowly woke up in a slight haze before entering the shower.

Life was all so perfect for a short time, but beds were not something I would see very much of in 1984.

Thursday 23 December

I have only known Phyllis for three weeks now. It was one of those scenarios when people move into a village and parents compare notes of what their children are doing, and where they live. Are they married, and children? No not in this case. 'He's going to Australia,' having decided the domestic life can wait.

'Oh that's interesting when is he going, on the ninth, well he will be in Perth for Christmas. I'm going to be there to see my daughter and son in law on the twentieth, why not ask him to come around to say hello. I can give him their address; it would be so nice to see him out there. What another from this quaint little village where we plan to spend our retirement!'

I had walked up our lane in the dark and through the small iron-gate, before ringing the doorbell. It was a nice little cottage where a previous occupant had been the 'enemy' of my childhood, a happy go lucky sort of chap, who was nice as pie, but boy could he talk and talk! It was nothing to get half way home from school, only to hear those dreaded words 'we have to collect some hay.'

This was easy enough, unless Luther walked around the corner. At which point another hour was invariably lost and good fishing time in the summer. All this was serious stuff, and invariably resulted in me walking home and now late. Ah good old Luther, how could I forget the man with the bionic lip!

Right then in the dark Australia still seemed somewhat distant and irrelevant to my life, yet here we were light years away, when the door opened and Phyllis asked me into their nice piece of English heritage, all cosy and wooden, with the kitchen gliding nicely into the dinning room area. I liked the place and could never imagine this being anywhere else, with a fire burning brightly.

"Oh do look us up, our son Guy is also there at the moment with my daughter. George my husband will be flying out there with me, unfortunately he had to go to a meeting this evening," she remarked.

"Thank you very much I would like that, it will be nice to mentally compare us sitting here and then in Australia," I said.

Martin and myself now walked along the scorched banks of the Swan River, and then stood watching a girl struggle with her windsurf, from the Narrows Bridge, connecting us with the northern suburbs and strangely intrigued by her efforts. When to my right we heard a splash in the water and noted some youths preparing to dive off the top likewise.

"Thirty feet is nothing, in Melbourne we dive off rocks one hundred feet high," one remarked.

"Good luck then, and do a belly flop for me!" I replied.

We now kept walking and backtracked our way along the river and I wondered if we could have swum over. But of course not, the currents might have been too great, and would conclude the end of these lines before they have really begun. At least there are no crocodiles here, or are there? The kids seem to think not, but I'm sure, it has been known. This is Australia and the land of crocs, when swimming might best be curtailed and what a thought!

When we arrived at our destination the family were all present, having enjoyed dinner together, and had prepared for our early evening visit, with a few stubby of beer protected by a cooler around the can. Swan is the local brew, with each state having its own brand of lager, the chemicals that satisfy a need and keep the goodness from your heart.

The beer has prospered so well that Swan are advertising their new low alcoholic brand you can drink in vast quantities without losing your driving licence, or can invariably be divided by the locals who I have asked, "Now tell me which is the low alcohol glass," much to their confusion of taste and vision.

It seemed strange to be here in a little bit of England cast adrift, with English accents and even the Earl Grey just for us.

"It's to make you feel at home, I brought it out with me," Phyllis said, now sitting outside a chalet styled bungalow, surrounded by other houses, in what is a prime area to live in with a job just across the water.

I still liked our flat the better with its location. It is a pity we are not going to be able to stay, life without winter would be great here. The shop owner claimed it "never goes below 20°C."

Juliet and Brian apparently spent about six months travelling across Asia before settling in Perth for the past two years.

"A lot of people arrive here, and never venture any further east," he said, being one of those tall individuals you sometimes meet, with a placid nature. Juliet on the other hand remains anaemically white, having never ventured on a coastal beach in her life.

"No, I hate the sun," she remarked, as we all sat in a shady garden area, with a plastic roof to protect us from the unseasonable rain; it would soon move on and simply leave us to enjoy our Earl Grey.

Sunday 25 December

Christmas Day, what can I say, this 'is' a celebration and we are on the other side of the world, with my problems beginning to pile up. Walking back towards our flat I found it hard to imagine that the festive season has arrived. The humid temperatures do not echo a celebratory feel, simply walking around the city and looking up towards the heavens with the decoration banners glistening in the sun.

I soon began to think of snow, and that time when it began to fall on Christmas Eve and what fun it was. Before walking home with the snowflakes still fresh in the night air; just the once, but it happened and would do so again I'm sure; the last noel, the angel does sing, 'noel noel the angel does sing'…I wanted to be in church and sing those carols.

Instead the day just drifted on. Martin became more distant in the mind, and I rang home to say all was well: "Of course I already have my own pad, and things will work out nicely," or somehow that should read.

His opening chorus this morning sounded rather similar to "This is the worst Christmas I've ever had," as last night's merry cavalier has fallen off his high horse with a bump! I'd merely been to King's Park and didn't go night clubbing with the others; instead I mellowed in the early evening sun and reflected on our new life.

"It's about the only thing I can afford to do without an income," I remarked.

"Oh I don't know, I can't take it like I used to; all night and lots of beer, I'm falling apart! The girls are so lucky, they have been invited out for dinner, just think of all that food," he said.

"It's alright, you've still got me!" I replied, at which point we decided to exchange Christmas presents of a can of Swan lager each, and proceeded to cook our seasonal meal of two beef burgers, boiled potatoes, carrots, bread and an elegantly presented desert of hazel nuts in a bowl.

"You know Baz, you're some kind of cook!"

"No problem, it's all to do with the way you boil the spuds, it's taken years of practice!" I replied.

My evening was presently spent on our balcony, overshadowed by a skyscraper and its huge blue lettering BOND, which seems synonymous to Perth, and the man himself advertised across it. 'He' must like his own name, or rather brand name; my mind was still thinking like a business studies student.

I'm enjoying this life with my feet on the railing and pushing the plastic chair onto its hind legs with my right arm resting on our small metal-framed table. It's nothing special; the book I'm reading keeps me company with a small radio that blasts out repetitively *Thriller* by Michael Jackson, and appropriately, *Up Town Girl* by Billy Joel, the two biggest hits in Perth at the present time. Or is it just that Elton John's *Too Low For Zero* is the only other track in their record collection?

Martin has now gone off on his own to phone his folks, and a younger brother, who he seems to hold in such high esteem. This should pepper his enthusiasm, while I just sat here alone in the shadows and thought about my own feelings; that I've never been quite this broke before, struck adrift and without a lifeline in sight. Things could get desperate in about three week's time. I should feel worried, but I'm not. It's kind of nice here, just sitting back with my legs outstretched, another can of lager should help; the temperatures are still 20°C, even as midnight approaches...

Monday 26 December

Boxing Day has arrived and the great British tradition of the day after, or is it the compromise between religion and those that don't go to church? Why is it so called anyway, I doubt if any of us have ever thought about it. Do we really think about the birth of Christ, or is it just a time to snooze in front of the television, after a big feed up, and then communicate with those from afar who have crossed our path and we want to take along the mystery tour of life. The mind is like a piece of micro film that is moving slowly forward, and then once a year momentarily drops back to those memories and friendships that have shaped our lives in a positive light, of a chance meeting, a memorable holiday or even the camaraderie that student life once brought.

We therefore spent our day as separate lives. Martin with the girls and myself with the English contingent across the water, before we again joined up for a quick stroll through the pleasant temperatures and vegetation, towards the white arched entrance of Gloucester Park, where I was requested by the gatekeeper "To put your thongs on lad." A comment, which left me wondering what he meant and had I heard him right, what did he say; thongs is that?

"Your thongs," he repeated. At which I stared at him, as if to say what do you mean, when somebody behind me said: "They're in your hand."

"Oh you mean my flip flops!"

I was walking barefoot at the time and loved every second of it in this climate, and did as he asked…

This was always the time of a family outing to the greyhound racing at Hove. My grandmother was the gambler of the family, having discovered an interest at seventy and encouraged her offspring to follow suit. She started with the horses and soon became sharp as a hawk in picking out winners.

A Victorian attitude at heart, nobody ever spoke during the evening horse race results. The kitchen might be one of laughter with the grand children and their parents one moment. But at 6.45pm the room would descend into complete silence, without a pin being dropped. I certainly knew where my station was on these occasions and remembered the consequences of other more foolhardy extraverts who had said otherwise!

So one year as we sat freezing in the canteen, at the greyhound stadium, my grandfather looked a 'worried' man. 'Who is going to tell her?'

Our instructions were quite simple. There are twelve races, and we had to do a combination of one and six for each race, with the idea being to back the first two dogs of six in each race home. Obviously 'to win' would bring in more money, and I liked the sound of that, but somehow never managed to win a fortune; neither did my grandmother this year, when we missed the first race and lost her money on the next eleven! Then I do not need to confirm the result of the first race; she even backed three winners from her final sickbed, as the horses were read out for her to choose from.

I write here that this is not either of the mentioned sports; rather a more refined form of chariot racing around a 2,275 metre oval dirt track, under floodlights. Martin was quite keen on this idea and the chance to win, which I also had aspirations of myself, of winning some much needed funds to bolster my flagging supply and morale; or answering questions of 'why do you spend so much time in Kings Park!'

"It's a bit like Ben Hur's Roman chariots' race, how would you describe it?" I said.

"I don't know why you insist on writing an epistle on everything we do," he said.

"I'm not sure really; these are uncertain times and a lot is going to happen in the future. I might be able to make sense of it all, and then to piece something together. It will act as a reminder in years to come, when we have gone our separate ways," I replied.

In knowing that this was going to be a time of great adventure and that very soon a fresh impetus was about to blow through my life; that in time I will be able to look back on this trip with a feeling of great pride in my veins. The experience is something we could take with us through life's chequered waters, and has its twists and turns in abundance up ahead. I shall continue here, with Martin's description.

"The blinding floodlights, a sandy track skirting the dark oval track, and dodgy bookmakers. I mean that wasn't a horse we backed, more like a donkey!" he remarked.

Adios Marty had been our tip, a true-blooded 'thoroughbred' as we stood on the terrace opposite the finishing post and enjoying the moment.

"The winnings are already in our pockets, did you see his ears prick when he trotted by, a real winner; you see!" I said.

Martin was likewise excited when the runners came charging by, in what was a fast paced affair and all bunched together. That's it Marty give them stick, you can do it! "Come on Marty," where is he? Look for his number; I can't see him!

The horses soon glide by and trot away from us.

"Where's our horse?" he said, following the action, and wondering about our $5. When I looked back along the track, only to see him gliding along as if he was on a picnic and approaching the straight. What, he's already half a lap behind after the first; we are lost! I don't believe that, he hasn't even reached us yet.

"He's doing a lap of honour!"

"Did you see that tooth-like smile when he passed us!" I replied, in seeing the funny side of our first bet.

Adios Marty did perk up to finish about eighth, when he finally realised this 'was' a race, and that we were depending on him, for our next stubby. But no, it was not to be; those mechanical pistons are rust laden without oil and were merely gliding along in its own time scale.

When the evening finally ground to an end, and the horses had returned to their stables, Adios was probably given an extra bale of hay, and with it our financial losses, which were shortly added to.

It is Marty I shall always remember though as I sat on a grass bank surrounded by cigarette stubs; simply watching the crowd pass by, with the empty crisp packets and a light sprinkling of losing ticket stubs strewn around me; rather like confetti in the night sky.

Wednesday 28 December

The Devon contingents have all gone to the small Rottnest Island, 11 by 5 km wide, for three days, 19 km offshore from Fremantle to camp. My own financial situation is far from healthy, with less than $200 in hand and a seemingly precarious situation looming. I felt the $23 spent on the boat crossing might be put to better use later on; not to mention the added expenses incurred on the island, such as the hiring of bicycles and any beverages consumed in the island's solitary tavern.

I therefore opened my guidebook and read that it was discovered by the Dutch explorer, Vlaming in 1696, who named it Rats Nest, in his description of the numerous Quokka, or minute Kangaroos, which can still be seen here to this very day. There will be plenty of opportunities in Queensland for such luxuries after our current plight has been rectified.

Rottnest was originally established as an Aboriginal prison in 1838 by the early settlers, who were opposed by the resident population, until its closure in 1903. Martin eventually described it as "Paradise without human beings; but inevitably tourism is creeping into the island and might possibly spoil it."

It has also just been confirmed over the radio that Australia, being a severely sports-minded country, narrowly defeated Sweden 3-2 in the Davies Cup Final, and have recorded a twenty-first such tennis victory since its inception in 1900. Pat Cash and John Fitzgerald played in the singles (one win each) with Mark Edmonson and Paul McNamee winning the doubles rubber. Cash was the eventual hero when he beat Joakim Nystrom 6-4 6-1 6-1 in the fourth rubber. Sweden's main stay was the two single wins by Matt Wilander.

The format for the men's team championship is comparatively simple to understand and runs on a knockout basis throughout the year. Two singles matches are played on day one, with the doubles splitting the reverse singles on day three, this time at Kooyong, Melbourne. These were the original rules and have remained as they were designed. Harvard student Dwight Davies commissioned the trophy, but the British Isles were the only country to accept the challenge. This though ended in a three nil defeat at the Longwood Cricket Club in Boston, Massachusetts. Australia and New Zealand also won four times combined early on, but New Zealand has never won in its own right.

There was a time when America, Britain, and Australia were its only three serious competitors, before the French in the 1920s momentarily became dominant. Britain again rose to the challenge in the 1930s with Fred Perry enjoying a grand slam of the games four major championships in 1936 (The Australian,

French and United States Opens and Wimbledon). Since when, the Australians have invariably remained competitive worldwide. Britain's sole moment of under-achievement lies with a final appearance in 1978, and John Lloyd's defeat, in the 1977 Australian Open, to American Vitas Gerralitus.

In a way then things 'never change.' Australia also won the first ever cricket Test match in Melbourne, played on Richmond Paddock and completed on March 17th 1877. The crowd that day was about 10,000 strong as the colonialists under Dave Gregory's combined Victorian's and New South Welshmen defeated England, captained by James Lillywhite, or the 'Professionals' by 45 runs, without the legendary W.G Grace at the time.

The coincidence here is that the Centenary Test, and 226 encounters later in March 1977, was watched by 60,000 people each day at the Melbourne Cricket Ground and ended with Dennis Lillee taking 11 wickets for 165 runs; Australia again won by 45 runs!

The origins of the present day Ashes tour can be traced back to a one off Test match in 1882, when Australia narrowly defeated England on home soil. The British press were outraged and claimed they were the worst in living memory. It was the *Sporting Times* that printed the following obituary to Cricket which read: In Affectionate Remembrance of English Cricket Which Died at the Oval on 29th August 1882. Deeply lamented by a large circle of sorrowing friends and acquaintances. R.I.P
N.B. The body will be cremated and the ashes taken to Australia.

In 1983 it is the America's Cup triumph that will be remembered here most fondly, and something else we Brits invented much to our own spectacular demise in 1851. The cup was originally known as the One Hundred Guinea Cup with fifteen British entrants up against a solitary American interloper, to race around the Isle of Wight.

The event was designed to celebrate the Great Exhibition, and encouraged by Prince Albert, who was later elevated to the title of Prince Consort in 1858, and husband to Queen Victoria. There are no prizes for guessing the winner though and the aptly named Schooner America, representing the New York Yacht Club that walked away with the trophy. They held onto it for another twenty-five successful defences, until local business tycoon Alan Bond's syndicate entered the fray and won the right to challenge for the America's Cup, with his controversial winged keel yacht Australia II.

In a way this was to become one of sport's greatest contests off the coast of New Port, Rhode Island. Australia II, led by John Bertrand, fought back from a 3-1 deficit to win the decider by 41 seconds. They had been 57 seconds adrift at one stage, and almost out of the race, in their quest to re-write the record books for the sport's most prestigious prize.

"Everybody has their day in the sun. This was ours and I'll never forget it," Alan Bond remarked, with all the expense and sophisticated designs to remain competitive.

Only the very rich could ever maintain any kind of challenge, which has so far remained beyond British shores, in this twelve-metre class. Prime Minister Bob Hawke, since Labor's election victory in March over Malcolm Fraser's incumbent Liberal Party, spoke for the nation in exalted frenzy in September, when he announced that anybody missing work the next day had a good reason for being hung over, and should not be dismissed by their employers because "We'd be a nation of zombies anyway!"

January 1984

We saw the New Year in with a fireworks display at Gloucester Park with Andy, a friend of Martin's who went to school with his brother. He has now moved out to Perth to be with his father and all the perks. Not to mention the university education; that has left him relaxed, and with one of those open-topped mini Moke's to breeze around town in for what seems to be one long hot summer here; so much so that I want to begin all over again in this environment and be a student. What a difference to Haringey High Street and a zebra crossing bleeper outside your bed sit window!

England will also be hangover time, slumped in the armchair and wondering why I drank that last drink or was it really worth it. New Years Eve is so over rated, 'nothing ever happens, never meet anybody. No never and now here I am full of remorse for my sins!'

'That's funny the sun is out, and the air is warm, I'm in Australia and the beach waits. There is none of this watching from afar at those sun-drenched souls being interviewed from down under and saying 'hi ma, love you!' I'm going to be there, yes I am, myself on the beach on New Years Day, oh those fools back on Brighton beach. The shingle beach that is and their cold morning swim!'

We are off to the sand and to surf a breaker and another harrowing experience, of a spellbinding thrust forward on top of a wave, lying flat, and then to look down at the sand.

Where's the wave? I'm floating, just hang on and don't fall off, this is bloody dangerous!

The shoreline then rushes up to meet me and the water engulfs my life, with the board tied to an ankle and doing cart wheels in the torrents of abuse that cast me out of control beneath the waves, and across the sand in opening up the pores of my skin for another day of careful adjustment…

Wednesday 4 January

On a more serious note nothing seems to have gone right for us on the job front, although perhaps we have not tried hard enough. The girls have done nicely out of their waitress jobs and look great it has to be admitted, in giving them just a slight advantage over us in the magnetic appeal stakes, coupled with fresh smiles.

They also arrived before the students were clambering for work and the city centre became somewhat empty. Being so isolated, the passing trade is remote to perk up the casual migrants dwindling resources, as we tried the shops, bars, restaurants, agencies, newspapers, and at the Commonwealth Employment Services (CES), who had next to nothing available for their own, let alone us, it appeared on our various visits.

The students have taken up the slack since November, which has supplied us with the leftovers of being over-qualified, too old, or even too young and "Too honest," Martin remarked.

"Hey steady on, do you want to get us a bad reputation!" I replied.

We therefore registered ourselves unemployed, which in a way is probably accurate. No money, income and prospects. We have been swapped for an Australian who has probably done the same in England. I might even have been paying for it, had I done what most of my contemporaries have and found a job! Besides it is a one off. We are under twenty-six, and this will be our only such chance. It was really now or never and I had chosen now.

The signing of the forms and a social security interview

brought us some good news of sorts that we qualify under the following criteria:

    1. Hold Working Visa.

    2. Have lived in the UK for the past year.

    3. Took less than thirteen weeks to reach Australia.

"All of which will be checked out in England, via the Australian Embassy, although Christmas has slowed things up," an official informed us.

Time has passed by quickly, the rest and relaxation has done me good as we began to analyse our immediate prospects of achieving the objectives we set out with. The trains across the Nullarbor Plain to Adelaide are all fully booked up until January 23rd and would leave us with almost three weeks to twiddle our fingers.

Even Martin now only has a little over $400 to his name. This has left us with no alternative, but to spend $75 on a coach trip. Our random enquires at some large trucking organisations also came to no avail.

Hitchhiking did cross our minds at one point but "It's going to be pretty hot out there, even the pavements are scorching and unbearable in bare feet," Martin remarked, with the common sense that illustrated our plight.

We are better off moving eastwards first, and naturally decided us against this option or delayed what was seemingly the inevitable. We might even have rented a car, which could be left in Adelaide; this we again found out of our budget.

"Alright the coach to Adelaide will give us more alternatives," I replied.

My lack of preparation has already become evident; the now or never mentality can only go so far. It is obviously going to be an insecure existence from 'here on in,' and the kind of challenge we both seem comfortable with, in this our changing environment. We would certainly have to wise up and very quickly indeed, in our search for the hidden answers that lie ahead.

Thursday 5 January

Connie, a contact of Martin's, kindly took us both out for a drive around Perth's outer reaches this morning, together with her three young children. She seemed particularly fascinated by all the modern houses built, and confessed as much to us that she would like to move from the coastal town of Scarborough. Her husband though is very content where they are and feels at ease with the rushing tides; being an ex-surfboard champion, his slowly greying beard is now in keeping with his fisherman's environment.

"That's the thing with the sea, once it is in the blood it's hard to shift," I remarked.

The houses here invariably seem very modern with only a few derelict buildings to be seen in Fremantle, on the Indian Ocean. Signs of a prosperous boom can be seen everywhere. For example, Perth residents supposedly boast the highest ratio of yacht owners in Australia. Property prices can be particularly high, and especially in Peppermint Grove, Victoria Avenue, which is reputedly Australia's most expensive residential retreat shadowing the Swan River; as for myself, I remained more interested in the seashells above Connie's front door, of their colonial styled retreat, and the words: 'Sussex by the sea.'

"Oh the previous owners put it there; we liked it, but that was ten years ago now," she said.

Perth in hindsight would undoubtedly remain my favourite Australian city due to its laid-back countrified atmosphere. Or is it merely because this is where it all began, and my first 'winter's' suntan. Indeed much of the 'world' has still to discover this alternative to Melbourne's glamorous lights, mainly because Adelaide in South Australia remains a mere 2,713 miles away by highway.

Out to sea one has to sail 3,600 miles before coming ashore in Mauritius. There was a time, when a segment of Western Australia politicians wanted to declare their own state's independence. In some instances it is even cheaper to holiday in Malaysia rather than Sydney.

The America's Cup though could have a profound effect on this heavenly atmosphere, because Perth will for the very first time become the focal point of a mass media spotlight. Tourists and rich businessmen's minds are about to be alerted to its vast potential; with so much attention some locals are echoing their own reservations that the capitalists might diminish this tranquil city's environment.

"It's going to be a commercial boom time here with an insurgence of outsiders," Brian had remarked. "Perhaps the best solution is for us to lose this time around, otherwise we would have to stage another defence in 1991?" (Kookaburra III 0 Stars and Stripes 4)

Saturday 7 January

Nothing can really prepare the mind for thirty-five hours cramped in a coach with nowhere to stretch the legs, or even to rest one's head. At least we had until 7pm to pack our worldly belongings, and dismantle the homely pictures on the wall. I am going to miss our balcony, with my feet stretched out on the wall with just a small glance of the river to our left. Unfortunately the rent man did not turn up, with our deposit minus the $42 outstanding with the electricity also to be deducted. I'm sure this will be sorted out in the future; otherwise it's good money wasted.

Connie collected us at 12.30pm for another drive around, this time south towards Albany. Martin had hitchhiked there on one of his solo missions previously, and is something that he seems intent on doing at various times. It is actually older than Perth, having been formed in 1826 as a coaling station for ships bound along the east coast.

This afternoon we merely enjoyed the Stirling Range, with its arid vegetation and picnic facilities. Before she dropped us off at the coach station and said to call her if we get in trouble. Connie has also given us the phone number of an old school friend who is married in Adelaide.

"It will give me the excuse for a chat, as I last saw her five years ago," she remarked.

The coach left Hayes Street and then followed the river for a short while. It gave us the chance to stand up and momentarily see our red-bricked domain, so out of place with its surroundings, but so perfect in every other respect.

I now remembered the time when the wind blew the kitchen door shut as I put out the rubbish. It might not have been a problem at any other time. But with our neighbours all out, Martin was on Rottnest Island, and the local shopkeeper without keys, or even a ladder in sight. My alternatives were limited to forcing a small kitchen window open, then squeezing through a confined space and over the sink area; our kettle was happily whistling its tune of boiling water!

Drivers John and Michael are both friendly, in trying to bring some humour to the proceedings, with a little cabaret during our first hour together and preparing us for the inevitable tedious journey ahead. Darkness though was soon upon us, and then the daybreak of January 8th together with breakfast at Merredin. A small place where the Perth-Kalgoorlie railroad, reminds me of a much easier form of transport on the mind and legs; as I stretched my muscles in the early morning sun and admired the barren landscape full of wildlife, somewhere 'out there.' The land is still fertile enough to grow wheat, but it will all change further on beyond Southern Cross, 378 km into our journey, and then on to the Nullarbor Plain.

Driving across 2,700 km of almost nothingness is hard to imagine until you experience it. The Nullarbor remains an oasis of treeless scrubland, burnt grass and reddish dirt, all a direct result of temperatures climbing daily into the 30ºC bracket. The terrain is obviously useless to farmers without irrigation; no food can be grown here to support the communities, while the nature life appears almost non-existent, apart from a mass of irritating insects.

One can only imagine the kind of panic Edward John Eyre must have felt amid this inhospitable terrain in 1841, when with his companion John Baxter they set out to reach the centre of Australia from Adelaide, and decided to give up at Mount Hopeless in preference to heading west towards Albany.

It sounds easy enough here. 'You' just have to head towards the sunset each night, without food or water with two Aboriginal guides, who would eventually kill your companion. But Eyre didn't know that at the time. Rather like a mountaineer, he never considered the dangers of not coming back alive or the adverse elements.

This 'should' in theory be the Eyre Baxter Highway, but true to tradition we only seem to remember the 'winners.' In this instance it was Eyre, who struggled on to Rossiter Bay where he stumbled across a French whaling ship, with provisions enough to continue his journey. It took him five months to complete his epic crossing.

Our next two communities remain on the map, for the reason that they were once gold mining towns of the 1890s. Being discovered in the wake of the original find at Southern Cross in 1887, just before Coolgardie. This was much to the government's delight that it might kick-start the economy and with it brings in some much-needed settlers to the region.

Coolgardie, with a population reaching 15,000 and Kalgoorlie, now with 23,000 inhabitants, were the boomtowns, most recipient to prospectors from far and wide. Now there is only one major operation at Mount Charlotte, near Paddy Hannan's original find, where he found his gold lying on the surface; all of which was not bad for a stopover on route from Coolgardie to another strike. However others were not so fortunate and have had to extract it from the ground and then the rocks.

"It's no good we need a goldmine of our own, but where to begin." I remarked. "There must be acres of untouched land out here, or deposits waiting to be found?"

I'm not going to try and make this journey sound adventurous, or even interesting. Simply squashed into a confined space can never be described as such. Once a lift is obtained there is obviously a good chance to hitch right across, because what else is there here and where would people go?

Communications though came slowly to Western Australia, or through the natural progression of time. Accordingly a telegraph line was connected in 1879. The initial bicycle crossing came in 1896, with its four-wheeled engine equivalent in 1912; and must have been rather interesting without any kind of metal road. At least the terrain is pretty flat, with only bush to negotiate. In 1941 necessity brought upon by the war, meant the beginnings of the unsealed Trans-Continental Highway that was eventually sealed in 1969; the South Australian section was completed in 1976.

"That's only eight years ago, so much change in such a small space of time. This place is really beginning to take and off," Martin remarked.

The Nullarbor ends rather dramatically on the coast of the Australian Bight, where our coach driver stopped momentarily for us to experience the white cliffs; to visualise the rocky waters, and ships being torn apart by sailing too close. Our route though only touches the outskirts of the Nullarbor, which seemed desolate enough; the Eyre Highway in South Australia lies further inland.

It's all a bit confusing. They have modernised our coastal route through the small Aboriginal settlement of Eucla; the Indian-Pacific rail line runs about 150 km inland across the Nullarbor's central heartbeat. At one point it stretches for a world record 500 km in a straight line of engineering ingenuity. Perhaps only matched by the 557 km water pipelines from the Reservoir near Perth, 400 metres higher than Kalgoorlie, in order to enable the old gold miners to service their needs and was completed in 1903.

On the South Australian border we were asked to put our watches back 45 minutes, when entering the intermediate time zone between the two states; it then continues until Caiguna, in which case I opted for Adelaide's time one and a half hours ahead of Perth. In a way its true time does not matter out here. We had nothing else to do but watch it get dark for the second time; at which point daylight would finally bring with it a dose of South Australian hospitality.

3. South Australia

South Australia is somewhat surprisingly the driest Commonwealth State, while even WA doesn't possess such a large proportion of desert. Look at the map and it is Adelaide you note first, instead of the state line, or even north towards the Northern Territories. Here 1.3 million currently people live, with 900,000 in Adelaide.

It is also the most urbanized of states, with only pockets of people seen before we reached the suburbs, barring the coastal resorts. SA though is no place to become stranded on foot, alone, and without water, although the Barossa and Clare Valleys remain green and fertile. This is where a quarter of the country's wine is produced. It's historically attributed to fifteen German families who can be traced back towards 1842. And like so many settlers preferred to remain true to their own culture, that has been passed down through the generations to such an extent that a form of German Barossa Deutch is still spoken in the valley.

Monday 9 January

We arrived in Adelaide at 8am, naturally tired, unshaven and in need of fresh breath. Somehow it always seems impossible to sleep in such circumstances, and yet here we are now, 'half' way across Australia. On Air India, at various stages there had been the chance of stretching across three seats, but not here, the coach was fully booked up and there were no stewardesses to wake me up at 4am, to ask if I would like a beer or even whisky!

Neither Martin, nor myself though, spoke much to each other or to our fellow passengers. It was as if we were just concentrating

on playing out time from the outset, and both no doubt wondering what might happen next.

Our first priority was to find the youth hostel in Gillis Street before 9.30am, which gave us time enough to check in and leave our packs in safe keeping, before exploring the city. Adelaide is very much on line with Perth in atmosphere, although its architecture remains more consistent with the original colonial stone masonry rather than skyscraper in context, reliant on a potential financial boom to balance its books. This is an old money city, both conservative in nature and independent of Sydney's business entrepreneurs, or Brisbane's massive natural resources.

Adelaide was named after Queen Adelaide of Saxe-Meningen, the wife of Britain's reigning monarch King William IV, the brother of George IV who died without leaving an heir. It has to be noted that William never considered himself as a future sovereign, and it was only when his elder brother Frederick died in 1827, that history bestowed upon him such a possibility in 1830. George IV only produced one heir, Princess Charlotte with Queen Caroline of Brunswick in 1817, who died at birth.

It was for these combined reasons that William found himself in the unique position of having to find a wife should he become the heir, even though his actress partner Mrs Dorothy Jordan bore him ten illegitimate children. They all lived at Bushey until the relationship floundered and William decided to face up to his pending responsibilities. Mrs Jordan though would die a pauper's death cast adrift in France to avoid her creditors; such was the Duke of Clarence's excessive lifestyle.

William though had found himself in a growingly complex situation that meant he needed to find England a potential Queen, in assuming that he might outlive his brothers. Although deeply in love with Miss Wykeham, an English heiress, it was Parliament who refused to sanction their marriage. This was at a time when royalty was invariably encouraged to inter-marry across Europe and forge harmonious alliances. Therefore at aged fifty-two and with a number of refusals, Princess Adelaide of the German Duchy of Saxe-Meiningen, whom he had never met, arrived in London in July 1818 to become his future wife; she would again fail to provide an heir, when two small girls were to die in their infancy. But in all other respects Adelaide served her royal connections with both dignity and loyalty.

The Duke wrote to his eldest son about his future marriage: 'The Princess of Saxe-Meiningen is doomed, poor, dear, innocent, young creature, to be my wife I cannot, I will not, I must not ill use her… What time may produce in my heart I cannot tell, but at present I think and exist only for Miss Wykeham. But enough of your father's misery.'

It was in turn left to his departed brother Edward to provide an heir, and the Duke's eighteen year old daughter, Victoria, to carry forward the royal banner for the next sixty four years and finally into the twentieth century.

Adelaide itself expresses a clean, safe and peaceful environment, as we strolled around in the warm afternoon breeze. I liked the place, or the elegant Torrens River that is, with various tourist cruisers passing by; together with the domineering Festival Hall invariably referred to as a 'flattened version of the Sydney Opera House,' without glamour. It was also nice to receive some forwarded mail at the post office.

We then walked across the river to admire the Adelaide Oval, the scene of a recent Test match. I wanted to stroll to the centre square, and imagine myself opening the batting for England. Naturally I score an unbeaten century in raising my bat to acknowledge the crowd; unfortunately today though the huge iron gates are locked, giving us a clear view of the vast outfield and the stands in the background.

There was nothing else much to do now but to search out St Peter's Cathedral, completed in 1876. Here there is a wooden pulpit, with a circular staircase rising above the congregation. It also seemed appropriate to be wearing the Australian sporting colours of a yellow shirt with a green collar blending in nicely with my suntan. Out in front the pews are empty, and even Martin had momentarily disappeared outside, to leave me alone with my thoughts of thanking 'our maker' for this golden opportunity that life has brought my way.

It seems appropriate here to think of home cast in darkest winter. There is nothing I can do if anything should happen.

Weeks might pass by, before our correspondents catch up with us. Such is the uncertainty of our flight. I now said a silent prayer and then rejoined the radiant sunshine outside…it was time to make another phone call home.

Thursday 12 January

We have unanimously decided to forsake Adelaide work-wise and further our enquiries in Melbourne. The main fruit picking area is situated 80 km north of there, but unfortunately from now on we will have to start hitchhiking; public transport is out of my financial range, which now totals $23. Soon I shall have to borrow money from Martin although we should still get some dole money, coupled with our rent rebate. Things don't look too smart, but then they could be worse; at least we are moving in the 'right direction.'

In a way I always knew this was how things were going to turn out from the outset, when we arrived in Perth; picked up a leaflet and noted the harvest dates and their location. I had mentally prepared myself from that point and had only half-heartedly gone about the task of trying to find something else in the meantime. Another week, and perhaps we might again start to go forward. We have adapted quite well and have seen so much already, that we can hardly complain.

We then phoned Connie's contact; she has naturally enjoyed a chat with her long lost friend. They probably write and send Christmas cards. It's amazing how difficult we invariably find it to pick up a phone, but that's modern life and only when we have a reason. The best presents are inevitably those given for no reason at all, apart from to say hello, you're a friend who I like.

It seemed appropriate that these past three days were spent staying with John and Ross in the suburb of Brighton, who said to come over and stay, and that 'you are only too welcome.' Connie, it seems, has given us a glowing report for which we must be grateful. It was just this kind of encouragement that gave us the confidence to continue, for what might prove a difficult few weeks ahead.

John was on holiday away from the pressures of his marketing job in the city, which meant luckily he could drive us around Adelaide, in this the height of the holiday season. He seemed to be a jolly soul, who could take care of himself in the commercial world. His wife Ross was the salt of the earth and does him proud; they are a nice family who welcomed us with open arms.

"We are doing quite well here," John remarked. "The swimming pool, for instance, can be used for eight months of the year. I could have been further along the career ladder, but Ross and I travelled extensively, and then bought a campervan for Australia. You boys are going to learn so much."

I certainly liked the leisurely pool lifestyle; just strip off in the morning and go for a dip before breakfast and something I could quite easily get used to. As we took over the small living room of their 'colonial' styled house, nicely snuggled in a middle class district. It might not be an Australian expression though, with the country now rejecting any kind of honours from the Royal Crown, for instance, unlike New Zealand. But that I'm afraid is how things stand here and very nice too; just a short trip from the beach. It's safe to say, we are both impressed by the lifestyle and should I say their two children with me, and a new playmate in the pool. Even if I did spend most of my time sitting in an orange blow-up plastic dingy, with a tin of beer in my hand soaking up the sun!

On Wednesday we drove out to Mount Croft, 7 km, into the Adelaide Hills, and 771 metres high. In a way this was the highlight of our trip here, seeing how the terrain looks. It also gave us an idea of what to expect when we finally leave. On either side of the road lay charcoaled tree trunks and occasionally a gutted house, or the stark reminders of a forest fire deliberately started.

"Smoke could even be smelled in Adelaide," Ross remarked.

"Anybody hurt?" I said.

"No, not seriously, just smoke fumes, but there are now daily warnings on the risks of fire," she replied.

During the hot spells there is often a total fire ban, such is the risk and fear of even one spark to any surrounding forestry and towns. Lookout towers have been especially erected on Mount Croft to alert the fire services immediately of any suspicious smoke signals, such is the seriousness of a potential catastrophe.

It is Ash Wednesday, February 16th 1983, which will be particularly remembered here, and in Victoria, when fires fuelled by 40°C temperatures and gale force winds claimed over seventy lives; people got caught up in the dramatic severity of the occasion, with numerous fire fighters also dying as they tried to stem its flow. The fires formed a semi-circle around Melbourne, and even reached the coastal areas west towards Warrnambool, together with the Adelaide Hills.

It is hard to imagine the dramas that unfolded on such a perfect day, or even that people would deliberately endanger the surrounding wildlife and its domain.

"It's something we have to live with in Australia, especially now, fires can easily result from lightening, or carelessness. Then there is the reflective glass; we just have to hope they can be put out quickly, and kept under control," Ross remarked.

Adelaide can be seen in the distance spreading itself along numerous sandy coastlines. Between the rows of bricks and mortar much parkland is evident, with a cluster of high-rise buildings cramped together in the centre, casting their dreary shadows over a cosmopolitan society below...

Friday 13 January

Friday the thirteenth seems an apt time to begin my hitchhiking career. I'm not even sure if I would have pursued this idea if Martin had not been with me. The uncertainty of not knowing when or who might come our way could have been too much at first. He once thumbed around New Zealand, but I was definitely a 'rookie' at this kind of thing, in preferring to stand back while my friend held his outstretched hand in the air. My confidence, although not really nervous, was rather unsure of itself, or that anybody might actually stop for us!

John made sure we had an early start, with Ross cooking us a hearty breakfast, together with a packed lunch for the day. He also appeared confident that we would be fine, and that we will get a lift, in reaching our destination before dark.

"It's in our makeup, people like to be sociable and have the company for the journey, especially on a long haul. Many of the motorists will have been hitchhikers in the past, and know what you are all about," he remarked.

We were left south of Adelaide, at a small gravel area, nicely fit for about three cars to park, with plenty of time for an oncoming vehicle to make a judgment and pull off the road.

'So this really is it,' I thought, as we watched John turn around and smile before he drove back up the road, and left us in silence, standing there wondering what to do next.

This is not a busy highway, with a nice sprinkling of traffic passing by in three's, or as an individual going about their business. We now looked at each other for a couple of seconds cast in isolation, and the point of no return; of what shall we do, just stand here, or put our packs together in an orderly way for motorists to see. There's no point in just standing here, start to smile, people like a happy go lightly approach to life, and we are it! The Australians could not be less friendly, as I was soon to find out.

Lift number one, from a young fisherman, took us 2 km to the top of a hill.

"Lorry drivers will never stop for you back there, as they cannot pull away," he remarked.

Lift number two took us about twenty minutes to obtain, when a middle-aged duck farmer drove us 80 km towards Murray Bridge. From here Australia's greatest river, at 650 km long, can be viewed in its prime. It starts high up in the Snowy Mountains, close to Mount Kosciusko, and combines melting snow with the Murrumbidgee and Darling Rivers. The Murray has enough water to flow through the arid plains, to irrigate them, and eventually reaches the Southern Ocean, southwest of Adelaide near Goolwa. The Murray-Darling basin is in turn one of Australia's most prosperous agricultural regions, the river forms the NSW-Victoria border in part, away from the usual straight line.

Lift number three took almost an hour to obtain, but eventually a young couple drove us to Tailem Bend, 21 km, near to the Murray's mouth.

Lift number four at 12.30pm turned out to be the jackpot, as Chris and Libby were driving their Volvo down to Melbourne for a wedding ceremony.

"You know, I once spent four hours trying to hitchhike from that spot. I didn't want anybody to experience that," Chris said, as he handed over a stubby of Cooper's lager.

"So what's it like in Greenland, a bit cold, isn't it?" he kept saying.

Chris had obviously misheard the word England from the backseat, but the novelty seemed to work in our favour.

"Oh, a bit frosty at times, a few trees and snow in the winter," I remarked, much to his interest. "The problem now is the lack of daylight, besides once a traveller has seen the world, there is always Greenland. You must come and stay!"

"That's a long way, I don't know about that," he replied.

"You'll be alright, summers are quite pleasant," I said, and wondered what I might say if he asked me for my address, so I decided to quit while ahead!

My first impression of Victoria, the garden state, relates to an abundance of fertile farmland, attributable to higher rainfall levels than in South Australia. This has made it a rich pasture for sheep, horses and cattle, for instance, to fill their bulging stomachs. I'm told the coastal route along the Pacific Highway towards Melbourne is one of those great cliff top treasures worth a detour in anybody's life. But in our present circumstance, we felt the direct route via Ballarat, Victoria's largest inland town, best served our purposes.

At another time it might have been worth staying here for the night, instead of our quick pit stop to view its numerous colonial styled buildings. It was here in November 1854, that the local gold diggers formed their Ballarat Reform League to canvas for full civic rights and the abolition of a monthly licence fee scaling the dizzy heights of 30 shillings. This did not even bring with it the 'right to vote,' and the chance of owning their own claims, or even police protection. All of which led to the infiltration of corrupt practices, much to the prospector's own detriment and frustration. In turn they constructed the Eureka Stockade of logs and tried to organize a protest, which led to 200 people gathering inside.

On 3rd December the police and troops attacked the protesting miners and massacred thirty of their number at a loss of five government forces. For what must have stirred considerable anger among the colonialists, and put the authorities under intense pressure in the immediate aftermath. Of why this can have ever happened, and that Australians must never be seen to shoot each other again in such circumstances.

All though was not lost in martyrdom, when the licence was in turn abolished in 1855, and replaced by a 'Miner's Right,' which came with the right to vote and land enclosure.

"Do you want to stay here, or continue with us, only we can't stay too long, as we promised to be in Melbourne before 8pm," Chris said.

Reluctant to lose our lift we decided to continue the journey; we also have two contacts that might prove useful in providing a floor to sleep on, or even point us in the right direction.

"I think we would like to continue," Martin replied.

In little over twelve hours we had managed to meet numerous interesting people, and travelled 720 km free of charge, at a saving on coaches of $76. Not that with a combined $6 in cash between us, we had much choice in the matter. Even the campsite charges were $7 a night which meant pitching our tent in a nearby field shortly before dusk, and 'praying' that nobody would disturb us during the night.

Snuggled in my sleeping bag, I began to think about our self-inflicted plight, and considered this to be an important stepping-stone in our quest for more stability. It has been an insecure experience so far and one that seems to be going down to the wire.

"You know Martin, I doubt if we are going to look back now," I remarked, with a growing confidence.

"Sure why not, things will turn out fine, the pressure will spur us on," he replied, and wondering why I ever doubted our hitchhikers outlook to Australia.

4. Victoria

Victoria is the smallest mainland state, founded by the 'Van Dieman's,' who arrived here and organised themselves into the Port Philip Association. They then bought 700,000 hectares of land to farm from the Aboriginals in return for blankets and knives in forging much friendlier relations with the natives.

On their isolated island the settlers had the upper hand. Here in 'Bear Grass' though they remained within sight of Sydney but still out of the Governor's 3,000 km protective ring, and were in turn not protected by law; the area had already failed once in 1803, due to mismanagement and the settlers duly moved further south.

Although a number of whalers had used the bay in the meantime. It was not until 1835 that further settlers arrived, to organize themselves into such a disciplined unit, that the governor was bound in his own judgment to take them seriously. In the return for official recognition, it was agreed to rename their settlement in 1837, for the acknowledgement of Lord Melbourne, Britain's Whig elected Prime Minister.

Saturday 14 January

Daybreak had arrived when I woke, and asked Martin the time. It was 6.30am; already the inhabitants of the field had rummaged us. I thought it was empty and so did the horses outside, who began to investigate their intruder, as if to say that tent was not there last night. 'Who, why, and where did it come from?'

They stood quite still outside almost in a circle.

"Hey Martin, we're surrounded," I said, looking out of the flap.

There were about a dozen of the enemy munching around our vicinity.

"Come on we have to get up, the owners might be along in a minute, and you know what these horse people are like, up with the larks!"

We now spent twenty minutes packing everything away, and took the first of a whole string of liberties that lie ahead of us by creeping into the local campsite for a shower, without the proprietor's knowledge. We then began hitchhiking again in the rush hour, which provided us with the final piece of our journey into the centre, where we had deliberately avoided last night.

My first concern was the size of my pack and walking around in scorching heat. In a way this was our first piece of strenuous exercise we have experienced here, which has admittedly come as a shock to our leg and shoulder muscles; my body soon became dehydrated and in need of constant fluid intakes.

Melbourne is a much larger city than either Perth or Adelaide in its make up; and the people-orientated streets, with non-stop traffic congestion. For instance the Greek population here numbers some 70,000, making it reputedly the largest outside Greece. The city is full of interesting contrasts and high-rise buildings supplemented with industrial output. Admittedly pollution has been kept under control. But I still didn't like its heartbeat after our more laid back environments of late and hankered for my swimming pool lifestyle.

Perhaps it's the solid architecture of Victorian times that is so unappealing, or our own situation. In a way I'm looking forward to going back to my rural 'routes,' with nothing to think about, a fixed abode, and an income to alleviate the situation. It's not all gloomy though. The city obviously has an active nightlife to be enjoyed, as well as a great deal of parkland, and especially on either side of the Yarra for a nice picnic. However, Melbourne is better known as the unofficial sporting capital of Australia.

In 1956 the Melbourne Cricket Ground was used as the central stadium for a highly successful Olympic Game's. It is also used each September when huge crowds attend the Australian Rules Football Grand Final; the equivalent to English soccer's Football Association (FA) Challenge Cup Final. It is a game closely related to Irish Gaelic Football, and played on an oval pitch with double upright goalposts with six points for an inner goal and one point for an outer. Eighteen players are on the pitch at any given time, with two able to interchange from the bench; players are allowed to handle the ball with one hand and punch it with the other, or run and bounce it every fifteen metres, although a player can be tackled above the knee and below the shoulder.

Basically this remains Victorian, rather than an Australian game, while Rugby League and Union are more popular in Sydney and Brisbane. The most recent Grand Final was competed for by twelve teams in the Victorian Football League (later expanded and re-branded as the Australian Football League), including the Sydney Swans, was on September 24th when 110,333 fans watched Hawthorn defeat Essenden by 20 (120 points) goals and 20 (20 points) outer for a total of 140 points against (8:9) 57 points. The unique thing here is that during the three years that this trip encompasses Essendon won the next two finals against Hawthorn by 105 (14:21) to 81 (12:9) in 1984 (attendance 92,685) and by 170 (26:14) to 92 (14:8) in 1985 (attendance 100,042), to reclaim a crown they last held in 1965.

Only last year 84,000 spectators watched Australia play England in a one-day international cricket match. This is the world's largest such venue, with its covered oval shaped balconies reaching towards the sky. In a weeks time we would see Australia defeat Pakistan in a one-day match by 43 runs. A crowd of 24,273 attended and yet we were still dwarfed with the upper reaches all closed with an oasis of empty seats, such is the magnitude of the place.

Australia's national sports day though remains the first Tuesday in November for the Melbourne Cup horse race when the nation grinds to halt for a few minutes, similar to the Epsom Derby in its hey day. A mid week fixture tends to leave a great race with the sporting focus, rather than a weekend slot that might get lost among the various team sports results and those actually taking part on a more amateur level.

The first winner was Archer in 1861; it beat a field of seventeen in what is still the slowest winning time of 3 minutes 52 seconds. He triumphed by a record 8 lengths the next year by cutting five seconds off his time. This compares with the 1983 winners time, by the aptly named Kiwi, of 3.18. But it is Archer I shall relate to here because only Cliff Young might be able to compete with his feat of walking 550 miles to the course from his stables, and then actually win the race.

On May 3rd the 61-year-old potato farmer from the Otway Ranges ran into the record books by winning the inaugural Sydney to Melbourne Marathon, in five days and fifteen hours. His mother said afterwards that it was time he retired: "As he is getting too old!"

Sunday 15 January

Yesterday's scorching heat was replaced by a deluge of torrential rain, which found Martin and myself huddled beneath a concrete canopy outside Melbourne Zoo. Between us we managed to buy three packets of crisps with our remaining 99 cents. Apart from that, all we could afford to do until the banks open is watch an ever worsening rainstorm; we planned to camp on a piece of waste ground opposite.

"Why did you ask me to come on this trek, halfway around the world?" I remarked, in a wistful kind of way.

"I didn't, you volunteered," he replied.

"Good point that…"

Monday 16 January

After washing in the basins of the nearby schools playground, we walked into the city, where Martin withdrew some money from his ANZ bank account; my own balance is slowly moving towards 'the red.' Inevitably my only concern is to find an income of sorts, with no sign of our deposit from Perth in the post as yet, or a social security cheque. We therefore decided to make some enquires, at the government offices, and were informed that United Kingdom working visa holders were ineligible for payments, in which case we filled in the necessary forms.

"Could you check with Perth, they seemed adamant about our rights," I said to an official, when behind us in the queue, a Scottish traveller began comparing notes with us and insisted: "You're right, Australians do the same in England, we have an agreement. I also arrived on December 9th in Perth."

"What time was that?" I said.

"At about 6am, you might have seen me rolled out in my sleeping bag," he replied.

My mind then flicked back to that solitary figure curled up in the airport entrance and much to Martin's apparent surprise, as we saw sunlight.

"Hey look Baz, they're even sleeping rough out here!"

Tuesday 17 January

Hitchhiking a lift out of Melbourne proved to be a precarious business even though a contact of ours left us on the highway at 9am, to give the day some much needed impetus in our search for work. However after two hours of standing still like a pair of lemons uninvited to a party we decided to split up.

Our confidence or ambition cannot have been too high, as for some reason we decided to meet up at the half way point of Seymour, rather than our actual planned destination. We then flipped a coin to decide that it was my turn to start walking up the highway.

Ten minutes later and my first lift was to be an elderly gentleman, in an open topped yute, who spent our 20 km together telling me everything that was wrong with his family, and England itself, or something I could do without.

"Just look on the positive, there's good everywhere if you

look hard enough," I remarked, and smiled as I got out of the car, in wishing him all the best.

Five minutes elapsed and a Ford motor dealer stopped, who was going all the way to Shepparton. He also mentioned the possibility of a job on a neighbouring farm fruit picking when I had to think again, and especially in our perilous financial position.

"You will never find it on your own, we are very much out on a limb," Peter remarked.

Unfortunately Martin had not arrived at Seymour post office, which meant leaving him a letter there in the hope that he might ask about his friend to the postmaster. It was a gamble admittedly, but when you are minus your last bean and nickel, the risk is worth it. We had not mentioned anything like this, which I confess only confused matters in that you should never change your mind and do as you agreed, otherwise nobody will ever rely on your word again. But this was a special case and something I dare not let out of our grasp in waving goodbye to the possible solution to many of our troubles.

We eventually arrived at the wooden farmhouse at 3pm surrounded by arid vegetation and a dusty landscape, with a willow tree looking splendid in the sunlight. Peter was right. I would never have found this without his help. I might have searched aimlessly, and wondering if I was going in the right direction. The farmer was fortunately in and said to come back on Sunday, when he was hoping to start on Monday if the fruit ripened somewhat more.

"You can move into the bunkhouse, there are already three people waiting for the picking to start, if you want to meet or even join them now," he replied, to my questions.

"That's very kind of you, but my friend is still on route, and I have to find him now to see when he wants to come out here,"

I replied.

Peter then offered to drop me off in 'Shep,' where I thanked him for his help, and phoned Seymour post office. They informed me that they had seen him, but no he had not collected his message. Fortunately they would keep an eye out for him, especially as Martin has our tent, with mine left in Melbourne for the time being.

My immediate prospects appeared to be park bench orientated, and something I have missed out in life to date, but there would be plenty of times to rectify it at this rate. There was no way anybody might sleep in the undergrowth with snakes so prominent, or even to light a fire for that matter. One spark, and the vegetation between here and neighbouring Mooroopna might go up in smoke. Now all I could do was wait and hope that my two loose ends could be brought together in one evening.

In a way something always turns up, it's a case of having to make it happen, and a situation that I am going to have to get used to or go home prematurely. Even that is not really an option to consider. Besides this is a good country. The time is right in my life, I'm staying put, and want to become part of it!

Martin turned up at around 8pm and was slightly aggrieved on first impressions, with my change of plans. He had apparently tracked me down via two German girls who remembered seeing me walking around, an hour ago, and naturally wanted an explanation.

"Why didn't you wait?" he said.

"I'm sorry, we have a job," I replied.

Wednesday 18 January

Shepparton is situated in the heart of the Goulburn Valley, amidst a prosperous area of irrigated land ideal for growing fruit and vegetables. Pleasant in nature it is well laid out with a boating lake situated a short walk from the town centre. I quite liked it, just relaxing in the park and contented that the tide might begin to turn.

Waiting for something to happen seemed unnecessary, especially as we still have some of our kit in Melbourne with Jan and Cal, who welcomed us as a friend of theirs, or another of Martin's contacts in collecting addresses. We have slept on the floor of their small flat, soon to be house when they get married in April. Jan is a nurse while Cal works as an engineer in a factory, arriving first and working late to save money. It all sounded 'quite boring' to my mind, but Jan will make him such a nice wife, that I was soon beginning to see the logic of his ways.

"We have done Europe together two years ago. This is not the end of our travels, there will be time in the future," he remarked.

When things are desperate, and let's just say with me counting the cents and not dollars. It is safe to say we would not be eating in a café, or anything else even close to it, with the thorny question of food and what to eat. One of us though noted in a guidebook something about the local cannery and that for $2 we could buy a giant can of reject peaches, which will keep us fit and healthy for another day. This would also enable us to take our remaining provisions with us on our journey south.

Sunday 22 January

Martin arrived in Shepparton about an hour before me this morning, when he received a lift, which was actually going to 'Shep' itself, rather than my own three separate journeys. The town was fairly deserted; I also knew Martin had the head start this time, having disappeared when my lift stopped and said: "Your friend has already gone, I saw a motorist stop for him further up and thought to pick you up, if you were still here on the way back."

I was glad of that, within half an hour we were both up and running, and this time with no halfway house. The bench in the park was the place to be, and there he was asleep on my perch, waiting to begin the next phase of our travels, or the salvage operation, that has seen us both in something of a financial slump, and ready for tomorrow morning. It couldn't come too quickly for me that is, and now all we had to do was to begin our 14 km hike, in the hot afternoon sun. We could have waited, but both concluded it might be better to begin, just in case we get lost.

"I hope you can remember the way," Martin remarked.

"Yes but only on foot, I could not explain it to a motorist," I replied.

We now started our journey with a walk through the forest, and began to notice the mosquitoes at their rampant best. One thing at the top of our list will have to be anti-mosquitoes spray before long. The water would attract them wholesale. What with soap, suntan oil and the spray, I'm wondering what my skin is likely to resemble after the sun has beaten down on it for the next two months. There is no substitute for the moist atmosphere of the English countryside and noted my light brown arms, once anaemically white.

There is a road route, but one look at the map told us they both run parallel, and that the leaves will put us in the shade, with something nicer to look at. The track being bone dry except for the oddity of an isolated puddle or two, made me wonder how this could happen in such a climate. Before we reached the much smaller town of Mooroopna, and a pleasant enough place, all built of wooden colonial styled buildings. The surprising thing here was the close proximity to the trees of many of the houses, which were just ripe for a fire to sweep through large sections of the houses, in wreaking their trails of destruction.

"This place would go up in minutes, why don't they cut back the trees?" Martin said.

"Perhaps they think they are safe, and prefer it that way," I replied.

We then began what was to be a long silent walk out of town, and where we soon found ourselves on the open highway. Staring aimlessly into the distance, with the sun beating down on the tarmac and melting it in places, such was its intensity. Another hour and things would soon begin to become more bearable. We had plenty of water and a straight road, I remembered some trees on the horizon and eventually said: "It is just beyond those."

There is nothing like doing things the hard way in adapting to the climate; to our left a railway line runs parallel with our route. I'm not sure how many empty carriages the goods train pulled, but perhaps a hundred or so. The driver tooted his horn and I raised my arm to wave, cast adrift in no man's land.

In time we made good progress, as we rotated the lead, towards those distant trees deep in thought and staring down at the gravel besides the road. It was easier on the feet and not so heat consuming. On my small radio, a familiar voice seemed to sum up our plight, singing their latest hit single *Radio Ga Ga,* with the vocals of Freddie Mercury and Queen.

"Are you sure you know where you are going?" Martin remarked.

"Just beyond the trees, trust me," I replied.

"That's the problem!"

The sun was slowly setting over the horizon when we finally arrived at Naygoondy Farm, along a gravel road named after the resident grower. The farmer was out, but his wife said to make

"Yourself at home. The electricity is on, and there is fresh water, but don't drink the water from the ditch, it is polluted with rubbish, and insects…my husband said to expect two English lads."

In the pickers' kitchen half a dozen scruffy individuals were slowly drinking themselves into a drunken haze. For a solitary moment of awkward silence I assumed that we didn't belong here amongst this 'rabble,' but what right have I got to think these derogatory remarks. Besides I'm certainly the poorest person here, and possibly in the 'whole' of Australia for that matter.

"How long have you been here?" I said.

"About a week, this time last year there were pears galore; this could be the worst season for over twenty years," one replied, at which an old grey haired man in desperate need of both a shave and fresh clothes grabbed my arm from behind, and proceeded to show us around our new billets. He also appeared particularly uncouth in his mannerisms and general language about "Those drunken bastards in there."

Two days later he disappeared leaving his few belongings on the farm to be eventually burnt. Nobody could be sure; I gather he made his way to the local hospital and died shortly after, as a lonely man, living his lonely existence, and alone in death. He may not have been the most polite or pleasant person to meet out here.

"But he had one overriding redemption," I remarked.

"What's that?" Martin said, after it became clear he would not be coming back.

"Quite simple really, he liked us."

One look at our room brought a gasp from my lips, which instantly turned into a dusty cough. In front of us lay three rickety old beds, grimy mattresses and a three-legged chest of drawers. Sleeping in this mess made me realise just how squalid the third world conditions are so often to live in, and can only help us to understand their plight.

The problem is that the place is left for nine months of the year, and it really depends on how the last tenants left it; when the dust is annually cleared away or how the farmer views his responsibilities and with a little more effort, I should add.

Everything appears to be in a chronic state of decay and filth. The showers are door-less, and there are no light bulbs anywhere, apart from in the kitchen, which in turn is polluted with stale beer and cigarette stubs. The area is also swarming with blood-sucking mosquitoes, millions of flies and poisonous snakes to contend with in the grass.

At the end of our block, which resembles an old cowshed, we found a comparatively clean two bedded square room, with a missing pane of glass, some daylight through the cracked walls and a broken mirror, now being the most distinctive elements of our new living quarters.

I then tried my bed and the dust began to swirl in the evening air followed by a cleaning session. It's the best we could do in the circumstances, which only illustrated why this would only be a place to sleep, with no balcony in sight or sheets. I would wake at first light and extract myself from the redundant springs that were designed, it seems, a very long time ago when the first settlers arrived to plant the orchards.

Monday 23 January

Eager to earn some long awaited money, our enthusiasm was soon dispelled by the news that the pears are not ripe, due to a lack of sunshine!

"Last year was a bumper harvest, we had already started two

weeks since," the farmer said.

Typical. We did try picking those pears which measure 2⅝ inches wide, but when a container holds half a ton of fruit, scrimping around for solitary pears with our pickers measuring ring can be a pretty tedious experience. At the end of six hot hours of climbing ladders, we had earned a combined wage of $15, or $7.50 each.

"You know, this is pointless I'm going back to Melbourne to find out what has happened to our social security money," Martin explained.

He left soon after breakfast in the morning, with me preparing for another search in the orchard, when it soon became glaringly obvious that things were not exactly going to plan, but I would have to stick it out. Any money was better than nothing. I was also in place to earn something and eat without spending. The situation is certainly not good, but it looked a lot worse this time last week.

Wednesday 25 January

Further heavy rain delayed my resumption of pear picking until the orchard had finally dried out by mid-day. I then made good progress, filling three quarters of a bin, before a deluge of rain further curtailed my aspirations in earning $15 today. Known as the Pom around the hut I'm getting on quite well with everybody who are all helpful and show me where things are kept.

In a way this is their life, to follow the seasons and be merry! Few appear to have any fixed abode, apart from Gary, a thirty-year old dropout, who claims to work on his parent's farm, and is here because this is a rather "slow time" for them. But without money and a reluctance to even buy any shaving foam, in preference to saddle soap, his life as ever revolves around a stubby of beer.

"Don't listen to him, he even tried to sell his parents farm without them knowing," one remarked, in his sixties, with the sign of a man who has been following the seasons without his roots for many years now.

He will probably also conclude his life in a hospital bed, with alcohol on his breath. Whatever the truth, I am unlikely to ever know the answer to this question, or really want to for that matter. With $2 to my name, tonight's expedition towards the pleasantly sounding Toolamba is unfortunately going to happen without me.

Thursday 26 January

Martin returned this afternoon unexpectedly, with the workforce all sitting around doing nothing, except resting in the shade and contemplating another day off, due to the Australia Day Bank holiday. He brought with it the news that we are not entitled to any benefits as such, but this was not quite as important now with this base. The pears would ripen and the money will flow in, if only by a trickle, then we can reassess the situation.

"Perth had given us the wrong information, we only have six months visas and not twelve month ones," he said.

This though all seemed decidedly odd, that our fellow travellers should be given these concessions and not us.

"What about the others?"

"Melbourne thought the money would have to be repaid," he said.

"But Perth checked with London in all cases, they told us," I said.

"Somebody is certainly wrong?" he replied, much to my disappointment, but at least we now knew where we were on this count.

Saturday 28 January

Neither of us wanted to sit out the holiday weekend, which meant a halt being brought to our picking activities, owing to the closure of the fruit depots. This is due to a law paying us twice our daily rate of $9 an hour plus $15 a bin by the farmer. After some deliberations we decided to hitch east towards the Victorian Alps, best known for their skiing. No roads actually run through this area, which makes a circular route impossible.

We had no real problem and with time on our hands, it did not matter where life took us. For once we had a carefree manner that left us in the small town of Benalla, and an ideal setting to launch ourselves into the mountains from. It was in nearby Glenravan, in 1880, that the Kelly Gang's blood shooting days came to an abrupt end, when police surrounded and burnt down the local hotel, where three of its four members perished.

For some reason Ned Kelly, captured wearing an armoured helmet and later hanged, has become a cult figure throughout Australia, similar to America's Billy the Kid. Books and films have invariably been produced about his outlaw activities, which left we noted, three dead police corpses in Mansfield's graveyard in 1878.

One of the intriguing footnotes to the local museum and the ruins of his family dwelling, near Greta, is that Kelly, then 25, was hanged in Melbourne on November 11th. The presiding Judge, Sir Redmond Barrie also died on November 23rd after a very short illness. At his dying breath he might have given a thought to Ned's rather ironic words directed towards him, at his trial: "I dare say the day will come when we shall all have to go to a bigger court than this. Then we will see who is right, and who is wrong."

At Jameson, a small junction retreat, we obtained an invite

from Adam and Damien, two students from Melbourne, to join them and a dozen friends in a wood for the night. I'm sure he meant county more like, judging by the distance that we drove down a forest track and hit the bumps. There would be no point in calling the breakdown vehicles out in winter, with the snow prevalent, and yet where we are working on the low-lying land, the temperatures are into the nineties.

"We all come up here twice a year where nobody disturbs us; you can set up your tent anywhere about," Adam remarked, when we arrived, and said to join them around the fire.

In the dark nobody really noticed us rummaging around the campsite. A couple smooched in the shadows, while others opened a carton of beer, and then handed me one in typical Australian fashion. I felt quite at ease with these surroundings, somewhere amongst the mountain's and who knows where. We then gathered some firewood and stoked the fire in an attempt to fit in. Nobody had much to say, as we sat cross-legged and declined a 'joint' being passed around, similar to the pipes of peace… I soon found myself staring into the naked heat, slowly warming my cheeks now bright red with contentment.

Sunday 29 January

We washed our greasy skin in a fresh flowing stream, where last night we had patiently watched a fisherman snatch a ten-inch trout from the jaws of darkness. Above and all around steep pine covered hilltops shadow our every movement.

In this area prospectors are still panning or dredging for gold in an almost forlorn hope that their dreams might become reality. We tried to imagine ourselves doing likewise, and dredging for gold, gold, I've found gold! But no it was a piece of coloured mineral in disguise, besides we have pears to pick and what good is a goldmine to us?

"Well as you mention it, a strike might come in useful," Martin remarked.

"Yes but what would we do with all that money!" I replied.

We now grabbed a lift out of this place in the morning. Fortune was shining bright, when one asked us how long we were staying, and that his friend would drop us back on the highway when they went to buy provisions. I didn't want to hang about though, this was time lost and a small window for us to use more positively.

This in turn led us to Gough's Bay, which stretches for about twenty miles through mountainous terrain, and from here illustrates the story of last year's drought. Much of the surrounding vegetation is still left barren and indeed a complete wood near the lakeside resembles a dead skeleton of its glorious past.

We have nothing to report here, sat upon a mound and reading our books in the afternoon sun. There are people, but not too many, with a small trickle to the kiosk below. The water is a hive of activity, which made me feel quite envious, watching the water skiers and powerboat drivers having the time of their lives, bouncing across the waves.

It is hot and humid, with the sun momentarily hiding behind a cloud, and soon coming out to play, on what seems to be the most perfect of moments. Then without warning, in no time the clouds filled the sky with a flash of lightning. Followed shortly after by a huge crack of thunder, which instantly signalled the end of today's sport; it was time to hitchhike back towards the orchards.

Friday 3 February

The pear-picking season is at last in full swing, and with it the influx of a combination of young people doing the same as us; travelling around Australia on the shoestring of all shoestrings and an occasional student. One of which Tony, from Canberra, has just spent a week hitching to Ayers Rock, in the centre, and enthused about this at every such moment he could, and how next year he is travelling to Europe.

"I'm telling everyone to meet me on the steps of the Acropolis on April 1st," he said, when we met in the kitchen, and decided to walk across the scorched looking meadow with long grass.

Fortunately I wore my army styled trousers, with the socks as ever tucked over the bottoms, in trade mark style people invariably mention, and reply "It's something I have always done," or would continue to do so. It was especially important after this hike, which took us onto a gravel road, and in effect meets the original road we struggled along when we arrived. My friend has one of those pleasant easygoing natures, and weighs about a third of my body weight again, together with a towering presence over my shoulder. He's from a Greek background; his parents emigrated out here some fifteen years ago.

"Oh nobody is going to mess around with me, being this size," he said, with a smile, and a very nice person I should say to have on your side, for which I must add my gratitude.

The idea had been to make our way into Toolamba, for a well-earned drink at the Junction Hotel, and to get to know some of my newfound friends, or particularly the Australians in their own country. I can talk to the English at home, but this is a time to mingle. It is hardly a town, rather a road junction with a level crossing, the post office store, a dozen houses, and more open than Mooroopna without the surrounding trees.

Two cars then came our way and we gently moved over onto the light grassed verge, with the dust being sprayed up; my vision was momentarily blurred by the dipped lights in the gloom.

"Lookout!" Tony shouted, as he instinctively grabbed my arm half out of its socket and wrenched me across the road, as if his life depended upon it, or mine that is. What's going on, it all happened in a flash. One moment the dust and then I'm being dragged across the gravel, with my feet half off the ground.

I then glanced at the Australian, who looked straight through me, with my eyes following his, and the sight of a Brown Tiger snake slithering into the grass.

"You were lucky, I looked down and saw it moving between your feet. I'm sorry about the arm, it's all I could think of in an instant," he said.

"Wow," I replied.

"You would have about five hours to reach hospital, or risk cutting the poison out yourself," he said, somewhat relieved.

"I think, the first drink's definitely on me," I remarked, still staring at the dried grass and thinking of what had just taken place, or might have…

The hotel was as you can imagine nothing special, cast in the wilds, and probably only ever alive at this time of the year when the pickers are about and have money to spend, or the older Australians following the seasons, rather than those here for a short spell.

It was fun and we all blended in nicely at the bar, with a bit of banter, and one asking another younger man if he knew him, which backtracked to a pub in Adelaide, and not his native Tasmania. This was another place I had to visit; there's nothing like the right time and this was it. We chatted and I was finally grateful for a lift. There is none of this late night drinking mentality among us, rather a couple of lagers, and a lift would do us fine in the back of an open topped truck, with my hair gliding in the night air.

I presently sat talking to Terry in our kitchen until 3am. This whiff of a social life had left me wanting to continue, as everybody soon splintered off to bed; the two of us sat across the table, and swapped stories of our lives, or that mine was slowly beginning to flourish. I also learnt how his experiences of armed combat in Vietnam had affected him, and wondered why these young men had been put through this ordeal.

"Screwed up my life," he said.

Terry's friendly manner and grey ash coloured beard gives him a kind of charisma which one has to admire, even W.G Grace would have been proud of his bristles. Yet here is a man who drinks, smokes and cannot find work outside of seasonal employment, or a true-blooded Australian if ever there was one, who I could never imagine being anything else. Put Terry into any other environment and he would be like a fish out of water.

We then started conversing about snakes, and in particular an instance last season, when a young couple left their baby in its pram only for them to return in time to see a copperhead arched in the air above their young offspring.

"Life just stood still, when five of us remained motionless. The tension was almost unbearable. I just couldn't think, in not wanting to be the one to scare the snake into a panic," Terry remarked.

"What happened?" I said.

"Now there's a strange thing, the farmer's twelve year old son, and too young to understand fear or any possible consequences, instinctively walked up from behind us with a scythe and thrust the blade through its neck, killing it instantly. My hands still sweat when I think of what might have happened," he replied.

Saturday 4 February

Simply put, this is hard work in the blazing sun all day when not being used to it. At least we are adapting nicely with the floppy hat, climbing our long ladders, which arch out into a stand that can either be rested against the tree, or set up as a v-shaped structure to rest our pouch on the top, although the leaves tend to shield us from the sun and keep our temperatures down.

Martin and myself are again working together. There is nothing in our work rate, as we wondered how a professional picker managed to hit the dizzy heights of five bins, when we have only averaged two each a day, with a line of twenty six trees instead of last year's average of three trees per bin.

It's just our luck, when we at first size picked, and then stripped the trees bare. Unlike one unpopular soul who stood on the ground, stripped a row of trees and thought the rest of us were going to do the hard bit for him. That is until the foreman told him different and the row was his alone, until it was finally picked.

"It's a hard enough job, without you leaving us the loose ends," one of the older Australians remarked at him through the trees, in what was charitable piece of diplomacy to keep the peace. I gather the culprit left the next day, when he realised how difficult things were going to be here, with a series of long walks or flagging the tractor driver down to move his bin further up the line.

On the other hand things have greatly improved with an influx of much needed fresh blood to bolster our numbers up to about twenty-five. We now include travellers, students, unemployed, and inevitably the lost souls of society. Labour turnover can be in excess of one hundred during these few weeks. We now have Australians, French, German, New

Zealander's and half a dozen fellow poms. Nobody though is entirely sure of the origins of this Australian terminology, when perhaps Prisoners of Her Majesty's Service, or Pohms, might be the closest idea.

Sunday 5 February

It has to be reported that the Australian cricket team has been experiencing stage fright during the past week as the West Indies have proceeded to teach them a lesson in the art of one day cricket matches. Naturally the English contingents have delighted in informing their counterparts at every relevant moment! Sport invariably goes in cycles, with the game changing and the television companies becoming more powerful in dictating when games are played.

This all has its roots in the late 1970s when Kerry Packer formed a breakaway World Series cricket tournament. It also brought the Sussex and England captain Tony Greig to the forefront of cricket politics, when he resigned the captaincy, and threw his lot in with Channel Nine. The revenue increases, not only to the players, also blew away the cobwebs of a sport operating in the dark age of time, who once called their players gentlemen and professional. This was at a time when each had to use separate entrances onto the pitch, such was the structure of the game at its infancy, in England. But not now I should add, the various factions have made up and compromised their two forms of cricket.

The calendar still encompasses a series of Test matches, and also a three-team one-day event with the top two playing a best out of three final after Christmas. The Australians though have suffered on the pitch lately, with the loss of so many players, to the short-lived rival tour and which has stifled the natural progression of the conveyor belt of talent.

On numerous occasions players were brought through too early, or were simply not good enough for Test cricket. These cricketers had been fast tracked up through the state game and into the international arena. It will be interesting to see how the new sports academy in Canberra will fare in preparing the future generations for the challenges ahead.

Sport should be about friendly rivalry and the bringing together of people for the settling of old scores in jest, as we all began a few days of banter, just to let them Aussies know where their station is in life. It's their way and they would have to take it!

This all led us to an international challenge match in a nearby field where we mowed out a strip twenty-two yards long, and confiscated two cricket bats and a tennis ball from the farmer's son. Before we all proceeded to roast ourselves alive in the 33°C heat.

England's self-appointed captain, yours truly, managed to lose the toss with the Queen's head facing up in the dirt, which allowed Australia, who have even sneaked a New Zealander into their ranks to bat first. The rules were simple; everybody fields and no deliberate dropped catches, while English bowl at Australians and vice versa.

The Toolamba 'Test match' got off to an electrifying start from the visitors' point of view, with the Australians soon all out, and their batsmen one by one walking off in 'shame' at having let the side down. It was nothing to do with a divot or two, or once the ball hit the ground it might go anywhere. This was just great, thirteen all out in twenty minutes, even the mosquitoes were buzzing!

I'm not sure if Gary had decided to commit suicide, or was just over hot when he jumped in the lurgy green ditch, between the huts and the orchard, or could even understand his language at that. But that's what he did.

"Ah shit I was trying to take a short cut, this cricket is shit," he fumed, and then complained about his cuts, or what about the snakes!

"Ah shit," he repeated.

It was soon time to get the reply underway, and who better to open the batting than myself, with an elegant cover drive, a misplaced hook intended to clear the canal, and the defensive play of the 'highest calibre.'

Australia has admittedly produced the greatest Test batsman of all time, Don Bradman, who averaged an amazing 99 during his 52 Test match appearances, between 1928 and 1948, in a sport where nobody else has even come within a third of, and certainly makes him the greatest batsman who ever lived.

My first delivery down under was firmly extracted to the boundary for four runs. The next missed our wooden crate wicket by a hair's breadth, or too close for comfort, and then the third was 'magnificently' caught just in front of a murky looking canal boundary.

"I was aiming for Gary!"

Ironically Bradman required only four runs in his final Test match innings, at the London Oval in 1948, to cement a legendary international average of one hundred. On that occasion, Australia only batted the first innings. Perhaps a second attempt might have harvested the said number of digits, or that fate had scripted his cricket epitaph. The crowd naturally gave him an emotional applause, and England's players even shouted 'three cheers,' when a living legend they knew was soon to pass into the history books. He was shortly to become a knight, or simply The Don to future generations.

Bradman survived the first ball from Warwickshire's leg

spinner, Eric Hollnes. But unfortunately he edged the second delivery, a googly, onto his stumps and just firmly enough to dislodge the bails, in possibly sport's cruellest of anti-climaxes. Don Bradman then slowly trundled from the field before a disbelieving crowd. No doubt bewildered by the disappointment, he refuted the claims that his concentration had waned during this emotional finale to the greatest of all Test careers. Instead he preferred to praise the little known Hollnes, who himself retired with fourteen one hundred wicket hauls in an English county season to his name.

Martin though soon followed 'his leader's' fine example by being bowled through his legs for the princely sum of three runs, which in my calculations left the rest of the team with a big zero between them! England had been caught on a dodgy wicket that had been doctored. I'm learning fast about excuses and that it was not our fault, or the first rule of the football manager being interviewed, and that the official was biased!

We had been routed for seven all out, giving us a deficit of six and big runs by our standards. Their bowlers were quite magnificent. The Don would have said so, and that sounds good enough for me.

We then all walked back to the pavilion, which looked rather like the kitchen, with Gary still complaining about his injury and out of the game. The Australians were not worried though, they thought they could do better in the second innings, and told us so!

This only fired the troops on even more and the home side was soon in desperate disarray, with a fine display of medium paced daisy cutters. I even bowled their opener grey beard, for a golden duck, in what seemed to knock the stuffing out of their rearguard, in being finally eclipsed for twelve all out. This left us needing nineteen to win, with a new opening partnership. Forget

Australia's successful 404 for three wickets run chase, at Headingly in 1948. This was serious stuff and pride was undoubtedly at stake when neither side wanted to give up their bragging rights!

A nail biting finish was in prospect when the scoreboard read: 'No score for one wicket.' I might even have to bat it seemed, and the embarrassment would be all mine at the crease, if I failed with this pass the responsibility kind of act, otherwise known as giving everybody their turn or a chance to shine.

Fortunately our batting line up soon managed to rediscover their grip on the proceedings. There would be no more early alarm bells with a couple of hook shots, the wicket keeper missed a straightforward chance, and then a fielder lost the ball in the grass! This all gave our fine young men the chance of taking advantage of running an extra run, together with a wide that the umpire kindly gave us, and about two feet from the batsman's outstretched willow.

Those Aussies soon began to look like a worn out bunch of hot air in the afternoon heat! We had lulled them into false sense of security, and then our batsmen sliced and nudged their way towards a memorable four wicket win over 'the old enemy,' to regain the Ashes in the most emphatic fashion; in the evening we all celebrated at the Junction Hotel full of banter, but then I have to report, this *is* Australia.

Wednesday 8 February

The best of the pears have now been picked and a crop the farmer claims is the most "disappointing harvest" he has ever known in over twenty years. In effect we are left with a small proportion of fruit in the orchard and too many hands chasing their diminished returns. Making enough money is now becoming increasingly difficult, that it has prompted most of us to look for more work, while still continuing our endeavours here. Four of my fellow pickers have also decided to work on a neighbouring farm where the trees are still covered in pears and have about two weeks work left.

My mind remains very undecided on what cause of action to take. Stay put, and then hope for some peach picking, enquire at the next farm, or even look for some grape picking in Mildura, which according to our phone calls will yield us employment. How much can we earn there? Nobody really knows as yet, which is why I have decided to stay put, until my mind is made up, perhaps by other people's results. At least here I can live cheaply and earn some money to travel on with. The farmer has increased the price from $12.50 a bin to $15. But I doubt if this will act as an incentive because filling the bins is now going to take an extra two hours at least.

Friday 10 February

Things seemed different last night when Martin began to voice his reservations about staying here and "hitting our heads against a brick wall." He wanted to go back to Melbourne to see the girls who have now left Perth and begun their sweep around the coast. It might be nice by realizing the "futility of our efforts" here, and that getting away may prove beneficial to finding another source of income?

"Perhaps we can then make for fresh pastures," he remarked.

Life on the road can pose an uncertain obstacle, besides my 'savings' still only amount to $10, although on a more positive note I have at least paid him back his $44. This in itself might have been far more had it not been for almost every cent having to be accounted for.

It was Martin who was offered a job on a neighbour's farm, while walking back from Toolamba after posting a letter, and leaving me to explore the orchard. He seems quite dispirited, so I reasoned this might be his best option when trying to turn things around.

"The trees actually have some pears on them, you can go over there this afternoon and pick a bin, I'll be back next weekend," he said.

These are insecure times, but I have learned that loyalty counts for very little when money is concerned. The grower told us that his brother-in-law will need some help on his farm shortly, and that he would recommend us to him due to "Your conscientious efforts."

This only added self-doubt to my prompt actions of guilty feelings. I desperately needed a competitive wage, due to a shortened season, or lifeline that should be. But also felt our under-handed tactics seemed a slight betrayal, in not seeing the job through to its conclusion. However these thoughts would change later on when the pickers who remained 'loyal' were not offered such an inducement.

"There was never any chance that we would be needed," a young Australian later told me. Not that anybody could ever blame the farmer for looking after his own self-interests. He has a family to care for and no doubt his 'understanding' bank manager to please, so why should he be interested in our self-inflicted problem. His concern is for the harvest, and the most important part of his financial year.

Saturday 18 February

Saturday mornings were invariably spent in Sheparation's sparsely populated shopping precinct, buying my provisions for the week, and spending time with my colleagues who remain friendly and in the same boat. It's rather nice just wondering around and then bumping into somebody you know doing the same thing. Before we all meet up for a drink, and then pile into our 'open tops' for the return journey, or the camaraderie that such moments bring.

This can be looked back on with a warm feeling of thought, that I was actually one of them for a short time, and not just a pom abroad. There is nothing much to Shep and one visit is very much like another.

At one time I even found myself looking through a second hand bookshop for new reading material and a fresh author.

"What you buy books. You borrow or steal books, but you never buy them!" Terry memorably said, shortly after.

It was on one of these occasions I also found myself walking out of a supermarket, and about one hundred yards up the 'high street,' without noticing the three items in my Irish friend's hand.

"Oh damn it, I've done it again," he remarked.

"Why's that?" I replied.

"I've not paid for these," he said.

At which point I had some unjustified thoughts that he would not now bother because nobody had even noticed us walk out.

"Wait here I'll be back in two minutes," he remarked, having soon impressed his apprentice of his honest intention. It's an insecure thought that we could have been accused of shoplifting without realizing it, until shortly after the event had actually occurred.

Our new fixed abode is at the Bon Terra orchards, nearby within walking distance of Naygoondy. In the evenings I have invariably walked over. But this seems to be out now, as the original employer appears reluctant to have his previous regime around for social reasons, rather than work. There are seven of us here, who are now going on to Atwood's for a further two weeks. The electricity at Naygoondy is also about to be switched off on Tuesday for another year, and something we have lacked here at Bon Terra with a constant diet of sandwiches. I am now looking forward to my next cooked meal and tonight's barbeque with some of the pickers.

My only negative moment here came when John, a Dutchman, threatened to take one of my beer cans when his had been stolen, much against my own wishes. That's two wrongs don't make a right. But he seemed adamant, at which point I took the four tins out of the fridge and was reluctant to share my weeks supply; besides there is not much else to look forward to. After a hard day's slog in the sun the thought of a deep chill in my throat is motivation in itself.

Yesterday I put $156 in the bank. This was three bins short of its total in shortfalls, which the foreman has promised to sort out. Right now $36 is a lot of money to me. What with receiving $93 from Andy in Perth, who has sent on my flat deposit money, things are improving, especially with at least two weeks work left. I now have some kind of breathing space. The patient is slowly making a recovery and is now looking towards a healthy future.

Sunday 19 February

Martin returned this afternoon, somewhat pensive of his situation. Perhaps he regrets 'lighting off' as his finances have plummeted to $100, while mine have soared in comparison to $300.

"What do you want to do?" I said.

He has found it more difficult to fit in with our surroundings here. It was easier for me, having attended a state school, and to relate to the down-to-earth fraternity than possibly a public school background that might not prepare you for, and especially in this social environment. It really came down to horses for courses on this score.

"Tomorrow our travelling 'circus of pear pickers' is moving to another farm. Then it is Tasmania for me, now the money is beginning to come in," I remarked.

Martin wasn't confident. In the morning he left alone for fresh horizons and was still unsure of his thoughts, or what to do next.

"Let me know of your plans at our Melbourne address," he said, as we shook hands in the sunlight.

"Adios and good luck," I replied, now somewhat more at ease with my own circumstances.

I then watched him get in the back of a truck for the beginning of his journey to where, even he does not know. This life can be like that at times, in going with the flow, and then he was gone beyond and out of sight. I felt quite sad and wondered if this was it, the end of the team, or would things finally spin around and see us travelling together once more?

Saturday 25 February

It has to be recorded that my living accommodation, although not the most hygienic imaginable, is admittedly better than our last place. This did not even have a cooker, and other such facilities while our hut roof also leaked at times of nightly rain. Here we have two square shaped bedrooms.

In my section, Charles, a post advanced level student from England and Daryl, one of the numerous boozers, occupy the other bunks. He appears to be one of those sad cases in life, lost and nowhere to go, with a quiet demeanour about him.

"After I tired of a civil service job, and failed to make the grade as a modern artist, I tried my hand at gold mining in Victoria's Alpine region," he said, as we sat in the kitchen one time.

"Did you find any?" I remarked.

"Oh yes, I panned the streams until the snow arrived," he replied, in a matter of fact way. He seemed gentle and kind, only lacking confidence.

"Here," he said, taking a small transparent capsule out of his breast pocket: "You can have this, that's real Victorian gold panned last winter."

"Why thanks very much, I'll treasure it," I replied.

Now still in the prime of life, Daryl remains a pale shadow at 32 years of age. His few belongings consist of a toothbrush, and possibly four pieces of spare clothing. I doubt if he even owns a comb, when a good meal and nourishment ought to be his priority. Somehow you knew this was never going to be the case, rather his money will continue to be spent on a substitute for a life unfulfilled.

I also have to record that the mornings at first light, or when the larks began to stir my sleep, was an experience in itself. Beginning with an incessant example of a chronic smokers cough, it signals me to roll over and glance at Daryl opposite, lying on his back, with eyes still closed.

At 6.30am, his left hand stretches out and slowly extracts a thin white rizzler from its packet, strategically placed on a small bedside table, coupled with some tobacco. This in turn is, one handed, swivelled around his fingers into a roll-up.

I never spoke each morning, and the marvel in my sleep never dulled of inspiration. Daryl's hand then moved towards his mouth, in licking both ends together, while slowly placing the 'cigarette' firmly between his lips.

Fortunately a match was always close by, as three puffs of smoke soon followed before he finally opened his eyes, soothingly relaxed, and staring at the wooden planked ceiling, with its decorative cobwebs intact, still without words.

"Good morning Daryl," I remark, who would slowly acknowledge my presence; before finishing his smoke and finally to sit up on the side of his bed, wearing a pale white tee shirt and pants to match. Those thin bandy legs would then be rested on the dusty floorboards, and in turn a can of Fosters was offered my way, but not for me. He then proceeded to consume it for breakfast…

Sunday 26 February

The peaceful tranquillity of my wondrous sleep was shattered at 1.30am by a howling Alsatian performing some kind of Indian war dance around our hut, with us wondering what is happening in the dark, well Charles and myself that is. Daryl seemed to be out for the count, and was without a concern in the world.

"What's going on, why is the dog in here?"

'What's wrong with that dog, where is the candle, oh good Charles you have one, here shine it on the floor, there's something under the bed the dog is concerned with. It's a pity we have no electricity, that's right under the bed. I'll get on my knees, and run if it's a snake. Here in that corner there is something. I can't make it out, now look Charles, look at that 'hey Daryl' wake up Venus is under your bed. You're a father! But this only stirred a groggy response, and as he was now awake he might as well have a smoke.'

"Look under your bed."

"What's that," he replied, without interest.

In the shadows we could see a small black coat still not yet dry, and much to the excitement of her adoring audience that she had given birth to a solitary pup in the dark…

Saturday 3 March

The curtain has 'finally' arrived with an end of term time feeling that we will never all be together again, when the last pear has now been picked for the season. I could have done better in any other year than this; March has arrived and at least I am solvent, with a little bit of leeway. Not much, but enough to sleep easy for the next week or two.

The social life in the huts has deteriorated somewhat in the past week with the alcohol taking over from the more wholesome of us as the day draws to a close. Each night a number of pickers all arrive back drunk; two of which fell out the back of a van last night, and slept on the ground. Such was the state that things have descended to.

Then there was young James, an English school leaver, who we had to carry out of the pub legless and leave to sleep the effects off. The only problem was that he woke up in the late evening, and left his 'deposit' outside Adrian's tent, who claimed that he had "never" seen anything quite like it! He then walked into the kitchen with his trousers and pants down to his ankles, and asked two English sisters the time, without ever remembering a thing about it, before collapsing in a heap of dazed tomorrows on his bunk!

I began the morning by packing my belongings, and watching little Venus walking around our hut and then fall through the door. 'I don't know,' the children of today they grow up so quick! Outside I rather hoped we might have one of those camaraderie sessions looking back over the past six weeks, which has seen some of us through from day one until now. But it was not to be, when Chris asked if I wanted a lift into Mooroopna and I had to say yes.

The decision to leave had been made and the place would be deserted in a day or two, with everybody now going in their different directions, for wherever that meant, or whichever bar Terry and the Irishman would find themselves in next. There was no future there for me, but I'll miss them with a fondness that is bonded out of these situations.

Chris is from Queensland; he worked in the cannery last winter and earned 26k, but could not understand where "the money went." I should also mention he brought his attractive wife along, and that they have a house somewhere in Brisbane, as their base to start a family.

There have been all kinds of people here, as the flow goes, and we are all the better for it, rather like those initial student days that are so full of variation and people from different backgrounds with much to learn. I shortly left Chris and Terry pouring gasoline into a can at the garage, where three hundred metres from the finishing line we ran out of fuel, and had to walk the last stretch.

"Good luck," Terry said, shaking my hand.

"Yes it's been fun," I replied, and began my hike. This time as if I have been doing it all my life, and now had veteran status. The thought of catching a bus never really occurred to me, I'm simply a hitchhiker now.

Life began easy enough on this stretch. Ten minutes and Paul, my lift, eventually dropped me in the Melbourne suburb of Springvale, after an easy day's joy ride. I could have 'parked' up earlier, but reasoned it might be better to worry about a place to stay when I get there, and with a ferry to catch shortly. It might be better to play 'safe' and go all the way, now that the offer was there for me to take up.

I had planned to see Ian, who had hoped to come with us originally. However, his hip disability would have made our life down under impossible for him to keep pace. He worked with Paul at the dental estimates board in Eastbourne, checking the various forms in regular monotony. A mistake that came to light afterwards was for him to leave shortly before his fifth anniversary in the job, which would have enabled him to claim his pension fund back; that has now been lost in the bureaucratic black hole. In any case, it's still pretty tough having to tell a friend he can't come with you, when his heart was set on this trek.

"I'm sorry, we will see you out there when we are set. You will never be able to do the walking that it will entail," I said.

Besides we could not afford to do it any other way, or if I am honest wanted to. This is Australia and our best option. Money would only have taken away much of the adventure, that I had set my sights on from the outset, and in the back of my mind felt reluctance in Perth to find anything that might have gone against this attitude.

I soon tried to phone Ian's uncle Ted, who has moved without giving a forwarding address, which in turn also left me stuck in the heart of a vast concrete jungle, or not really knowing what to do, and another self-inflicted situation. Ian is here somewhere, and perhaps my letter will be forwarded.

Now I would have to hike through an assortment of little alleyways and building estates. My choice seemed quite simple, as nightfall descended amid a 'freezing' autumn sky, and that was to find a camping spot. The only available open space was seemingly on a football pitch, and I wondered if it might be safe late on?

Certainly there was nobody to be seen anywhere, no life, and no movement, except for the lights in the high-rise blocks. The area was like a churned up paddy field, with too many stud marks that left me with the choice of sleeping between the goalposts, on the only piece of flat grass available. Yet still nobody moved, the birds are asleep, and the match was played. I could sleep in peace tonight…

5. Tasmania

Tasmania's Aboriginal heritage is something neither the Australian settlers, nor the British Empire, for that matter could feel unduly proud of. These native people, it is thought, became separated from the mainland over 10,000 years ago, when rising ocean levels following the closing stages of the last ice age, in effect cut Tasmania off from the mainland Australia.

They lived by hunting and fishing, and were also often stripped naked in these inhospitable surroundings. But unfortunately they soon began to lose their hunting grounds upon the arrival of their white counterparts. Bushrangers, farmers and even convicts alike rounded them up, as if they were on a rabbit hunt, and quite often shot them rather like vermin.

By the 1830s the forty-four survivors were shipped out to Flinders Island, where they remained like a group of homeless refugees, until they were permitted to return in 1847. Their tragic demise was severed in 1874, when the last full-blooded male died in Hobart's Dog and Partridge Tavern. The race finally became extinct with the death of Truganini, also known as Lalla Rooth, who originated from the Bruny Island Tribe, shortly afterwards.

Today the population is mainly situated towards the east and northern coastlines, where the terrain is at its most fertile. The Midlands region is normally compared to a re-creation of green England, and the memories of which many settlers naturally thrived on.

By contrast the southwest and the western coasts are as wild as the infamous Tasmanian devil, a black squat like small dog with a fierce screech to scare the early European settlers. It is the world's largest surviving carnivorous marsupial with a thick set, and a short but thick tail. It has been extinct on the mainland for about 600 years when the Aboriginal are thought to have introduced the dingo as their great rival. The west coast is virtually untouched, with Strahan being the only port of any size located on this entire stretch. Inland the forests and mountains remain dense in vegetation, although very beautiful.

This area was recently turned into a conservationist battlefield between naturalists and the reputed profiteers bent on flooding an ever-increasing amount of nature's resources, in the quest for hydroelectric power. Tasmanians have often felt enraged by their exclusion on various Australian maps. But in this instance, the island found itself on almost every news item back home at least.

In December 1982 more than ninety anti-dam protesters were arrested, as hundreds of people arrived to fight the government plans to dam the Gordon River below its junction with the Franklin, as part of these developments. They even spent about $2,000 a day in bringing in new protesters and supplies, including the influential help of British botanist Dr David Bellamy, who was flown in to add conviction and publicity to the cause. Indeed when he was subsequently arrested in a boat with his fellow supporters on the river which resulted in him spending his fiftieth birthday behind bars, the die was cast together with the eye-catching headlines that came with it.

Crossing The Bass Strait is a fourteen-hour overnight voyage, which prompted me to spend $69 instead of $58. The idea of sleeping between clean white sheets for the first time since leaving England seemed too good an opportunity to miss out on.

Tuesday 6 March

Standing onboard and leaning against the side rails is so often the first memory people have of any new destination. My first sight of Tasmania is very similar to these thoughts, in being just that, a harbour town surrounded by a high backdrop, and functional. It is simply a place to get your bearings, and prepare with some much needed provisions. I should also acknowledge the city status, due to Devonport's population now exceeding 20,000 people, and a rather sleepy baptism into island life.

My first impression concerns shop prices, which seem to be generally higher than Victoria's equivalent. For example, a small Philips radio bought in Shepparton for $7 has a retail price of $19, where my tent is advertised at $55 compared with its purchase price of $29 in Perth. This, I am informed, is reflected by reputedly the world's highest transportation costs across The Bass Strait. I now decided to begin my journey east, and slightly inland to what is the most likely destination worth checking out, before heading south. This was quite an easy journey, although what with looking around to check things out, the afternoon had already arrived when an elderly fisherman, homeward bound, stopped for my outstretched thumb.

"Last year, I picked up a hitchhiker who pulled a gun on me and demanded money together with my car keys," he said.

"What happened?" I asked.

"The armed robber was a bit dim you see. I've lived here all my life, in which case I parked behind the police station, and told him that I'd be back with the cash," he replied.

"Nice one, did he catch on?"

"No, not until the police handcuffed him. Apparently he was one of Tasmania's most wanted criminals," he remarked.

Launceston was ablaze with lighting along both sides of the

River Tamar, where I decided to try and avoid youth hostel fees. One glance across the landscape told me that darkness could only be seen on the dominant gorge, which left me with little choice. I then began the great climb skywards, and stopped at one point to pass the time of night with a group of friendly possums that took very little notice of my shady presence, even after photographing them with a flash. Eventually I found a small patch of wasteland sandwiched between numerous houses, where setting up camp appeared safe enough until a nearby dog decided to awaken the neighbourhood of my arrival.

'Damn that dog, is this waste ground, or part of a garden?'

This was public property, it seemed, squeezed either side of the path, and rarely used in the dark, if ever. In these circumstances it is only ever guesswork, as I crouched low in some shadows and felt my heart doubling its beat in anxious stutters; half expecting an owner, or a busy body to investigate the dog's mutterings, or at least to bring it in, but no nothing stirred.

I then sat on the ground and gently prepared my tent, which could be erected on all fours, and being green is almost invisible in the dark. What I didn't want was to be seen against a night sky in silhouette form, and to bring attention to myself. It was going to be a strange night, without movement huddled in the dark hidden from the dog that fortunately knew its territory, as I know mine.

Wednesday 7 March

Launceston takes its name from the said town in Cornwall, England, where no doubt some of the settlers arrived from, and needed a name to make themselves feel more at home. They also called their local hotel The Cornwall. It was from here that John

Fawkner the landlord put forward his plan to colonize Victoria in 1835. It is now the second largest in Tasmania, being 64 km inland, and 200 km north of Hobart. The first settlers arrived in the area in 1804, with the town then named Patersonia in 1805 on its foundation. Nowadays it is called the garden city, due to its abundance of parks, and a zoo.

What really springs to mind is the Cataract Gorge and the paddle steamer that regularly glides up the South Esk River, and meets the Tamar. It was a pleasant enough morning taking in the sights, and walking along the footpath into the gorge, to enjoy its sights. After which I decided to make an adjustment to my image with my hair slowly encroaching over my eyes of late. The red, white and blue headband certainly adds some colour, but a 'hippish' image is not going to entice passing motorists to my outstretched thumb. Social pressure now led me to a local hair salon, and in turn to washing my scalp in some public toilets, much to the local's amusement!

It is a fairly straight run from Launceston to Hobart, which meant travelling along the Midlands Highway, when obtaining a lift was easy enough. This time with two pensioners, who asked me to tell them if I wanted to be dropped off on route, otherwise they could take me most of the way.

The fertility and agricultural potential had encouraged early settlers to plant English trees and hedges in an effort to acclimatize to their new surroundings. It has, in turn, provided a fairly uneventful pilgrimage for hitchhikers, who are likely to come across a string of solid settlements of less than one thousand inhabitants; like Oatlands, Ross, Campbelltown, and Bothwell for example, but precisely nothing to hang around for or to be stranded at.

The one striking element is the signs of a once prosperous area of rolling hills and valleys now scorched by drought, and desperately starved of any extensive irrigation system. Progress was quick, but after Melbourne I have decided against deliberately putting myself in an isolated position.

"I'll drop you on the outskirts at Bridgewater near some parkland. You can get a bus in the morning along the Derwent and into Hobart," the husband said.

I soon thanked them and began walking up the road, just as darkness had descended.

It is amazing to think a chain gang of 160 convicts, once moved a reputed two million tons of stone to build the causeway, which is still the main crossing point on the river. Fortunately it was a warm evening, without the sign of rain, and I decided to camp just back from the road, in full view of a flyover, and the passing police cars. Nobody made any enquires though, when the whole vicinity was apparently cordoned off in an attempt to catch the culprits of a nearby burglary.

Thursday 8 March

Hobart on the south coast may seem an unlikely place to house Tasmania's capital. This has led to further widespread development, even though there may be strong merits in having it more centralized, and nearer mainland Australia. It is the smallest state capital, pretty easy going, and possesses few of the inner city hang ups, such as pollution, petrol fumes and rush hour congestion, which constantly dog Melbourne's internal workings.

More important, is that Hobart's long history has been preserved and kept to a manageable size since its formation in 1804. In a way with its mountain backdrop, and easily negotiated streets, it is hard not to like the place, apart from perhaps in the winter when the temperatures hover around the freezing point.

To counterbalance this there are plenty of historic buildings scattered about to keep the eye occupied, and the mind's imagination full of 19th Century charm.

Linking both sides of the Derwent River, and in turn my route to the Tasmania Peninsula is a fine example of Australian engineering, The Tasman Bridge.

On January 5th 1975 a bulk carrier, the Lake Illawarra, rammed into a bridge pylon, having been outside of the marked shipping lane, and sank. This in turn resulted in the Tasman's partial collapse and numerous cars falling into the water below. Two were even left hanging from a collapsed span, only for their drivers to be saved from death through the gravity of mere inches. In all twelve people reportedly died in the accident, including seven crewmen from the Australian National Line carrier and five motorists, who were trapped inside their submerged cars. Police boats and divers also rescued several people.

"A doctor's body never has been recovered, they just found his driving licence," a local remarked.

"That's a bit sad for his family," I replied.

"Yes, at least one of the vehicles is supposedly part of the rebuilt structure, because removing it posed too many engineering difficulties," he said.

The weather was somewhat overcast by afternoon when I decided against staying here for the night. Besides with the fruit picking Huon Valley to the west, I will have to hitch through here again via the small town of Sorrell that now turns south along the Arthur Highway.

Hitchhiking, as with most major cities, is difficult at the best of times. This meant another one of my long route marches towards the outskirts, and a gravel surface lay-by, where vehicles could stop safely. About one minute later a dilapidated car pulled up, with a small fishing boat on its trailer.

"Where are you going?" Mick said.

"Port Arthur," I replied.

"Hop in then, we could do with a third set of hands," Paul, his younger brother remarked.

"Why's that?"

"Fishing in our boat, the company would be good for us, three's more a party," Mick added.

"Oh alright," I said, the company will also be welcome, with an option of a return journey close at hand, as we drove through Dunally.

It was nearby that Abel Tasman became the first white man to touch these shores in November 1642. He named it Van Dieman's Land, after The President of the Dutch East Indies Shipping Company. It was officially renamed in 1856, as Tasmania in recognition of the explorer, rather than his employer.

I was not sure where we were going, the two brothers and myself, and both typically Australian. I might have been anybody, but it also has to be added here I could not scare a ghost in the dark with my boyish looks, and slight frame without an ounce of muscle. Half way between Taranna and my destination, we turned off into a forest track, and began to head towards Cape Hauy, which looks out onto Fortesque Bay. This is a trek, about 12 km, of bumps and slow progress and that 'nobody would ever find me down here.' Disappearance could be total, even the clouds looked blacker than ink, at which point I began to question a snap decision of trusting my new companions.

But I need not have worried…

Life soon found us at the edge of the water, and shielded by the trees. We then gathered together some lighting wood, and unloaded the small boat, with an outboard motor to see us into the middle of the bay. From here, and cast adrift, the car looked remarkably warm from my standpoint, with us shortly to be immersed in a deluge of torrential rain.

I have to mention that Paul and Mick were not the most dedicated of fishermen, who were more interested in their 'tinnies' than catching fish. At least there would be no twelve hour slog tomorrow, as a couple of fish were soon caught and the boys became impressed by my efforts to catch their tea.

"What are we doing here, it's freezing," I said out loud, as a cooda made haste with my bait and hook. I tried a strike only to find the weights remained in the wind, 'this is nippy nip nip!'

"Have you got another hook?" I asked Mick, who in turn looked at Paul.

"No, that's our only one."

"Do you mean you've travelled to no man's land with one hook, one rod and a boat?" I said.

"I'm afraid so, it's been a busy week," he replied.

"You berks!"

Darkness fell and I was just glad to put foot on firm land, to light a fire and then dry my drenched clothing. It has certainly been an experience with two people I have only known for about seven hours. Now here we are preparing for a cramped nights sleep. Myself on the backseat as my new friends occupy the front. I then notice a possum outside as he rummages among the hot ashes for the remnants of our evening meal.

Friday 9 March

We cooked breakfast in the morning, by revitalizing the fire, and then hitched up the boat, with a mist still descended over the bay. I rather hoped they had used up their enthusiasm for the time being, and that we could continue out of the forest and then left onto Port Arthur, 150 km southwest of Hobart. This has been an interesting diversion, simply cast adrift. But it will be nice to be back in the main stream of life, and then continue back towards Hobart.

"You can stay at my place if you like, then we can go out in the evening," Paul remarked.

"Let me think about it, I still want to see if there is anything here for me to see first," I replied.

Port Arthur was originally used, from 1830 to 1877, as a penal colony of a well-planned and solidly constructed nature, situated besides the bay. Conditions for these hardened criminals must have been almost unbearable, especially in the wet cold wintry months of June, July and August; escape was an unheard of achievement. Many tried, but nobody ever made it past Eaglehawk Neck, a narrow point of the isthmus 'between earth and hell,' 19 km north of Port Arthur, where ferocious dogs lay in wait, chained across this narrow stretch of land. Swimming or commandeering a boat was one's only real alternative to a life of misery and an unmarked grave. Today one in six Tasmanians are supposedly descended from these convicts.

In the late 19th Century a fire swept through the prison leaving only a sandstone shell as living testament to its darkest history. However, the church, model prison, watchtower and asylum have been preserved to attract 20th Century tourists from the 'four corners' of the globe to spend their much needed dollars, and on sunny days to picnic on the open waterside grassland.

Time was of an essence with me, and with a lift and shelter, the smartest option was to take up Paul's offer and spend some time in Hobart. I can at least have a taster for the nightlife, and understand some of its workings.

The real difference between the two brothers was simply

Mick was married, and Paul was single, with just a hint of a distant spring not quite in place. In this I mean who else would walk around the supermarket in broad daylight, eat the chocolate and assume nobody would notice, they didn't, but this was slowly becoming a cause for concern. What is he going to do next, set me up with the girlfriend's younger sister when we go to a bar? Then for some reason get himself paralytic on a mixture of rum and vodka, with the car outside.

At about 3am I found myself trying to awaken my new buddy slumped forward against the dashboard, while his car remained silent. I had done the right thing and relied on orange juice, with an emergency on the horizon, and now it had arrived. Besides, I needed some homeward guidance.

"Paul," I said: "How do you start it?"

"Bump start, I'll sit in the driver's seat and push the accelerator," he murmured.

I wasn't sure he was capable of even raising his head. But then reasoned that I had little choice as I put shoulder to metal, which surprisingly had the desired effect of igniting the engine.

"Here, let me drive, you can guide us," I said, opening the driver's door; at which point he hit the accelerator.

"I'm alright, it's only a mile," he replied.

I now had an instant decision to make alone in the dark. Jump into a moving car or let the fool drive off. The rucksack was at his house, although my passport remained close at hand. However tracking down somebody named Paul with fair hair and about twenty seven, might pose even the local police force some problems, and then of course only in the morning when he had sobered up. I didn't really like the look of my prospects right then, and so made the decision to jump aboard, for what was a surprisingly adept piece of driving, considering the state he was in.

It naturally felt good to find my feet on motionless ground ten minutes later. Paul had somehow managed the drive home, in relative comfort and redundant of a mishap, or a mounted pavement. How I'm not sure, for all he seemed capable of was to stagger into his house and fall across the threshold. He would be alright in the morning, with the assistance of black coffee; but for now I helped him onto his double bed and removed his shoes, when his girlfriend and her sister turned up, only to be confronted with somebody they hardly knew, and a man who seemed to be in a half crazed drunken stew.

The girl then had a few minutes alone with him, while I chatted to the sister, both pleasant and attractive at eighteen. It was a pity I will not be around from here on in, as I wished them good luck in the future, and made the coffee. Paul was now oblivious to the world and its workings. A nice guy really, but a fool to himself. I would merely check he was awake in the morning, and let myself out into the open air.

Monday 12 March

The Huon Valley is located in the peninsula directly below Hobart, and is the centre of Tasmania's apple growing industry. They also seem to be having as bad a year, as the Victorian pears, without much sign of activity in the commonwealth offices. I did though see a job advertised for picking fruit, which turned out to be at the winery just outside Cygnet, at the far end. This was something I was reluctant to do when it turned out to be for a blackberry expedition in return for the princely return of 30 cents per punnet, but an income better than nothing. In my circumstances, that $600 of mine would soon be diluted, especially with a return ticket to the mainland still to be bought.

During the night my tent proved its worth in dry clothing by keeping the overhead thunderstorm at bay. Life was going to be rather primitive here with no cooking facilities, hot water or even company. I'm going to get quite lonely, especially as the nearest shop is three miles away, while rain will see me twiddling my fingers undercover. This might prove to be the low point of my time down under. Tomorrow morning I will break camp before daybreak, and make my way back up the muddy farm track, without explanation, and continue on my way. There are plenty of blackberries in England...

Wednesday 14 March

I have made no real progress over these two days. It would be nice to lament my bad luck, but that would be inaccurate in searching out the area. Firstly towards Huonville, via a school bus and the local postman, where I noticed the many orchards again seemed very thin of apples at this the height of season, which admittedly dampened my enthusiasm. At $11 a bin, with no relevant accommodation and those pear-picking memories still fresh in mind, I again decided to abandon this idea forthwith. There is nothing to this small town that can be reported, indeed for some reason, it was simply decided to abandon these job-hunting efforts and regroup my thoughts in Hobart. I can always come back for a second attempt, if all else fail. Things are still comparatively healthy.

I therefore headed towards Dover, a nice little coastal town, without the famous white cliffs, south of here. The north of England is also represented by Southport, looking out at its own bay. But it is the small town of Hastings I finally found myself in wandering around aimlessly, and notching up another highway. This time I discovered Adamson Peak amid another rainstorm. All of which meant sheltering in a nearby swimming pool lodge, where I made a fire in a barbeque area, and watched the rain falling for about two hours, without anything else to do.

The notice board records that the water: 'Stays at a constant temperature of 27°C due to diverted spring water. Cold water (14°C) is acid from natural tannins where the various streams interlock. It is interesting to compare the natural waters' tea colour when the spring water is almost transparent.'

After following a guided tour around the Newgate Caves to see some skilfully illuminated stalagmites and stalactites, I caught a lift back to Hobart with Steve and Debbie, a young Queensland couple, who even persuaded me to make use of their spare $30 a night hotel room.

"The company we work for made a mistake by booking two singles. You are welcome to take advantage of it, nobody will mind," Steve remarked.

"Thank you very much," I replied.

It certainly solves two problems with one stone, and in effect that should be three. When in the late afternoon, amid a slowly fading light, we drove up the barren, almost desolate slopes of Mount Wellington (1270 metres) towards its gale force summit, barely with time to see our objective in the wind.

Far below I could see Hobart surrounded majestically with rising mountain ranges and an elegant succession of bays and inlets, enabling the Derwent Estuary to claim its worth rivalling Sydney's apparent waterway of riches; suddenly in an instant the mists appeared to fall over our heads as Hobart below began its disappearing act before my eyes, and I realised that nobody can claim to have seen Tasmania without experiencing such a beauty of delight.

Thursday 15 March

I left the hotel early on, and thanked my friends for their thoughtful gesture, before retracing my footsteps over the Tasman Bridge; and began my days hitchhiking opposite Mick's lay-by; this time towards the small town of Richmond, and just 27 km northeast of Hobart.

This was not one of my most successful of days in terms of progress, as it took me time and three lifts to complete the task, with a spot of walking for good measure. I also began to get a few distant looks, or to my imagination, with one in particular driving past and noting my appearance. This was at odds with their mature years when life was indeed invariably difficult and standards more defined in marriage and social structures, when people stayed together for life, but how things have changed. It was here I had some creative thoughts, and began to note the following, as if people from another era might have remarked to their spouse:

'Oh no, there's another one of those hitchhikers. What an existence! Haven't they got a home, or has the young generation lost its pride to better themselves, instead of begging a cheap lift, and scrounging more like. Why can't they find some work like we had to? Perhaps then I could respect them. In my day we had to improve our lot by sheer hard graft, but now they expect everything to be given to them on a silver tray. Why some ever attended school I'll never know. Anyway I'm just glad that I shan't be here to clear up the mess, after this bunch have had their day!'

I shortly arrived in Richmond, which had the usual stream of day-trippers who come here every day from their hotels to walk across the bridge, constructed in 1824 at the time of the town's foundation. But it is not much in comparison to its namesake,

Richmond on Thames, with its swanky setting, and expensive lifestyles of the rich and famous; the pop stars, and their chauffeur driven limousines parked outside expensive restaurants, together with a bill to match.

There is the river gushing by, as you stand alongside the Ship Inn and chat among yourselves with a drink in hand. The people are always there on a Friday night standing outside, or sitting on a lush green bank with their misplaced plastic glasses strewn about, and cigarette stubs with the sprinkling of rubbish all around, just down from the bridge. London traffic also roars overhead, with the boatyards in full flow below, and the occasional pleasure cruiser gliding past. The high tide invariably comes right up to the edges, in this most vibrant of settings.

I thought of all this, and so far away from here. The surrounding countryside is arid, and so lifeless, that the river remains bone dry and without water. There was no need to worry about getting wet feet as I jumped off the bank and walked into the centre. I felt somewhat disappointed without the flow underneath the sandstone structure, now isolated and really quite charming, just waiting for a tidal wave of water to re-ignite its being, or a sense of purpose.

I now did as 'everybody' does here and take a picture through the arches of St Johns, built in 1836. This is the oldest Catholic Church in Australia, perched on a small rise. I had to try a number of times in deciding on how many arches, and the distance away, but it didn't matter. I had time in these hot temperatures to please myself; where the tourists begin to walk away for their dinnertime tipple, or for a trip to the local jail that dates back to 1825.

You see; there were a lot of convicts around here at the time…

Friday 16 March

I made my way due west this morning through Bridgewater, and into the familiar sounding New Norfolk; named as such by the Norfolk Islander's who abandoned their settlement in 1808. They were reallocated here, which now gives them a very English feel to their surrounds, with it being the centre of the hop growing area. This was of recent relevance to me and that perhaps something might crop up to my advantage.

By now I was getting a little tired of this job-hunting lark; also the town is without a CES employment office. The nearest is further down the Derwent towards Hobart, at Glenorchy. 'Problems, problems,' with the many hop farms seen either side of the river. I drew a blank on my initial enquires, but at least a local grower directed me towards the small town of Bushy Park: "Where you might be lucky," he remarked.

Temptation told me to pack up this useless traipsing around and to hitch on to Queenstown, an old mining town, which admittedly caught me in two minds, when those doubts started to creep in. Perhaps I might actually find a job. After all in my favour, is that I have just completed the hop harvest in Kent only six months ago. This should help convince somebody of my worth, and its relevance, or that I was more likely to stay the course than the usual array of rookies who think the hop harvest is a picnic waiting to happen.

I now went out onto the road and began my journey up the valley in noting the scorched surrounding hills, and wondered if this was going to be worthwhile without such nourishment. This has been a particularly long drought lasting for the past two years, and where the local growers have more than ever before relied on a system of irrigation to protect their livelihood.

My lift was about forty-five, lived here during his upbringing and only recently returned to his family home, after what seems to have been his recent divorce. Indeed I am not even sure if Dave has ever left this island before. It's a bit isolated and means a real get up and go attitude is needed, rather than the opportunity to nip over to France for a daytrip.

"How long are you staying?"

"That depends on the work situation."

"I'll take you up to the estate manager's office, I know him, a decent kind that will help if he can," Dave replied.

"Well thanks very much, an introduction can only help," I said.

Bushy Park turned out to be situated in a dip, with the hop vines surrounding the town in a square shape, and all green with nourishment, at its heart. This will do, a nice homely place to live with a touch of England in the autumn.

"I'm sorry, all the jobs have been allocated weeks ago," the estate manager replied, to my enquiry.

"It was just a thought," I said, and admittedly somewhat disappointed.

"Look, why don't you camp on our showground until Monday, then report to us at about 10am. There is always somebody who doesn't turn up, I'll make you first reserve." he said.

"Thank you," I replied, with an upbeat tone to my voice.

"See you first thing Monday."

Saturday 24 March

Fortune has certainly been kind to me, as I found myself employed in the hop kiln during the unearthly hours of 10.30pm to 6.30am, which might explain why the allotted employee decided against this task. The shift consists of Les, an experienced hop drier nearing retirement and myself, his able assistant.

My job is simply to look after the ground floor, where the hops are pressed into sacks, which I am responsible for fixing onto the machine and for stitching them together or possibly the easiest job imaginable. The hops are dried upstairs and laid out across the floor, in an even carpet, all green and somewhat greasy on your hands, which fortunately neither of us needs to touch.

Looking across this huge expanse from the day's efforts, it is hard to imagine we are left with only three giant bails at the end of the evening, or around the early hours that is. This is the problem, the drying has to be continuous throughout the harvest time to keep pace and to know when the hops are dry, but not overheated, which is where Les comes in. It is his decision; he constantly checks the four kilns and decides when the time is right.

In a way this is a one man job, apart from the fact that a second pair of hands is needed to hold the bales downstairs and give the signal to switch on and off the conveyor belt. Les works upstairs checking the hops and decides if they are dry enough to continue. Too much heat, and like all leaves the nourishment would be turned to a crisp leaf and be wasted. In an essence, this was the most important stage of the whole process, and where the owners knew a lot of money could be lost if it is not done properly.

I naturally feel pretty pleased with a job that is now paying $6.50 an hour. There is no heavy lifting, time to get bored or even being scratched from the hop vines that never actually reach this stage. More importantly working indoors keeps me out of the elements, where work goes on regardless. Past experience tells me that cutting down vines, and transporting them with tractors and trailer, or merely hanging the vines on hooks for the thrashing machine can be sheer misery in rainstorms, and freezing on the hands during the early daylight hours.

It has to be admitted that a sudden change to the biological pattern of life has soon thrown my entire body into a kind of turmoil that will have to be adjusted to over the course of time, and a reoccurring pattern of trying to sleep in the day. By 3am, on my first watch, I was feeling groggy and deadbeat; without having had any prior warning of my job until the afternoon, I could hardy risk saying 'not until tomorrow!'

My only alarm arrived one night when the owner came around on a surprise visit, to find me slumped on the side of the hops, with Les simply staring into the lurgy green.

"That's no good," the farmer remarked, at two hours before dawn.

"He's alright," Les replied.

"Are you sure?" he persisted.

"Quite so," Les said, much to my gratitude, the fatigue would invariably soon wear off when breakfast time approached.

Sleeping in the tent pitched besides a fresh flowing stream during the day is particularly difficult, due to a rush of mid-day sunshine. Then come Saturday morning I felt physically exhausted. Little things like climbing stairs became such an effort that walking 4 km to and from work, on my 'quicksand' existence, made the trek seem more like 4 miles. Next week I shall be more prepared as Jarv, my only neighbour, has lent me an alarm clock! Previously I have been too worried about oversleeping and losing my job to get any shuteye.

The showground is quite spacious in its layout and provides us with ample space to camp an army in if need be. With only one other tent pitched besides the river, I had decided to do likewise. I could not see anyone, but the company might be useful. I could always find an excuse to move if need be, or that a couple might want their privacy a little more than me breathing down their neck. But this was not necessary, when my new friend turned out to be an ex-university student who decided that examinations were not for him.

"Instead I borrowed the money for the flight. A friend had already sorted out this job for me before I left," he said.

"How long are you staying in Australia?" I asked, during one of our mid-evening conversations, and cross-legged around his Bunsen burner.

"Oh, not long. I want to get home for a concert in about five week's time. I'll be able to repay the airfare then," he said.

"Don't you want to see anything else of Australia, or even explore Tasmania?"

"No not really. I just got off the plane, and caught the bus to Bushy Park. Perhaps I might spend a couple of days in Hobart," he replied.

"But why?"

"Because my parents kept saying I should do something with my life, in which case I decided to keep out of the way and lie low for a month," he said.

"Then enjoy the spring back home… nice one," I remarked.

Sunday 25 March

I had a spare day to enjoy the comforts of a secure lifestyle for once, on the veranda with Dave, my original lift into Bushy Park at his house. His life has hit a psychological low point, while he comes to terms with the death of his elderly mother. The problem also concerns their old colonial house, which must be sold for death duties, in order to fulfil a Will that takes account of his thirteen brothers and sisters.

It was certainly good to soak in a hot bath, and to relax my thoughts away from the greasy hop aroma of my tent, or the cold flow of my daily dip into the local river besides our tents. I'm told the water is clean and drinkable. But you never know a bug might find its way into my system. And what about my cloths, the dark green slime is going to be an interesting experience for the local washing machines!

We drove around in the afternoon and spent our time admiring the surrounding countryside, strangely arid in its environment with Bushy Park's green oasis cast adrift. In a way this is a small 'English village' rather than an Australian town, with two small stores and a post office. I was also quiet intrigued to read that the first person to settle in the Styx valley was A.W.H Humphrey who arrived here in about 1812, when the settlement became known as Humphreyville for a short time, before the name was changed to Bushy Park. The Hops arrived when Ebenezer Shoobridge moved here in 1867; he therefore continued his father's business interests and made Bushy Park the centre of the Tasmanian hop harvest. His father, William, arrived in Van Dieman's Land in 1822 with some plants and is thought to have been the first man to grow hops in Tasmania, although this has never been confirmed.

Dave is a bit distant though, with his mind cast in the shadows of the recent past. Any moral support I can give seemed appropriate. Besides everybody steps into a pothole at sometime in life, and after all it was Dave who put in a good word for me at the estate office, in lending my face relevance to the current situation.

"You know only a couple of years back I had a wife and four lovely children to watch grow up," he remarked.

"And now?" I said, "You still have your kids."

"I'm not sure, perhaps I might start a new life in Sydney,

where my aunt lives," he replied, and obviously lacking the confidence that divorce brings with it.

"Time is a great healer," I said.

"Sure appreciate your company lad, you seem to have such a fresh attitude towards life, are you sure you have never been married?" he said.

"No never, too young," I replied.

"Here have a look at these photographs, this is my eldest son who is twenty two now," he remarked, as I listened in the light breeze and enjoyed the atmosphere of an English woodland on the mountain slopes before us.

Sunday 1 April

By working different shifts this meant that Jarv and myself only had Sundays to explore the surrounding area, or simply sit outside our tents and discuss all the intricacies of life; to the larger picture, and something that I found both refreshing and enlightening, together with some of his observations. In some respects we were rowing in the same direction, but with different approaches that I could relate to, over a brew each evening before I went off to the kiln and my ally Les.

We decided to hitchhike 110 km west this morning through some sparsely motorised parkland to the oddly constructed small town of Strathgordon. This is one of those functional places without people or the sign of a shop; rather inhabitants seem to work here and stay indoors, or have their families elsewhere. Certainly there is nothing much to do except wait for the hunting season to arrive, only to get lost in the wilderness. Almost every building is prefabricated in order to accommodate the workforce of the nearby Gordon Dam, further on through this conservation area bisecting Lake Gordon, and Lake Pedder to the south; the

Franklin is north of here on the other side of Mount Humboldt.

This was one of those enthusiastic ventures that had it gone wrong might have cost me my job, but as it happened, two lifts in easy fashion was all we needed to do the trip, there and back before 6pm. It was here that we were able to travel one thousand metres underground in a specially constructed coach which can be steered from both the front and the back, due to the impossibility of turning around in a dead-end tunnel. The end product is an illuminated dungeon, with the generating room oddly cut off from the rest of society, and really worth our efforts.

"Good idea of yours," Jarv remarked.

The island has the largest hydroelectric power station in the country to date, and generates some ten per cent of Australia's power base; even more than its equivalent in the Snowy Mountains. The inevitable controversy has been going on concerning environmental groups, and green peace issues ever since the first construction on the Great Lake in 1911; followed by the Derwent, Forth, Gordon, and Mersey dams. It was the flooding of the Pedder that first attracted the outcries that irreplaceable damage was being done to this wild domain. Big business was driving on this self willed destruction, against the thoughts of the people of Tasmania and an argument which is set to run and run for some considerable time to come yet.

It was a nice stroll, in the early autumn leaves, with the sunlight shining bright as we made our way back towards the showground, and over a fresh flowing stream fit nicely for a children's game of Pooh sticks. We couldn't resist, and neither should we have, the water was flowing nicely as two adults indulged themselves in a bit of stick racing and the thoughts of a dumb bear famous for his exploits on Ashdown Forest, or just around the corner from my Sussex hidey hole. We tried to convince two youngsters, but they didn't seem to know anything about watching sticks floating under a bridge, and that the fastest stick won. What was even worse, they were not even interested.

"You haven't lived!" I remarked; then noted the horse chestnut tree nearby and the old English traditional art of conkers, whereby string is tied through its centre. The participants then proceed to bash each other's target in turn, until one remains smashed amongst the freshly fallen leaves.

"An old trick is to soak them in vinegar, it hardens the shell," I said, and somewhat surprised that the traditional terms of strings has also somehow been missed out on the backwaters of Tasmanian life.

"Didn't you learn anything at school!"

And still a blank face, no two blank faces starred at this alien being.

"What happens if neither breaks?" one said, and equally baffled by my enthusiasm at such matters, but at least he spoke, which was an improvement. This was hard work; they grow up too soon around here.

"Oh, that's simple we pull the opponent's string out of his hand and stamp on their conker!" I replied, but they didn't laugh.

It was time to go.

Sunday 8 April

Not wanting to sit around and waste our time we decided to undertake a far shorter journey west, towards the Mount Field National Park. This has some 16,212 hectares of mountain rising 1,524 metres in height together with forestry of exquisite beauty, wild canyons, lakes and an uncountable number of waterfalls, mountain streams and shady ferns for us to explore.

Through the forest we followed a clearly marked path, dotted with red painted cans on sticks. There would be no chance of getting lost unlike on other routes into the wilderness. Underfoot the rugged rocky surface slowed us down considerably due to the risks of twisting or breaking an ankle and never a good idea to hurry at such times, rather best to set an easier goal. The rain also tried to dampen our spirits. But today we were not to be dismayed, as Beatles' mania struck these slopes coupled with The Rolling Stones supporting our vocal chords. It wasn't a pretty sound lost in the wind, but it made us happy and passed some of the more mundane moments.

The summit of Mount Field East was in the tradition of all desolate mountain regions; wet, cold and miserable, as we finally crouched in a small rock constructed shelter for our daily dosage of bread and jam sandwiches.

"This is more like it," I remarked, and wondered why he didn't seem so interested in broadening his Australian outlook, after encompassing the past two Sundays with renewed enthusiasm.

"Darkness is only three hours away, I think the mist is about to set in," Jarv almost shouted, with the wind howling aloud.

"A quick photograph, then it's heads down before the storm sets in, the clouds are looking ominous," I replied, and wondered as ever, why I found myself in such an inhospitable climate. When we again reached the safety of life below the darkness had drifted away and again reached our base in the autumn glow of another fine day.

Tuesday 10 April

The casual workforces, of perhaps 20 people, were laid off at 2.30pm, because Bushy Park's regular contingent could now finish the harvesting themselves. During these final ten working days I ended up doing a double shift due to three different people relinquishing their services by not actually turning up, much to my delight on each occasion. Besides, the sands of time were extremely limited from my point of view. Sixteen-hour days have proved to be a pretty shattering experience on about five hours sleep, with a counterbalance to my finance that has now rocketed to an unprecedented $1,600.

"It's OK I can do both shifts, the eyes will recover," I remarked.

Les had very little to say most of the time, but it was not difficult to like him. After three weeks together he felt a kind of bond towards me from afar, with the enthusiasm to keep going and wanted me to remember my time here, with the fond memories that I undoubtedly have. I don't even know if he is married, only that he has spent his life among the hop vines and appreciated the company. He might retire soon, but this is probably a way of life that has seen him outside for most of it, judging by his windswept looks.

"When did you start?" he said, as he silently went about his job of rolling a white sack across the floor. Les dipped an iron brand of black paint on it, in the sign of a black horse rearing into the air, with the word Coniston underneath, then three stars and finally at the bottom 19.3.84.

He then wrapped it up in giving it to me as a souvenir, and one of those memorabilia, that are worth so much more than money can buy. Back home I shall put it on display and people will wonder why. But then you have to be here to see and remember, which is what this lifestyle is all about. The people and their variations that I have become so accustomed to, and long shall it remain so.

Friday 13 April

Bushy Park has now been turned into a barren remnant of three weeks, since fields full of twelve foot high hop vines have been replaced by a sea of upright poles connected with pieces of twine, which once created a canopy of fresh green hops. Our mammoth farewell campfire bash last night somehow dwindled to Jarv and myself munching ourselves silly on beef burgers in the company of a couple of Tasmanian biker boys, who had little to say through their heavy beards, and were more intrigued by our presence than anything else. For them the outside world did not seem to exist.

"I may stay in Tasmania for a couple of weeks, but I need to be back by the May bank holiday," Jarv remarked.

Even Dave failed to turn up due to another family funeral. I guess life is like that sometimes. Nothing much undue happens in most of our lives, and then suddenly out of nowhere the domino effect begins an unprecedented run of misfortune. I now wished him luck as he sat in his car watching us break camp, and somewhat distant of my voice.

"Chin up, Dave. I'll write to you," I said, but his troubled mind hardly registered, still in deep thought. I felt sorry and tried to smile, which he acknowledged during this rather distant farewell performance from behind the wheel, with the window down. He didn't even get out of the car, and then he was gone… driving off across the showground.

Saturday 14 April

This morning I managed to reach the small east coast town of Swansea located on Oyster Bay, by cutting across, and joining the Tasman Highway along the coastline. Yesterday the place might have been bursting with life, but this morning a blustery sea breeze has reduced Swansea into a sullen mass of sleepy pedestrians wandering around aimlessly in one's and two's.

There is not much to keep one here, except for a pioneer's museum depicting life since the 1820s and how people used to cope before the invention of communications and the supermarket; rather it proved a refreshing pit stop before an 'Irish' family gave me a lift in their campervan, Mum, Dad and their thirty-year old son, since they had seen me sitting on some steps drinking a litre of milk in the town. Then saw me on the outskirts of nowhere, and admired my attitude that said, get up and go.

"Thirty km in four hours seems pretty slow going," Paul said.

"That's how it goes sometimes, be patient and see what happens. I've got a couple of days to spare as yet," I said.

By dusk we had reached the long coastal beachfront of Scamander, where I pitched the tent besides my campervan friends on a sandy verge.

"You want to watch where you camp, that green's almost invisible. Other motorists parking up might run you over," one remarked.

"Thanks, I'll remember that," I replied, and a very good point. It's happened to other hikers, in which case I'd better be more careful in the future.

I shortly joined Paul in the campervan; his parents went to bed fairly early on to catch up on their sleep, which left us to swap tales, when I could see he was glad of being outside his parental guidance.

"Never go on holiday with your parents, they never stop giving you advice," he said, as if to say this was the last time.

Indeed talk of The Philippines sparked some interesting ideas for future plans. My only regret to date has been that we didn't make use of a stopover on our flight to Australia, not that we could have afforded one. Even so it is something to keep in mind or try to rectify next time around, and was an opportunity missed that I'm keen to make up for.

"You've got to be very careful all the time, never walk up any dark alleys by yourself," he said.

"I thought the people were supposed to be friendly," I remarked.

"Oh they are, and too friendly at times. I bought a girl for the night, only to discover her going through my trousers in the early hours," he replied.

"What did you do?"

"I just gave her one of those looks as if to say, don't even think about it," he said, in a thoughtful way.

"And a real lady of the night!"

"Yes, I hid my wallet under the bed, so there was nothing for her to steal," he said.

"She left early the next morning for the agreed amount."

Sunday 15 April

I began my day very much as I finished with my campervan family, who seemed to like the variation that another voice brought to their trip, around this island. The next place up ahead is the largest on this coast, St Helens, with less than a thousand inhabitants. It is a fair bet that most people know each other around here, or have moved away for the duration. The most important catch is crayfish, which is the main source of income for the families to live on. But again there is nothing left for me to see. With a lift in tow, it seemed wise to stay onboard for as long as possible, when my route starts to draw inland towards the forested slopes, and dairy valleys of Tasmania's northeast corner.

I remained with my new friends for the morning as they stopped for a picnic lunch at Ringarooma Bridge before driving on to Scotsdale, with its idyllic setting, and the parting of our ways. Bert wanted to do something north of here in Bridport, a beachfront resort, while Paul remained quiet in thought with his parents in earshot, more than like feeling suffocated.

I don't know his situation, past, or even his job, only they came from the mainland, and that he gave me the idea of visiting the Philippines. Sometimes parents tend to pull up their off-spring in contradictions, or even through inquisitive interest, which any detached individual could say without the slightest sign of relevance to them. Mothers often want their sons married, secure in their own eyes, and invariably forget the bigger picture of a person's own thoughts and aspirations. They see tying their lives to such commitments, sometimes with blinkered vision, and that this just might not be the one to be relied upon!

Tuesday 17 April

Hitchhiking beyond Launceston, where I re-visited my possum friends and completed the 434 km round trip from Hobart, and along the north coast has admittedly provided a rather tame finale to my time in Tasmania, especially when daylight draws to an end by 5.30pm, for unfortunately winter is rapidly approaching these shores, and with it my thoughts of a warmer climate.

Industrial Burnie, with its paper mills, came and went in an afternoon while at Somerset I did consider a 200 km excursion trip towards Queenstown. But then why risk missing the ferry on Thursday. The job is done and I have seen a nice cross section of what the island has to offer. It has fed my memory bank with a host full of positives in achieving the two objectives I set out with.

Nonchalant Smithtown signals an end to any kind of habitation worth speaking of. This in turn meant backtracking 22 km, amid a dull drizzle to Stanley, an uninspiring name, and a rather uninspiring few days really, or damp squid-like.

A giant nut shaped mount volcanic in origin, and composed of hard blue basalt dominates my memory here. This rises to 152 metres high over a murky looking Bass Strait, which shadows the town. Its flat top area is approximately forty hectares in size, and takes about half an hour to walk around via an easily recognizable footpath running through thick grass, the odd tree, and patches of scrub to surround my relaxed body.

I now sat on a rock, and enjoyed the refreshing sea breeze as it sweeps through my brown hair, and entangling the curls into a knotted mass; my mind now begins to focus itself on mainland Australia. Martin is out there somewhere, and how has he fared. We are certainly a long way from home, it's only now that I begin to think about him and did he receive my letter. Things were certainly 'touch and go' in the pear orchards for a time, but somehow we managed to find that last dollar, and a valuable few days that kept us above water. It is certainly nice to be in the black, and back with the real world.

The rains soon had the final say; when descending I found myself on the flat and walking through the gloom, with the clouds looking more beast, than friend. I will now have to camp under a tree, and then find a nice piece of safety above Devonport, to lay up early in preparation for the ferry's nightly crossing.

6. Canberra

I did not have much of a game plan when I walked down the tow plank at that precise moment. The post office would have to be first, anything might have happened in the past six weeks. Tasmania had left me out of contact with the world I once knew, when a hand waved itself out of the crowd, and caught the eye. For once I was glad to admit it was not a virgin damsel, or anything like it, but Martin in person.

"What are you doing here?"

It was a great moment, as we shook hands.

"I had to see some friends in Melbourne and thought to hang around when I got your letter," he replied.

He now explained that when he left he did not have a clue what to do. It was more a case of being fed up with the orchards, and not getting anywhere rather than our company of fruit pickers. This eventually led him to Myrtleford, a small winery town southeast of Shepparton, and towards the mountains.

"It's been a back breaking experience bending over all day. The early mornings are beginning to freeze up now, so I'm glad my immediate financial worries are on hold," he remarked, in obvious relief.

"Let's not hang around Melbourne, those clouds make this place grey in character," I remarked, at which point I decided that my post will have to be forwarded on to Sydney. The news will have to wait; what we really need to do now is to reach the edge of the city and at least find some space to camp on if need be.

The Sydney Road is perhaps 10 km from Melbourne's city centre, where hitching is possible and naturally we had many

subjects to converse on.

"I'm getting slightly fed up with this hiking lark, New Zealand can be left out this time, besides I did it before," he said.

"So you're leaving me to soldier on alone, I'll look up your friends when the time comes, it's too far for me to return; the opportunity might never arise again," I replied, and none too surprised.

Martin then went on to tell me about a Philippine woman, who gave him a lift after leaving the pear orchards.

"On route we stopped at this huge colonial mansion, where I was invited into a marital squabble involving her husband and his ex-Australian wife," he remarked.

An argument raged across the conference table for over ten minutes concerning maintenance payments. The fat, slightly balding, husband even turned on my friend at one stage with a 'you've got yourself in a right mess mate' comment, before he ended the proceedings with an impertinent door slamming show of stubbornness.

"Hang on a minute, I do believe we've got a lift at last," I interrupted.

"I'm only going to the edge of Melbourne," the young man said.

"No problem, every metre saves the holes in our boots!"

We were dropped in a prime position for tomorrow.

"Anyway after the old misery left," Marty continued in the fading light. "The Australian woman cooked us a king-sized meal. Her plan was to drop me on the highway and then collect me an hour later, after no doubt the 'two wives' had settled a few arguments."

"It all sounds a bit odd," I said.

"Crazy really, but it saved any embarrassment, and I got to sleep in a real bed for a change," he said, as we began to notice the ever-darkening clouds overhead.

Hitching any further was pointless in the dark, we had achieved our objective, and now a piece of waste ground would serve our purpose nicely. We were indeed in for a drenching, when we put one tent up and squeezed into our damp environment. There was nobody about, and nobody cared; this was a night to stay inside, if only under canvas, with a spin dryer unbeknown to us a stone's throw away.

Saturday 21 April

We were soon back on the highway, nicely out of the rush hour traffic, and made early progress this morning in staying together. Our lives are much more relaxed than in January, and time is not so important to us, with one day being very much the same as another.

By mid afternoon we had reached Wangaratta, east of Shepparton, where it seemed we might have to stay for the night, when preferring to sit in a café for an hour, with darkness now behind us. This is the gateway to the Alps, and Mount Buffalo, which acts as an interesting departure for the old gold mining towns and the wineries. It is also a short distance from Martin's tobacco farm, but he didn't seem interested in showing me around; I guess he is only too glad to be leaving Victoria at long last.

Our only concern is, with a population of 16,000 people, it makes this is a built up domain and in the dark could cause us problems. We then began our walk along a busy highway with the drivers thinking of their home life, or a night out. I had to check the day there and then; to note it is the weekend and even a bank holiday one at that.

Walking along I was surprised to see a fellow hitchhiker and simply nodded a hello, while Martin remarked: "You'll be lucky to reach Sydney tonight mate!"

"I bet he felt really encouraged by that," I replied, and was also somewhat pessimistic of our own chances of finding a safe place for tonight.

'Fortunately' Roger, a young air force trainee, presently picked up all three of us, with Martin and myself eventually clinging onto the backseats. It was one of those times when you just wanted the driver to concentrate on what he was doing, and hope that some of his over-taking was not as risky as it seemed from the backseat.

In many ways I was busy trying to think of an excuse why we might stop, and in daylight that is always an option. But not when you can't see a thing, and do not know the terrain. On the other hand it has to be admitted that the lights up ahead can so often prove misleading in the distance, due to the straight-line contours, and our inexperience behind the wheel in these parts.

None of us spoke, and let's just hope he stays on the road as I began to think of the 1950s movie star James Dean and his final wreck on the highway. Perhaps I'm exaggerating somewhat. Martin did later agree that Roger's driving had been too fast for the roads, which tend to be full of wildlife at any given time, but he also seemed less concerned.

"You can stay at my place tonight. I have plenty of space in the living room, you will never get a lift out of Wagga Wagga," Roger remarked, in the dark.

I however, was just glad to meet his parents who lived in a suburb, along one of these pleasant housing estates that tend to appear when the population begins to increase with an overflow looking to stay in the area. This turned into one of those 'embarrassing' moments, when people are looking forward to their son's imminent arrival, and can become his parents once more. His mother might even be looking forward to the dirty washing and an added meal on the table; not three complete strangers unexpectedly thrust upon themselves, who even their offspring had not seen in the light, standing behind their son at the front door.

"It's alright, they are all welcome," Roger's father said, and rather liked the adventure of it all, away from the norm, with tomorrow being Easter Day!

Sunday 22 April

Martin was not too interested in Canberra, having been there on an excursion trip from the tobacco plantation, and was far keener on a fresh impetus to his life, in making some new contacts for us, as an advanced 'party.' This suited me, another big city looms ahead, and if he can do the groundwork, who then could complain. We now arranged to meet up in Sydney on Sunday, which gave us both plenty of time to do whatever, and to hitch out of Wagga Wagga, at the heart of a busy farming community.

This also meant a split journey at the Yass turn off, where the Barton Highway, divides with the Hume. It is named after the explorer, Hamilton Hume, who lived in Yass for about forty years, which today is sparsely populated in terms of traffic. I now said goodbye to Marty, and watched his image disappear into the heat and crossed the road, to begin the walk, in giving myself a decent chance of being picked up and soon found a lay-by.

The traffic was indeed slow today, but this is a national holiday. In any case it still seemed strange standing there, and thinking that this is the main route into the capital of Australia, and what a place to put it! Sure enough things ran smoothly enough when a campervan stopped, with a father and son combination onboard, having driven up from Melbourne for a couple of days to see some of his family.

"My wife has stayed at home with our daughter who is not well with tonsillitis. She thought it might be good for us do a bit of bonding with our children individually otherwise we might all be miserable this Easter, and then ill afterwards. We will be back on Wednesday," the bearded father said, about fifty, with just a tint of grey now appearing. "Would you like to join us for a barbeque further on, it's just that we are going to pull up just short of the city, and then go on in the morning, so to avoid arriving late. We are early you see, my aunt is not expecting us until the morning."

"Sure why not," I replied, what is another day in the wider picture, and with hot dogs and beer thrown in for good measure! I was only too glad to keep them company, camp under a tree for the night and to enjoy a cup of tea in the morning.

"You've got to watch Fitzroy play the Sydney Swans on Saturday," the young son said. They are their local team, and the figment of a dream that will one day see them in the grand final.

"I only wish we could be there," his father remarked, with one of those wishful sighs that many married men seem to hold dear to their heart, and a spot of diversification.

Tuesday 24 April

Canberra was nice and calm when I walked the route towards my first objective this morning, the New Federal Parliament. It is being built to coincide with Australia's two hundred years centenary celebrations to be held in 1988. A model of the finished building, in a nearby museum, will certainly make it a Parliament to be proud of. But unfortunately the 1,200 workforces have been on strike for over eight weeks due to an industrial dispute concerning bonus payments at the completion date.

Directly in front stands the temporary Parliament, which has housed the various Australian governments since 1927. It has taken that long to develop the original design by the American Walter Burley Griffith in 1913. The planning came as a direct result of the Federation of Australia in 1901 and the need to have a permanent capital city.

It was not until 1908 that a site was diplomatically situated directly between Melbourne and Sydney; due to their intense rivalry that each should be Australia's capital.

Paul Maguire best illustrates this in his book *An Australian Journey* (1939):

'In 1920 the Prince of Wales laid a foundation stone of Parliament House. The stone stood upon Capital Hill until it was almost whittled away by souvenir hunters. Nowadays they are more careful of foundation stones in Canberra, which is largely a city of foundations-stones, and are inevitably carried off and locked up once they have been officially laid.'

The Australian Colonies Act of 1850 bestowed considerable self-government rights on each state, which developed separately, with little coordination taken into account. They introduced different laws, and even built railways with different gauge lines. Negotiations began in 1891 towards a Federation, which finally became a reality on January 1st 1901. The Commonwealth of Australia came into being, with Sir Edmund Barton as its first Prime Minster.

Australia is similar in political structure to Britain, and to a lesser extent, the United States, with its elected Senate and House of Representatives (Parliament), and a strong central government headed by the Prime Minister, and leader of the ruling party. Each state in turn, has its own government enjoying limited authority. Canberra is also responsible for its surrounding Australian Capital Territory, the Northern Territories and Australia's external Territories. As a step forward, to self-government, the Northern Territories Act with restricted powers, was established in July 1978. There are also roughly 900 local government bodies at city, town, municipality or county level.

The basic law of Australia is the country's Federal Constitution with the states also having their own 'watered down' version, whereby several different authorities govern sixteen million people. Australia is an independent country, and maintains a close relationship with Britain.

Queen Elizabeth II is also formally Queen of Australia, and the Head of State. A Governor General, and six state governors in turn represent her. All are designated by the respective powers and appointed by Her Majesty on their recommendation. Only in extraordinary circumstances does the governor act on the advice of the elected ministers, but they do hold 'reserve power' which enable them to act independently in cases of extreme crisis, as happened in 1974.

On this occasion, an emergency developed because the ruling Labor Party could not get the Bill to supply $170 million (money to run the country) through Parliament's Upper House, even though Billy Snedden's, Liberal Country party, were in effect breaking the Constitution. The ensuing election during May failed to break this deadlock with Gough Whitlam remaining Prime Minister.

Malcolm Fraser in turn became leader of the opposition, by replacing Snedden. He insisted that Labor's Lower House majority gave it the right to govern. Only in exceptional circumstances would he refuse, but then Fraser was not prepared to speculate what these issues might be.

The country was at low ebb with record inflation, taxation, rising unemployment, and industrial stoppages. Then came Whitlam's European tour in which he protested against Australia's recognition of the Soviet Union's incorporation of the Baltic States with some unfortunate comments concerning 'bloody Nazi bitches,' that resulted in Labor's state defeats in both Queensland and South Australia. Fraser now only needed an issue to force an election, which he chose to be the Government's loan raising activities.

Sir John Kerr, the Governor General, then appointed Fraser as acting Prime Minister, whose task it was to get the Supply Bill through Parliament with elections pending, but this led to unheard of controversy. Terms like 'Coup d'Etat,' and 'Putsch' were aired in the press, as the nation fumed over the Governor General intervening in such a delicate issue of who indeed runs Australia, and why not Whitlam to head a caretaker Government.

In effect, Britain's representative had sacked Australia's leading public figure. Whitlam told the crowd, which had assembled to hear the proclamation dissolving parliament: "Ladies and gentlemen, we'll may be say God Save the Queen, because nothing will save the Governor General!"

A heated conflict followed with talk of a general strike and 'blood in the gutters.' But all that eventually happened, during Fraser's overwhelming victorious campaign, was that a beer can was thrown from a crowd and hit him.

This has reputedly had its implications in that many Australians seem suspicious of Britain's Governor General and his influence over Australian politics. It is no coincidence that *God Save the Queen* has just been replaced, on April 19th, by *Advance Australian Fair* as the National Anthem.

Bob Hawke would even prefer a change of flag, but he also concedes: "This is a different matter, due to the number of war veterans who fought and saw comrades die under these colours." The Labor Party seem determined to propel Australia towards her own identity, and in time with a public vote of confidence, turn it into a Republic.

The song itself has a long history dating back to 1878; it was written by Peter Dodds McCormick (1835-1916) who grew up in Glasgow, Scotland, and arrived in Australia in 1855; his pen name is reported to have been Amicas in Latin meaning friend. He had been an apprentice joiner, but spent most of his working life in education, and enjoyed a musical life at the Presbyterian Church in Sydney. It was here on November 30th 1878, at a concert of the Highland Society, that Andrew Fairfax is thought to have sung its first public rendition.

The song's fame was finally sealed when it was sung by a choir of 10,000 at the inauguration of the Commonwealth in 1901, with a few amendments including 'Our youthful Commonwealth.' In recognition McCormick was awarded £100 for his composition in 1907. When he died in 1916, the *Sydney Herald* even recognized the song in his obituary as 'something in the nature of an Australian national anthem.' Below are the first three, of five, verses joined together to capture the spirit of the country's heritage. Its copyright ran out in 1966.

Advance Australian Fair

Australia's son, let us rejoice, for we are young and free. We've golden soil, and wealth for toil. Our home is girt by sea; our land abounds in nature's gifts of beauty rich and rare. In history's page let every stage Advance Australian Fair.

In joyful strains then let us sing, "Advance Australia Fair."

When gallant Cook from Albion sailed, to trace the wide oceans o'er. True British courage bore him on, till he landed on our shore. Then here he raised Old England's flag, the standard of the brave. With all her faults, we love her still. "Britannia rules the wave!" In joyful strains then let us sing "Advance Australian Fair."

Beneath our radiant South Cross we'll toil with hearts and hands, to make this Commonwealth of ours renowned of all the lands.

For those who've come across the seas we're boundless plains to share. With courage let us all combine "Advance Australia Fair."

Thursday 26 April

Canberra is certainly the cleanest city imaginable, with everything allotted its proper place, and none of the detracting black spots, which tend to be hidden down any side streets. Possibly this is because invariably people have well-paid government jobs, and can afford to spruce up the string of suburbs within which the city has been planned. The layout is also spacious, and being the capital visitors need to be impressed.

My nights were generally spent sleeping besides Lake Griffith, apart from when I looked up Tony in the suburbs, who said I could sleep on his floor. But he did not have time to show me around, with his exams just around the corner. Although he could get me a student card, which might come in useful at some stage, as every little bit helps. I appreciated his situation, and therefore claimed that I had to meet Martin earlier than planned. My distraction is the last thing he needed right now and was still comparatively fresh in my own mind.

For a major city, Canberra has an abundant amount of safe woodland to take refuge under. Autumn is on its way now, but remarkably everything has remained green throughout the hot summer of constant watering.

The highlight of my time here was undoubtedly Canberra's most popular tourist attraction. A giant war memorial, opened in 1941 that now looks out directly along Anzac Parade towards Parliament House on the opposite side of Lake Griffith. It commemorates the Australians who fought in both world wars alongside the Allies.

During the First World War (1914-18) when fewer than five million lived here, 417,000 Australians served in the armed forces; 322,000 of them were overseas in for example Gallipoli, Europe and Palestine; 60,000 were eventually killed. The most synonymous act was the disastrous consequences felt in the Dardanelle's, when the Australians were pinned down by the Turks, to the most horrendous of consequences on the beaches with the enemy holding the high ground.

In the 1939-45 war about one million, or 8 out of every 10 males between 18 and 35 years of age enlisted; 550,000 served overseas with the casualty rate on active service total at 34,300. No enemy force has actually ever landed in Australia, although Japanese planes did bomb Darwin extensively on February 19th 1942, which resulted in a combined civilian and armed forces death toll of 243. Eight ships, including USS Peary were destroyed, together with aircraft and military installations. The Labor Prime Minister John Curtin said at the time:

"We must face with fortitude the first onset and remember; we are Australians and will fight grimly and victoriously."

Housed here is an array of paintings, a number of Victoria Crosses, and old historic aircraft, including the German Albatross, Spitfire and a magnificent Lancaster bomber displayed in all its glory.

Outside a Japanese miniature submarine, which raided Sydney Harbour on June 1st 1942, greets tourists. This is in fact two made into one. The third is still hidden below the misty harbour waters, and perhaps the one, that never made it past the erected anti-torpedo nets, when becoming trapped. Its two-crew members elected to blow themselves up rather than surrender.

A second submarine was detected in Taylor Bay, which again resulted in a double suicide. Unfortunately though a third vessel managed to escape detection, until it got within five hundred yards of USS Chicago, before being spotted in its searchlights. However, by then the gunners could not get their guns low enough to inflict damage before the Japanese crew managed to fire two torpedoes, past the Chicago, and in turn blew out the hull of the nearby barracks ferry ship, Kuttabul, in all killing nineteen Australian seaman that night.

Saturday 28 April

In many respects five days in Canberra has been spent twiddling my fingers and lurking around the lakeside environment, or sat in the shopping mall without too much to stir the imagination. The city is purely functional and for people with a reason to be here or organised in other ways, but not for the backpacker with time to spare.

I was admittedly glad when Saturday arrived, and could begin my journey towards Sydney, where the bright lights wait. I hope Martin has made out, as I again found myself on the Hume Highway, further up from Yass. It was a nice day and things had gone smoothly enough, after my lift picked me up when walking out of the main drag, to put me in the right direction and what luck!

Ten minutes later and a young couple stopped.

"Hop in the back," the driver said, with her boyfriend in the front very quiet, who acknowledged my presence. Then they might be family or just student friends, but never assume anything of such. It was clear the young man had something on his mind though. A woman, 'it's bound to be,' and yet the girl seemed so naturally talkative and bubbly, or the girl next door many of us are looking for, but 'rarely' find.

Simply put I was enjoying the attention with that laid back approach and a smile, as the girl glanced over her shoulder and

I showed genuine interest in her as a person. I did not know what might be going on, but who cares, stick within the natural boundaries of conversation and enjoy the journey! I had no idea how far this would take me, but life is a jolly experience of passing strangers or of friends we have not met. It's always been one of my favourite sayings, and here I was to prove the old adjective true.

We continued in this way for about an hour, when the road slowly became more congested; the girl turned off and stopped just back from a bungalow, where I thought, 'this is it,' stranded in no man's land, and a cup of tea with a bit of luck. The young man still had not said anything, when he slowly got out and Kerry, I believe her name was, looked back and pleasantly said: "Stay here, he's the one who's leaving!"

I did not complain, and far from it, we all need a pleasant personality and a slim figure, but not what some might say sexy, no just nice with blue jeans and short brown hair. I liked her, and why not, this was the genuine article.

We would only be together until the journey's end, but sometimes that is enough in fuelling you with renewed faith in human nature, and that there are a lot of nice people out there waiting to be met. I now moved into the front seat, and watched from afar as the two said a few quiet words, or Kerry did, and the man said nothing it seemed; he rather listened and accepted without any kind of touch or emotion.

The girl then walked back towards the car with a heartbeat still at its level ratio and ignited the engine, with the guy looking on. The two of us acknowledged eye contact, and knew nothing of each other really, except that a complete stranger had now driven off in 'his' seat and was oblivious of why.

"That's my ex-boyfriend, he lives nearby," she said, to the stool pigeon, who for once did not mind.

"Sometimes it's best not to ask," I replied.

"It's alright, he's been sleeping around and now wants me back," she claimed.

Kerry seemed at ease with my presence, and naturally I wanted to open up my thoughts, and tell her that, 'he must be mad, or crazy even,' and that 'we're not all like that!' Her bold enthusiastic personality and dark looks made her one of those nice people who you always hope to meet in different circumstances, and yet sadly she will probably run back to her tormentor, rather than me!

7. New South Wales

I now had somebody nice to 'think' about for the next couple of hours, with one more lift into the centre of Sydney, where I knew Martin had booked me into the youth hostel for the night. We had arranged to meet after dark, as to not tie him down for the day in waiting for me to appear, as a result of the uncertainty which hitchhiking brings with it.

If I could not make it there would be a message waiting to cancel, but this was not necessary, when with good fortune I bumped into him on the way back from another gambling session. This time at the Randwick horse races, I gather he now has the bug.

"Did you win?"

"Nearly!" he replied, in almost instantly changing the subject.

I wanted to talk about Kerry; not that there was much to say though. She just left me besides the road and said goodbye. Before getting on with the rest of her life, and now Martin 'has' Lisa, he even mentioned San Diego and a phone call to America.

"So that explains it, you're a desperate man trying to gamble at the races to finance a trip to California!"

"Oh she's lovely, I met three of them in the youth hostel, and we went out around the Opera House. I've even sent her some flowers, to arrive when she gets home," he remarked.

"You sure work fast, I leave you alone for five days and you fall in love!"

"Well, you know how it is," he said.

"No, I don't!"

"You see it's like this, if I leave in August, it will be their summer vacation, and it might be the best time to drop by, when the students don't have any academic pressures," he remarked.

"What!"

"I'm going home by September," he said.

"Why you old smoothie, so you really are going to leave me to fend for myself," I replied, in acknowledging that with one other friend also having showed interest, and failing to motivate his finances past first base, with Ian here for three months, the original number of five, plus the two girls from Devon, was shortly to whittle down one. Then I really will be by myself, and in need of some fresh blood.

During the evening we strolled through the red light area of Kings Cross; it appeared full of strip joints and hookers encamped in the shadows, with their lives intoxicated by a rampant demand for their services. I'm not sure why they should feel the need to follow this path, when the strange vagaries of the unknown in your immediate proximity would put the doubt in most people's minds, but not these ladies of the night.

On this occasion I will forever remember the sad vision of a slim figure posing in a doorway, two steps high. We had been walking along slowly and avoiding other like-minded souls out for a walk amongst the crowds with my eyes noting more pavement slabs than anything else. Then some fishnet stockings caught my attention, and an impressively curved tight-fitting black skirt. I naturally felt inquisitive and glanced up slowly at a low cut white top. Her hair was jet black and nicely touched the shoulders without hiding her natural features, together with those dark eyes, lonely of mistrust. Her confidence had long since gone in these mysterious surrounds. The abundance of makeup could not disguise her years that have been spent on the streets. She would never see the low side of fifty again.

Sunday 29 April

Sydney, New South Wales, is both Australia's largest and oldest city, which may explain why roads have been designed so narrowly, winding and congested in comparison with its younger planned counterparts of Melbourne and Adelaide. The city's first settlement was developed on the spur of land from where South Sydney's side of the Harbour Bridge connects with the shore. It was an area once of squalor and violence that has now been reshaped into an Australian heritage site, known as The Rocks. The oldest building in Sydney is Camden Cottage dated 1816; where the site of the old public gallows can be found.

I have admittedly, never been a lover of the high life in polluted cities. Too many people tend to give me claustrophobia, coupled with the dire need to fill my lungs with fresh air. There is nothing so uninviting than having to battle one's way through streets full of shoppers overshadowed by skyscrapers, only to find your favourite park crammed with messy individuals, who throw their coke cans and crisp packets around like drags from a cigarette.

To me the essence of any country is away from the masses in calmer surroundings, where people matter as individuals, and not the latest media in thing, by which our environment is invariably influenced. This is only a personal preference and is disputed by millions of people around the globe, who would be likewise lost away from the throb of a mass of activity.

Sydney might be just another congested juggernaut to me, but even I have to admit the harbour is something special, when viewed from the famous Opera House. This was opened by Queen Elizabeth II on October 20th 1973, and is in turn dwarfed by an enormous Harbour Bridge linking North and South Sydney. On a sunny day it's an impressive sight, as the ferries and small launches pass by. At night in more peaceful and mysterious surroundings, the various coloured lighting around Sydney's most famous tourist attraction gives it a certain aura all of its own.

Martin had arranged to meet Clare and Sarah at the old port this morning.

When we arrived though we found out that the girls had changed their minds, in which case we had to backtrack our steps towards North Sydney Station to meet them, somewhere outside of a restaurant, supping cups of coffee, and discussing the various events of the past six months. This will prove to be our last such meeting in Australia. In a way it would have been nice to meet on the steps of the Opera House, for this is everybody's lingering memory.

One afternoon they turned up at Naygoondy Farm on a whim to say hello, and to experience orchard life first hand. Naturally they were without a roof, and it became the 'right' thing to offer Clare my bed, in return for that first night in Perth, when we could pitch the tents.

"Don't worry about the buzzing noise," I remarked.

"Fleas?"

"Well perhaps. But there's nothing to worry about. Just make sure you wear your shoes when walking around," I replied.

"Snakes!"

"Best to lock the door," I said.

"Men?"

"And desperate!"

"Oh she wouldn't mind!" Sarah remarked.

We therefore parted with a warm smile; I need not have worried though. Martin always seems to have a contact just around the corner. This time Chris and Jill, who know his parents back home, and are friends of theirs. Sometimes it's a bit confusing where everybody fits in, but they do. Our day finished fourteen stories up, overlooking the Opera House opposite, in a flat, and enjoying their hospitality.

"If you two like on Sunday I can take you both out on my yacht," Chris remarked.

How could we refuse!

Tuesday 1 May

No stay in Sydney is complete without a visit to the Blue Mountains, 65 km inland, and once considered impossible until 1813. In some respects this is the most interesting of areas to visit, with a 1,100 metres high point. It is the blue hazy mist created by oil given off by the eucalyptus trees, which gives this region its name, and with it our chance to get lost for a few days of mountainous bliss.

We initially made for Blackheath, a tourist hotspot; on the towns outskirts we intended to walk along the Evans Lookout Road, and then follow a footpath downwards, through Neats Glen. This is an overgrown area, with steps taking us to the bottom of the valley, follows the river along the Grand Canyon, and then for our rocky hill climb towards Evans Lookout itself; an exhausting climb with full packs admittedly, and memorable for its magnificent views of huge forest gorges, coupled with a creek running through its centre.

I could continue with these descriptions and fill three pages, but what is the point; my visions are complete of these three days with Martin's eventual plunge into Govetts Creek, on Thursday to celebrate his birthday, and his cries of 'it's freezing cold,' or something similar. He was a brave man, as I looked on and noted his face grimace with the chill and concluded that looks cannot deceive, it really was that cold!

"What next?" I remarked, as he dried himself in the sunlight.

"No more swimming, you wouldn't believe the difference in temperatures," he said.

"Oh yes I would!"

"OK then, how about returning to Blackheath for a round of drinks," he replied.

"Sounds good to me," I said, as we began our hike.

I'd like to report our international darts debut here, rather competing and winning did not go hand in hand. There was an open tournament being played in pairs, and we put our names down, but unfortunately lost without reaching a double on either occasion. It had been brief, and oh so brief at that, no doubt beaten by the favourites that is and eventual winners more like.

"Is that so?" Martin remarked.

"Well actually, yes they were pretty darn red hot," I replied.

"Or was it that we were that bad?"

"It's your birthday, they were that good!" I said.

Why we left our packs outside I'm not sure; perhaps we just wanted to be like two of the lad's without distractions. We had even pitched our tent in the local park among some rhododendron bushes; one had been left in Sydney, while our rucksacks had been hidden in a separate place for precautionary reasons, and the peace of mind it brought. What the local police force might have said is unclear had they known, indeed nobody knew us; the darts tournament would continue without us, as we walked in the dark.

Martin though seemed disappointed by his milestone, not in age, but without the flow of camaraderie and a hangover to embrace.

"Sorry it wasn't so special, but at least next years will seem so much the better for it," I replied.

"And always look on the bright side," he muttered.

"That's right, the bright side of life!" I said.
He didn't reply.

Friday 4 May

Darkness in Katoomba, the major town of the Blue Mountains,
found us wandering along some back streets, when a slow
drizzle began to fall. Unperturbed we decided to pitch our tent on
a small piece of waste ground, surrounded by houses. But
unfortunately the quicker we tried to erect our shelter, the more
the skewers and poles became lost in our haste to beat the
growing storm, which had by now turned into a torrential
downpour. Within two minutes everything we owned was
dripping wet, even our tent had become immersed under a flash
flood and laid in the puddles.

"It's no good, if we don't get into some warm dry clothing,
pneumonia will set in," I said, and stripped off my tee shirt,
which made things surprisingly slightly warmer, and more
reminiscent of a summer's day, without socks on, or bare except
for my shorts with Martin following suit.

I now looked at him, and then our tent on the ground with the
rain creating puddles across its surface. This made it impossible
to use in these circumstances, it had all happened so fast, and
now here we were in the most unlikely of situations. Perhaps we
should have stayed in the pub and made friends with the locals,
the barmaids were quite nice.

"Now what are we going to do?" Martin remarked.

"Only one thing we can do, try the nearest house for shelter
and hope they can help," I replied.

"Are you sure?"

"Yes quite so, this comes into the emergency category, we
can't stand here all night, without clothes," I remarked.

This was one of those times to step forward, and take a grip; a door is a door and people are the same everywhere. I doubt if they will ever meet another shirtless lost soul at their doorstep again; it might even be an adventure for them. We just hoped the owner was not elderly, or a female alone, that might be interesting! But fortunately not, we were met by a man in his thirties, with a pleasant expression, if not surprised.

"Excuse me could you help, the rain has caught us out," I remarked.

"How can I refuse, you have just interrupted our Salvation Army meeting, do come in. I'm sure there must be a towel somewhere, and a jumper…here let me make you some hot soup, then you can go and get your tent. I can hang it up for you, and dry your cloths in the spin dryer. My wife will be back soon, you can both sleep on the living room floor," Ian said, when we walked into the room, and rather brought proceedings to an end; with my brown arms, and more faded chest evident to the four female house guests sat in a row, wearing their 'Easter' bonnets; all middle aged and having been out collecting for their causes.

I noted the one at the end and wondered if she recognized me, and thought probably not. We last saw her an hour ago walking through a topless bar.

Sunday 6 May

Never one with sea legs, this was one of those days when the romance of a dream life across the ocean waves came down with a thump, and only confirmed a calmer existence on dry land, with the clouds up there, above and mighty inhospitable too. The day all started so well, in a nice warm flat, and a hearty breakfast to line the stomach. I was in good spirits as we walked down to the jetty, and prepared our vessel for what might be a ten-minute excursion trip, around the first buoy and back for a Sunday beer at the bar. 'Now show some enthusiasm; you can last, you can survive, think *Captain Blood* and the high seas!'

Martin had done some sailing before, not much though and enough to know that he should be all right, but this was to be my baptism of fire. I recall only too well a friend describing his first fishing trip, and never again! Now just stay busy, and learn to do the rigging. Of course this was a great opportunity, or one to be grateful of, and something I went at with the best of intentions; pull the ropes, tie the knots, keep everything safe, and double check the wind.

Chris our captain has been doing this for about twenty-five years. He apparently lived in London for a time, and now does a marketing job, or something similar in publishing. He was very kind and with such enthusiasm, it was a pity life has bestowed on me a dodgy stomach for such a thrilling climax to our time in Sydney.

Things were fine in the harbour, as we did fairly well as I followed Martin's lead and let him take care of anything related to technical jargon. Chris presently said to tie the safety harness on, then offered to sail out of Port Jackson, and beyond the two defensive headlands that surprisingly shielded us from the wind.

Life was still calm with the sea breeze, but this all came to a halt with the wave upon waves of torrential damage to my stomach. Our 37-metre vessel seemed to do cart wheels in the wind and rain fell to such an extent that it left me stranded in the corner of the boat, seasick, and redundant of strength, with Martin still in one piece and doing his bit for the team. To add insult a wave met us sideways and covered me in a deluge of abuse, with seawater being swallowed in part.

This was not how things were meant to be, in the bottom of a boat!

How long are we staying out here, at least let's get back into calmer waters and an inlet for soup; yes that would be great, and something Chris suggested I should admit here, when it became plainly obvious that one of his trusty seafarers was anything but enjoying himself.

"That was rough out there, and one of the worst I have known," he said, in a calmer setting, or was he just being kind. That was a pathetic effort, and I felt quite envious that Marty had shaped up so much better than me.

"Don't worry about it, even after all this time I still get the occasional bug," Chris remarked, who showed patience when I sat below and slowly began to feel more human. That's the problem, an instant destabilizing inside takes more than five minutes to remedy, with aspirins and a mixture to line the stomach; it was a full hour before the strength began to resemble normal service and never again!

During our remaining time I took over the helm for a memorable cruise around one of the world's greatest harbours, and past the aircraft carrier Melbourne. We then saluted Sydney's famous Opera House, and finally navigated a passage under the Harbour Bridge. Martin, in turn, took over on the return leg.

As the darkness slowly engulfed our craft, we had to start picking our way home through the various green and red warning lights to avoid running our vessel aground on the dangerous rocks, just below the water's surface.

"You know Marty, this is all just a dream," I remarked, looking up at the huge expanse of an iron structure overhead with us at the wheel.

"I'm going to wake up soon."

Tuesday 8 May

We hung around Sydney, on Monday morning, perhaps longer than anticipated and both agreed it was time to move on, and to leave the flat. Outstaying our welcome was uppermost in our minds when we finally caught a train to Hawkesbury River, and in turn found ourselves in the dark, before walking towards the Pacific Highway. It had been another one of those wet nights in a damp tent, with Martin's left in reserve.

This morning we found ourselves in the pretty company of two young nurses travelling inland somewhere, from Newcastle to see their boyfriends, and full of the spirits of an uncomplicated life. It's a shame we were not heading in the same direction, but instead we continued with our original plan to visit a reptile park full of venomous snakes, including my feared 'friend' the Brown Tiger snake.

We have now seen our first kangaroo jumping around, and almost shoulder-to-shoulder. Perhaps we will see some in the Outback, and none too sure of our plans. Then there was a beaky nosed ostrich roaming around, free to do as he pleases, and open spaces without cages. Australia is full of wildlife, and an education in itself with sharks and crocodiles further on ahead. It is also a dangerous place to become over-confident, what with mankind about as well we must not become too complacent. The trip has all gone so well, but you never know what is around the corner.

Gosford is situated on the northern shore of the Brisbane Water, about 100 km north of Sydney, and within the commuter belt for the ambitious. It is another sailor's delight with a yachting club on its coastal edge. On either side rich green trees add a park-like feel to the surrounding area, through where the heart of the commercial district runs, in a straight line.

During the afternoon we found ourselves sat in the centre outside of a supermarket; we took it in turns to do our shopping and to keep an eye on my tent tied between two trees on a small grass mound. This naturally attracted some interesting glances from the locals with the wind glancing through it.

"Are you going to camp there?" a small party of schoolgirls asked.

"Are there any police officers around here!" I replied.

It was one of those days.

Wednesday 9 May

We continued our trek north this morning after pitching our tents on a small bank besides a country lane, and something we really want to avoid, being so near to the coast and yet still 'inland.' It therefore came as a pleasant surprise when our lift towards Newcastle remarked that he has just returned to Australia after playing a few games for Blackpool in the English Football League. He now seems content to be back in settled employment.

Martin even received a lift, on one of his solo missions towards Melbourne, from a veteran of Everton's 1933 FA Cup winners, who defeated Manchester City 3-0; the vanquished returned in 1934 to beat Portsmouth 2-1.

In keeping with the grand traditions of English football's knock out competition, we soon found ourselves in 'Newcastle,' and triple winners in the 1950s. This is New South Wales's second largest city, even outnumbering both Hobart and Canberra. It was originally formed in 1804 on a peninsula, and was accordingly named Coal River at the mouth of the Hunter River, to house Sydney's most dangerous convicts.

Newcastle's image resembles its English counterpart, in

mind, if not vision. Being an industrial and commercial centre, it is dominated by the massive B.H.P steel works. They also export coal from the nearby mines in the Hunter Valley, which can be brought here by river, and then exported around the world. This also encourages other commercial enterprises to locate in the vicinity.

Neither of us though found anything to stimulate our interest buds, except for an hour spent in an almost deserted snooker hall. We now caught a train out to nearby Hexham, where we planned to reconnect our lives to the Pacific Highway, in the morning.

It was almost dark when a fellow 'commuter' suggested he give us a lift because we still had to get back on the 'right highway' north from here; he would show us the way when driving us 23 km towards Raymond Terrace, a small town with a sprinkling of early structures dating from the 1830/40s including a still in use court house.

"Then you have a straight run in the morning," he remarked.

We eventually camped behind the stands of the local football club, and saw nothing of the town itself, secure in knowledge that if the rains continued unabated, at least we would have somewhere to shelter our lives and protect us from the elements.

Thursday 10 May

Life on the road is full of uncertainties. There are no fixed rules, of who will pick us up or even how long we might wait for a lift of perhaps two miles, or it could be two hundred, there is no way of knowing. Hitchhiking can be a precarious business, especially towards the resort town of Port Macquarie, which began life as a convict settlement in 1821. They moved out nine years later, in preference to the surfers and people wanting to sit on long sandy beaches. This was one of those times when three frustrating hours passed by without any sign of interest from a motorist, or what there were on the road.

"Is this Sunday?"

"No Thursday, we might have to split up," Martin said.

"Sometimes I wish you had blonde hair and curves to match," I replied.

"It would help, but two guys has been easy enough so far," he said.

"Yes that's maybe, but I can still wish!" I remarked, when shortly a blue automatic pulled up slowly on the gravels hard shoulder.

"Hello boys, jump in," the elderly occupant remarked.

He must have been eighty pushing on eighty-five years of age.

"Been waiting long?" he said, as the car moved slowly on towards Tarree.

Ten minutes later it came to a slow halt next to some isolated toilets.

"Just a minute," he said, as the door was slowly opened and our lift began to shuffle across the highway, strangely thin of traffic. None the less dangerous, if that is you make a tortoise seem slick and much to our alarm bells from inside the car.

"We'd better help," Martin said, echoing my own deliberations.

"Here, let us stop the traffic, this road is dangerous, you could have parked on the opposite side," I remarked.

"It's clear."

We then both stood in the road, with myself walking towards the oncoming traffic, and Martin in the opposite direction, until he crossed and disappeared from view. Time though literally stood still on this afternoon, when the longest five minutes turned into fifteen minutes or more, I'm not sure.

"A morsel of wind might have blown him over," Marty said.

We might even have been parked for twenty minutes before he managed to make the return crossing and to find his seat once more… his car keys were still as he had left them, in the ignition.

Saturday 12 May

Good sound advice is always appreciated, as we listened intently to a flower power couple left over from San Francisco in the 1960s; driving their 'outdated' VW campervan, all cramped, with their worldly belongings in it, and heading to wherever they are going to, or they come from. Theirs was an attitude from another time, and the culture we missed out on in the 'summer of love' or at the Woodstock music festival in 1969; when 'peace and love man' was one of the idealistic sayings of a generation dominated by the war in Vietnam.

"You know what you should do?" the driver remarked, with his straight blond hair hiding his face. A gentle soul, who would hardly know how to raise his voice in anger, as we sat among their belongings, all squashed into a confined space.

"What's that?" I said, not understanding his chain of thought.

"You eat bananas, plant trees and make mud bricks to finance yourself."

"Thanks for the advice, but we're only in Australia for another few months," I replied.

"Oh, you should try it, we've been living this way for years," his wife remarked, in such a simple manner, that I do believe she meant it.

Sunday 13 May

After a hard day's hitchhiking towards Byron Bay we were a bit disgruntled to find the pubs closed; in turn this meant sharing a milkshake for our comforts. It has been quoted that Australians will do anything for a drink, which may explain why a well-informed government decided to curtail opening times to 6pm at the outbreak of the Great War in 1914. In turn they decided to deprive the nation of its alcohol until the 1950s, before this clearheaded law was finally laid to rest. The breweries didn't mind though, as revenue remained intact, while their overheads were cut.

Byron Bay turned into one of those typical tourist resorts, frequented by caravan parks, but with little to spark one's imagination. Its real claim to fame is the lighthouse on Cape Byron, the most easterly point on the mainland. Longhaired surfers also know it as the most important place to ride the waves on Watego's beach, where they tend to arrive frequently, and give the finest exponents of their art the trip of a lifetime.

Having experienced the pain of the battle, sunstroke, and seasickness, there was nothing left for me to damage! I had no fear now as we walked up the long sandy beach, further than the eye could see, where we decided to stay on the sand until sunup.

It was one of those nights when the waves kept charging up the shorefront, and seemed a temptation too much by charging into them in the darkness. Then from nowhere we would be attacked by another breaker, which were tested time and time again in thrusting us again and again across the sandy beach with such force that I ended up with a badly bruised shoulder for my efforts, or was it just the muscles, I couldn't really tell. Martin would have to help the walking wounded to put his pack on for the next three days of sporadic pain.

"I never realised being a beach bum was so demanding on the body, it seems to take me days to recover from each mishap," I soon remarked.

The whistle of the waves was lit by a full moon and moments of peaceful bliss without reply; I then looked slightly behind me and into the shadows; Marty was sound asleep on the sand dunes…

Tuesday 15 May

We made further slow progress this morning, and found ourselves in the small fishing port of Brunswick. This might not have registered much on our memory bank, had it not been for Malcolm, alone and having just been to the local store. He stopped on the outskirts and asked if we needed a lift, and that we could stay on his commune; it was only about two miles away if we liked. The day was still comparatively young and Martin did not seem to mind. After all this is why we are here; to see for ourselves, and besides it might also explain how we make mud bricks.

I looked at Martin, who nodded and we accepted.

"Why not it might be fun," I replied.

Malcolm continued to drive slowly into the commune with people aimlessly walking around the place, and going about their daily chores in a quiet kind of way, at ease with itself, or peace and harmony. There 'will' be nothing here for us to get worried about. Malcolm would have been only too pleased to have us join his merry band of free spirits cast away from the rest of society.

"You see, I regret my first thirty years spent on mother earth," he remarked.

"Why's that?"

"Oh, it's simple. I did the travelling thing and drank myself silly at times, in waking up with various girls, but that's when I discovered the Bible," he said.

"Sounds quite normal," I replied.

The entire congregation apparently consists of about 350 such ideologists, who mainly live in a number of wooden colonial huts and invariably cash in their welfare payments, to each other's mutual benefit?

"But who are they?" Martin said.

"Anybody, some are ex-shoplifters and two have been convicted of murder. People join us out of desperation. We have even had some travellers pass by like you who stay to learn our ways," he replied, in a soft tone that betrayed his lack of confidence. In helping to bring a predominantly thirty something group of people into an environment that can help them regain their often broken lives, and to shield them from the pressures of society that has often proved so difficult for them.

My curiosity was to get the better of me on this occasion, when we decided to accept an invitation to their mixed religious gathering, which in turn led us to an enlightening mix of an hour long singsong worship to Jesus the Lord.

"You don't have to attend, but you might find it interesting," Malcolm said.

All of which seemed very normal for a Sunday morning church service, except that the twelve men and women appeared totally transfixed with their eyes so shut, that I almost noted an air of obsession, and quite unnatural in its outlook.

"I can't handle this," I whispered, to Martin, during some religious mutterings, in bored frustration. Not that he replied or even looked my way, but later remarked out of earshot "The eyes had all turned towards your direction."

"I'm sorry for that," I apologized, and unsure that anybody

'could' have heard me under such a silent whisper. But also acknowledged that sometimes a thought is best left as just that.

Normality was restored somewhat when Helen, an attractive thirty year old divorcee took centre stage amongst our small group. She began to talk of her psychological pressures that she had experienced back in the bush, where she had immersed herself into the flower power fraternity. I wanted to speak up here and ask some questions concerning, how on earth could an attractive down-to-earth girl 'like yourself' find such circumstances. But then reasoned that once started, my enthusiasm might take over and dominate these 'pastoral' proceedings. Besides we are the outsiders here and don't know the 'score' among these people. Social politics might have a bearing, and I didn't want to step on anybody's toes, or draw attention to myself. I am a stranger in their midst, when Helen finally read my mind and answered the question.

"Only to become saved by the Lord," she remarked, as I soon began to lose interest. The opposition was far too 'powerful' for a mere mortal with a rucksack to compete against, which was kind of sad, because here was someone with a lot to offer the outside world.

It was quite an education of noting the normality in her mannerism, and the way she spoke. I was quietly impressed but we did not need saving or intended to venture around such an uncertain climate for more than one evening. For many this community life has enhanced their lives in a more meaningful direction that the camaraderie of others in the same boat has brought with them.

I could have stayed longer, and half admitted to myself from an experience point of view it might be worth it, but Marty did not seem keen. He could hardly leave here, and answer the sixty-four dollar question, of where did you last see him!

"I think we had best stay in our hut tonight to keep an eye on the rucksacks, and then move on at our first opportunity," he remarked, with a sign of concern.

"Tomorrow it is then," I replied.

8. Queensland

In 1824 a penal settlement was established on Moreton Bay, due to the good folk of Sydney wanting to rid themselves of their hardened criminal population. However this had to be abandoned due to water shortages and the Aboriginal warmongers trying to protect their lands. Brisbane then started to develop as Queensland's huge agriculture and mineral resources began to evolve in turning this into Australia's third largest city and independence from NSW in 1859.

Brisbane, with the 1980s skyscraper skyline, is still viewed in comparison with Perth's countrified atmosphere, and equally isolated from the political heartbeat of Australia. The 1982 Commonwealth Games were held here and drew the world's attention to its potential; it also enabled the city to build a modern sports infrastructure.

"The games were the best thing to ever happen here, now we have the facilities to train and compete on a level playing field," one local sportsman remarked.

Martin had wisely asked Adrienne for her address when she sat next to us on the flight out here, having boarded at Rome. I didn't really say much, when I huddled next to the window and tried to sleep in a futile attempt at feeling fresh when we finally arrived. All this forward planning was beyond me at the time, as these two 'brotherhood' of travellers conversed at various stages on route about their lives. It hardly echoed my own confidence when she mentioned having her valuables stolen at the station in Rome.

"I was standing alone waiting for a friend, when my attention was taken away from our luggage for a few seconds, but that was enough time to lose my credit cards and money. Fortunately my passport was in my pocket. That's why I had to take a later flight than originally booked," she remarked; a pleasant girl, who was almost nonplussed in her acceptance and did not even seem angry with the culprit.

"It was my own fault, I should have been watching more closely," she said, somewhat sportingly. This was something that turned into a fortunate stroke of luck when her flatmate, whose parents owned the spacious single storied wooden colonial house, had the idea of landscaping the garden.

"We have wanted to do it for sometime, how would you like a job?" she said.

"Yes please," I replied, knowing full well that Martin had just been for an interview to wash dishes, only to find him twentieth in line!

"I couldn't believe it," he remarked.

The garden has not been touched for years, since Liz's parents once lived here before moving inland, not plant wise anyway, with a lawn mower only brought out of service during the most 'desperate' of times. Still it will be nice for Liz, who we are told is likely to marry her boyfriend some time in the future, to have the makings of a garden to encompass their lives. And eventually see their children playing on a lawn, surrounded by freshly planted flowers.

We now began to transform our campsite with enthusiasm, and showed gratitude towards the task in hand. This was all new to us in landscape architecture, but slowly the green slope was topped of its grass, and then layered at two levels, in the hot daily sunshine.

"At least we're getting used to the climate," I said, as we managed to dig and concrete various uprights into the ground, ready for the cross sections to be wedged behind them to support the bank.

"It's a shame, we're never going to see the finished article, I'm sure it will look nice when the grass seed is sown," Martin replied.

It was against this backdrop that we settled into Brisbane suburbia literally sleeping on the job, and getting forever fitter in preparation for a spot of athletics. That's the problem with enthusiasm and opening one's mouth, there always comes a time when people are genuinely interested, and invite you to join in! Liz is a keen runner, and does some of these multi sports, while Jeremy is the cyclist.

"The trouble is Liz needs to lose weight," he said.

"There is nothing wrong her figure," I replied.

"No of course not, but if she wants to compete at a higher level that is different, especially on the long runs, she is just right for swimming, but it's a different discipline that's all," he said.

We travelled to Toowoomba on this occasion, 138 km inland, for the St Paul's School fun run. It is the region's largest town, on the edge of the Great Darling Range, and the Darling Downs, or plains stretching across some of the most fertile agricultural land in Australia. At times of drought, which occur sporadically, the valleys can also resemble a hayfield cut to a tinder, without nourishment for months or even years on end.

This all places farmers invariably at the mercy of the elements, and the problems it can incur, especially to livestock and their income in such unstable times. Liz's parents live here somewhere, and put us up for the night; I reasoned this was not going to be such an easy-going Sunday morning stroll I have been used to of late, rather something of a slog, and of course it was!

Martin it has to be recorded is a natural athlete, and somebody who actually runs for fun, and is really quite good.

"Why not give up the booze, late nights and concentrate on running for a couple of years, you might do well," I have often said to him. But no that makes it all too serious and he has often echoed, "I just want to enjoy it." He even turned up for the London Marathon with his 'own' number pinned to his bib, and joined in shortly after the start.

"It was easy, nobody noticed me slip under the rope. They even gave me a finisher's medal at the end and didn't bother to check my number," he once remarked; no doubt impressed by the first race when the leaders, American Dick Beardsley and Norwegian Inge Simonsen, ran past us in the crowd, outside Buckingham Palace, and crossed the line together for a well earned, and agreed upon, dead heat three years ago.

I have no such claims to fame or ever will have. My time to 'retire' was fast approaching when a 'ten' year old boy loomed up over my shoulder, slowly closing in on his prey from a distant horizon, when even a plump looking lady had waddled past without my stomach cramps; and to think we are scheduled to do this all again next Sunday!

My ego was finally shattered when I tried my last trick and put the pressure on the young upstart behind. This lasted for about two hundred metres, before I chose the most secluded stretch to 'let' him past, and then edge himself far into the distance.

I would save my energy for the finishing line, to convince any onlookers, into believing that this was actually my 'dummy' run for the real thing next time. Who am I fooling, only myself! Liz did us proud in winning the ladies' race in 29 minutes, with the men's winner clocking in at 23.30; Martin also recorded a respectable 27 minutes for the eight kilometres run.

On another couple of occasions we used other related contacts to acclimatize our thoughts. Firstly towards Surfers

Paradise, below Brisbane on the Gold Coast, and a 35 km stretch of coastline beginning at the New South Wales-Queensland border, and heading northwards. It is an almost continuous commercial resort, culminating in one big hangover from the recent property boom now stuttering to a halt. Our makeshift fixed abode was to be in a garage at a friend of Adrienne's.

Her parents have a restaurant here, but had nowhere for us to stay.

"Everyone was very good to her abroad, you will have a meal with us on the house!" her father remarked.

"Yes you tend to worry at the time, and wonder how they are getting on; it's such a long way away," her mother said.

These are the winter months with miles of beaches and almost inhabited. Originally in 1936 there was the Surfers Paradise Hotel, with a beer garden to entice people out of Brisbane and beyond. It's in the name; Surfers was all the rage with the girls when we arrived in Perth. But the place remains an overrated tourist brochure redundant in atmosphere.

The numerous skyscrapers have been built so close to the shore, or high, that we had to avoid the mid-afternoon shadows eclipsing our lives. It was nicer for us to experience the more idyllic Sunshine Coast north of Brisbane at Noosa Head.

Although the small resort is obviously geared towards tourists, I still found the old colonial charm present in its infancy, rather than Surfers more blatant virtues. Jeremy cycled here and used it as a training exercise, with Liz going on ahead in the car for the weekend, and said to join them. "The place is big enough for two more," and of course that is what we did.

It was here at Noosa that life changed for the better, and whether Martin really wanted the bunk bed, in leaving me with a hugely luxurious double, or that I decided it was payback time for sleeping on the settee I'm not sure. Apart from the Tasman

Ferry, which was a bit cramped and kept lunging from side to side, this was only my third night, after Hobart and Perth that I have actually slept in a bed reminiscent of hygiene since leaving England, and all at our hosts' expense I must add; it really was very good of them.

Monday 4 June

Decision time has crept up at an alarming rate of knots, when our working visa's run out on Friday, and with it a bit of pressure in making some hasty decisions. This can always be changed at a later date though. To renew them for a further six months, the authorities stipulate that an outward ticket must be shown with each application, which cost $30 in administrative fees regardless of whether our visa is reissued or not; after months of deliberation I have bought the following air tickets with one eye on visiting China; America has been put on hold for another time.

September 9th Sydney-Auckland;
January 9th Christchurch-Sydney.
March 6th Sydney-Manila;
March 16th Manila-Hong Kong.

Martin will be on the same flight to Auckland, but stays onboard for Los Angeles; we also have both veered away from our initial plans, and become sidetracked from the original objective concerning A-N.Z-C-U.S.A.

Tuesday 12 June

Liz and Jeremy dropped us off at the small town of Nambour, in time for us to visit the CES and to further our search. I again wondered where we might be if good people had not come our way. Brisbane is firmly behind us, when the search for work continues. As per usual the employment service was of little encouragement. The main strawberry growing area is around Pinewood close by.

Nambour soon disappears from the memory easily enough, rather than the Big Pineapple or even 6 km away the Big Cow, fifteen metres high and made of a fibreglass frame. They advertise the area, and can be climbed inside. Though first prize must go to the entrepreneur, who persuaded people to part with their hard earned dollars for the pink coloured storks, which invariably decorate gardens along the route. He made a small fortune I'm told, by hitting the right note at the right time. People eventually became bored of them, but there are still a number to be seen cast adrift along the route.

One of the problems that has crept up on us, and almost unnoticed in a way, is the fading daylight of winter at about 5pm. We have not had to worry about this with our accommodation taken care of beforehand since May 17th. Now we will have to take note of the elements once more, although temperatures on the coast remain pretty hospitable. We therefore returned to our old ways this evening by enjoying a couple of drinks in the local hotel. Before pitching one tent in a nearby field, and back to nature in readiness for normal service in the morning.

Wednesday 13 June

Our initial problems began when the main strawberry producers either did not need any Labour as "This is women's work," one replied, or to "Ask us in about three weeks, when the strawberries might be ripe." It wasn't a flat rejection, rather we were too early; in the mid morning sun we decided to backtrack our way towards Nambour, and then decide what to do next. It was now that the local sheriff stopped to have a word, all silently, and without fuss.

This was not one of those mad cop dashes through the streets to apprehend the villains of the piece, or anything like it. Rather we were just minding our own business, in keeping within the law, and then out of nowhere appeared trouble, for us at any rate that is.

"It's a bit obvious here boys, could you jump in the back. I'm taking you down to the police station," he remarked.

"Why's that?"

All over Australia we have been warned of Queensland's law enforcement approach, and that this might happen. Indeed it has been difficult to find any one to say a good word on their behalf. A lot of people have also met up with them, similar to us today, and were presumably received with the same response.

"Well the official line is that two people fitting your descriptions have been reported peddling drugs around nearby Pinewood," he replied.

'Thanks pal, and tell the other one,' I wanted to say. But as I wrote earlier there are times when discretion is the wisest cause of action, and of course if you are innocent there is nothing to worry about, is there?

Certainly Australia has a reputed major drug problem, which can never be won. The main stumbling block being that plants can easily be grown here, and particularly in Queensland, where temperatures remain warm, together with the vastness of its wilderness. It means that policing the entire area is merely unrealistic.

In about ten minutes we were parked outside the police station, and where we would like to have stayed. I don't know what Martin had on his mind; rather he would have been more confident with me than a few other individuals we have met so far. We then took the packs out of the boot, put them over our shoulders, and walked through the front door. We were then ushered into a small room.

It was here that two more uniforms were waiting with the keep net, and hoping to catch a backpacker red handed.

There was more than one reason for wanting to keep my mouth shut, and to do what they wanted. Simply put I did not trust them; no reasons really we were treated with good manners. But I still intended to watch like a hawk, and made it plain that is exactly how things stood. Martin was clean, and neither of us smokes the most basic of tobacco, and presumably it was the hashish that most interested them, as no crimes had been committed, or reported.

We were just the sardines between the bread; if anything were to be tried I wanted to see it at first glance, or in fact not let anyone be given the chance to plant anything we could not prove. If there was to be an allegation it had to be countered with a degree of confidence, which needed my utmost concentration.

"So boys do you smoke dope?" our friend asked, thinking he had the high ground and acting like it.

"No never touch it, nor does he," I replied.

We were clean, which is possibly why the whole episode seemed more of an enlightening experience than anything else. Perhaps if I had been with a stranger, I might not have been quite so confident. It's a negative thought that an individual might be innocently dragged into a trap through their friend's indiscretion, or just that two of you were going in the same direction.

Three against two, in a confined environment seemed unfair odds to me, when our rucksacks were then emptied and searched. The tents were taken apart, with an eye inspecting the poles; there was nothing, and nothing to see when we in turn were searched, and asked to take our shorts and socks off, then our top. This just left us standing there in our pants, with even less on than at our Salvation Army meeting, but no they did not want us to go any further. I was half expecting to be asked for the full strip, and had mentally prepared myself for the moment.

"Alright boys I can see you're not hiding anything," the police officer remarked, with his two colleagues about to be disappointed that we were not the bait to eat the hook.

We had admittedly been treated with respect of sorts, without having warranted this intrusion into our privacy, or perhaps the young officer was just looking for a promotion.

"Caught anybody before?" I remarked, on our return trip, when the offer of a cup of tea seemed somewhat remote.

"I've only picked up two other hitchhikers, and they both had marijuana hidden in their packs," he replied.

"What's the charge?" I said.

"About a $300 fine, two months imprisonment and deportation home. You two are the lucky ones," he replied.

I was not quite sure what to make of our unexpected visit to the police station. In a way any individual is at their mercy, and especially if we had been split up, which clearly was not the case here. Nambour though did not seem to hold the answers to our problems. It is one of those places with a rail route running through its heart and the signs of sugar cane its main financial ingredient, but that seemed about all. We had too many friends around here for my liking, and were now known to the local constabulary on the lookout.

We therefore elected to be dropped off on the highway, which was strange as hitchhiking appeared to be our only crime in keeping ourselves to our self; besides asking too many questions in a foreign land seemed somewhat too ambitious, with the cards all stacked against us. We now decided to head towards Gympie, and then onto Maryborough, two historic gold prospector communities turned affluent market towns. But the fruit was not ripe as yet.

It was between these two points that we received a lift from Stan, a weather beaten guy in his sixties, with a slight speech impediment problem. He was bean picking at Gunalda, a one pub, one shop town, and isolated on the map.

Stan, it is quite easy to imagine, has been doing this work all his life, and is probably lonely without marriage. He might have done the hops in Tasmania once, or regularly visits Victoria in January. It may sound bleak, but with a caravan and everything they might need in life, the laid back approach of the sundowners are to be envied.

"You can pitch camp next to my caravan, work starts at 7am; the job is yours for the taking," he enthused, even if it did mean getting up at 5.30am, and bright as a lark for such an unearthly hour of late.

Thursday 14 June

'Where's the sun?' I thought, standing there in the dark, with a hood over my head. These are not the temperatures we are used to, as Stan provided us with a hot cup of tea.

"Not bad Stan, blimey I'm cold," I replied.

"When do we start?"

"You have to see the farmer first, he knows you are here," he said.

We then walked into the field with the sun slowly beginning to warm up our lives and the farmer shortly put us to work at the end of a row, with the two of us working in total harmony. Stan was keen to begin, and a man in his element, he soon began to lose himself in the stringy leaves and plants that seemed to go on forever and a day. We had work, but what hard work this was to be, in searching through the jungle for every such small unit of vegetable.

My $14 would prove to be hard earned, over seven hours bisected by a lengthy rain delay, through the backbreaking exertions of international bean picking! The going rate is a sprightly 28 cents a kilo, in a country with a reputed average daily wage of about $40. This was hardly going to help us break even, then our time here will be gone, 'and so lads where have you been in the past three months, bean picking, did you say?'

Yes and what's wrong with bean picking, I like bean picking!

"That means we are never going to get ahead, if the rains continue, besides this is like tobacco picking all over again," Martin said, without enthusiasm.

I then looked over at Stan in his element, and a man following the seasons. In a way I felt envy at such a simple lifestyle, which he should be able to enjoy for a year or two yet, and who knows perhaps he has prepared himself financially for the time when he can no longer work the seasons and said: "You know, I do believe Stan actually enjoys this, in scratching his hands and storing the stringy greens away, we're rather like squirrels preparing for winter."

"Do you really want to stay here, this is only marking time, we might do better further on." Martin remarked.

"No you're right, breakeven is no use to us, let's cash in and move on at first light," I replied.

Friday 15 June

Bundaberg is a characteristic black spot of unemployment, where few jobs seem available. Although we only stayed here for a few hours, it did give us time to sniff out the local rum factory.

Martin still holds fond memories of his great 'bundies and coke' hangover from Christmas time, which invariably crops up in conversation, as if to say we will have to visit it, when the time comes. In a way we have detoured 50 km towards Hervey Bay, off the Bruce Highway, simply to take some photographs of each other with some rum boxes behind us; it should fill us with fond memories back home.

'Bundy' is more Outback than coastal bliss, and cast amid a dusty landscape. It was here that Bert Hinkler set a then world record for a continuous flight of 1270 km in length from Sydney to Bundaberg, his birthplace.

Hinkler must have been something special, with the enthusiasm of youth. He even completed his first takeoff in 1912, aged 19, in a home made glider on Mon Repos Beach. In 1921 his Baby Arvo was designed with numerous wires and a canvas covered shell, which in turn led to the formation of Qantas in 1922, or The Queensland and Northern Territories Aerial Service pioneered by Hudson Fysh and Paul McGuiness. This would demonstrate that an airline could be used for carrying mail and supplies to isolated areas of wilderness. They commenced operations at Winton, and then Longreach, on the route towards Mount Isa.

Qantas moved on in 1945, while Bert Hinkler, in 1928, completed the first solo flight between England and Australia. His house in Southampton, England, where he lived at the time of his death has recently been rescued from demolition, and since last year, found itself transferred to the Botanical Gardens here and now acts as a permanent reminder of Bundaberg's most famous son.

A young couple soon gave us a lift to a service station on the outskirts of Gin Gin together with a local tomato grower's telephone number. Unfortunately though he could only offer us two days work a week cucumber picking at $5.60 an hour. Admittedly this is good money by our present standards, but at a cost of five redundant days; we reasoned it made this an impractical idea.

Darkness soon crept up, and with it all our efforts today. The only people to stop for us either did not have enough room for our packs, or were police officers once more checking our passports, but not our belongings this time. Perhaps our names have been circulated as clean. We therefore eat at another service station, and chatted to some fellow hitchhikers who still seemed keen on chancing their luck. Then pitched one of our tents in a field near to the highway, ready for another try in the morning. But I really didn't mind, we were safe for the night and who knows where we might have ended up; time is still on our side.

Saturday 16 June

This stretch of our entire journey north, was perhaps the slowest we were to experience along the way; nothing comes to mind except standing besides the road and chatting about how long it will take us, and where we are heading for. It was already mid-morning before we managed our first lift, and this was only going onto the next town of Gladstone.

"Perhaps it's just this stretch, and that people have been scarred off by the police, or the rumours of those gone missing." Martin said.

"Well they certainly didn't vanish by themselves," I replied.

"Alright then if things are the same in the morning we will split up," he remarked, with my agreement.

Gladstone is another one of those dreary Australian towns with inhospitable looking parks, which seem to be Queensland's trademark. It lies on a basin floor with scorched hilltops shielding it from the Outback, below our lookout point; Bauxite ore is transported from Weipa, on the Cape York Peninsula, and processed in the aluminium plants. The coal yards in turn hardly add an air of fresh inspiration and beckon the tourists in their droves to clamber for hotel reservations. It is also ideal for sailing off to Heron Island, for a spot of snorkelling, and sun bathing.

Perhaps these unkind comments are the reason why we found ourselves serving an unscheduled one night's sentence in a local campsite, having given up hitchhiking in mid afternoon with little sign of a lift, instead of reaching the next destination.

Sunday 17 June

I think it was this lack of movement that persuaded us to jump in the back of a farmer's Ute; at least we will make some progress. But things were certainly not going to plan when at 2pm we found ourselves stranded in no man's land between Gladstone and Rockhampton. This was indeed our own fault as we accepted a lift, which in turn dropped us at the end of a farm drive.

"We should have known better than that," I remarked, when we decided to split up and try the individual approach.

It was my turn to start walking along the gravel highway, when Martin eventually got a lift. But he could not say anything due to there being only enough room for one person; he saw me struggling along the dusty roadside and reached our destination with plenty of time to spare.

One hour later and I still found myself walking along a never-ending insect infested kerb, covering my eyes every time a car shoots past, without good fortune coming my way. This is an ocean of dried dairy land, trees, snakes, insects and no houses.

Even the nearest cattle station is 18 km off my beaten track; it was quite a day.

Monday 18 June

Upon reaching Rockhampton we have now passed through the Tropic of Capricorn, or on its outskirts that inform travellers of such. I was not too impressed admittedly by Australia's beef capital, where a statue of a Bradford bull met us travelling north, into the southern approaches, while a Braham bull heralds those coming from the north; all in keeping with the traditions of the town, but then I'm constantly reminded that this is indeed a big country still developing an identity and culture.

The town has its roots in the over enthusiastic gold rush of 1858, which left hundreds of settlers stranded at an isolated point, 40 km inland, on the banks of the Fitzroy River, below Mount Archer, that prompted its formation; when a local stockman noted its location as a convenient port.

With no visible parks, greenery, and few benches, or tables with millions of ants living besides the water, there is nothing much to report.

"What a desolate place," Marty said, in the heat of an evening glow.

"Not good is it," I replied.

It was difficult to argue, and something of a reoccurring theme away from the water's edge. Progress has been made, but we must stay put until the morning in an official campsite; Rockhampton though is a town that is invariably used to launch holidaymakers towards far better things, just a short bus and ferry ride away.

Tuesday 19 June

So this is it our first island and one worth waiting for, it's taken us over six months to reach this point, or myself that should be. Martin had Rottnest and now we both have Great Kepple, 13 km offshore from the terminal at Yappon, and 40 km from Rocky. It has been the focal point of an advertising campaign, designed to entice people away from their normal way of life, and to take it easy in the sun, with slogans like: Get wrecked on Great Kepple! and After a holiday on Great Kepple you'll really need a holiday!

The island is 14 square km in size, with 18 km of sandy beaches; inland there are some lightly wooded rises and mud flats. It is only a short stroll along a few footpaths to some of the world's finest white sandy beaches, and almost deserted in places. The main resort is situated in one confined corner, of which the hotel is a focal point with camping and a youth hostel close by. The owners do not want to spoil its character, or is it that the local planners are intent on keeping this haven, as it should be. A little piece of paradise we can all enjoy without the financials coming along to build their beachside mansions to the detriment and character of the island.

I was impressed; this has real potential cast adrift, and especially in winter when there are not so many people about. The beaches would be full in summer, and the footpaths congested with bikinis and couples looking for seclusion. But here in winter it is almost deserted, and we found our day nicely curtailed on a deserted sandy surface without a soul in sight. What a place this would be to visit with a group of friends when sat under a palm tree and enjoying the surf with my feet in the sand, this really is 'the' life…

Obviously we met numerous holidaymakers during our short stay, but none were stranger than Arthur, a forty year old 'jockey,' when it transpired that we had a two hour wait for the ferry after we dismantled the tents in preference to another night's payment.

It was a nice day, and we had time to enjoy a beer and mellow out, when the man opposite began talking in riddles, as if to beckon us over. We had not seen him before, and judging by the state of him he might need the black coffee in the morning.

"Have you been here long?" I remarked.

"No just arrived, early this morning; my twin brother was murdered here four days ago," he replied.

"I haven't seen anything," I said.

"That's maybe, but I have come here to sort out the culprit."

"Who's that?"

"That would be telling, the police are on their way right now," he said, and then clicked his lips to the sound of an imaginary horse.

"I'm leaving on the next ferry, due to a racing appointment tonight, but you two watch out for anybody carrying a spear gun, that's how they killed him," he said.

This was our queue to leave early; Arthur preferred to stay, to soak in the sun and click his lips, and to find some more passing strangers, many of which had given him a wide berth as we spoke. We never did see him again, and certainly not on the ferry, where Martin voiced his opinion about him being a 'right nut case,' over a beer or one to avoid.

"All quite entertaining though," I replied in thought.

Naturally nobody had heard of this alleged murder, and even the police officers failed to emerge, in which case I must conclude that Arthur's only appointment was probably in his dreams; that have remained that way ever since his childhood and beyond, towards the glow of Great Kepple and cast along its long white sandy beaches.

Saturday 23 June

I was not sure of our prospects this morning with the slow flow of traffic, but nothing can ever be certain as things panned out nicely from near Rocky. That's the way sometimes; one day it is all a struggle, and the next two guys pick you up, offer us a hotel room for the night and a few beers into the bargain.

Richard the driver, in his thirties, runs the business venture while Clive, about ten years older, fits in somewhere in the bigger scheme of things; perhaps as the accountant, but it was not really clear. They are here to do some business relating to Richard's earth moving business in Port Moresby, Papua New Guinea (PNG), situated north of the Cape York Peninsula, and who seemed pretty friendly in their outlook. We now chatted on route, and the lads said to stay with them, in Mackay, when we can all go out "for a drink" and visit a nightclub.

"Sure why not," I agreed, knowing that Martin would only be too pleased, rather than spend another night in a tent with me!

"I can fly you to PNG free of charge, and put you both up," Richard said, over a beer shortly.

My head was slowly beginning to rotate; "here have another beer," they kept saying, and drank in rounds of two, without offering us the chance to say no, or even delve into our pockets. This is all I need, two hardened drinkers thinking I can keep up!

"How about the flight back, how much will it cost us?" I said.

"At an estimate about $183 each," Clive replied.

"It sounds rather tempting, is there any chance of a week's work in your earth moving business. It would be nice, but it will put our finances back towards the red," I said.

"Unfortunately the wage rates are much too low to allow white people on the workforce," he said.

"Why's that?"

"It would cause friction. Port Moresby is a dangerous place to be, especially at night," Richard said.

"It sounds tempting, besides the sea and on your beach front veranda, but it's out of our range," I replied.

"Did you mention a night club?" Martin remarked.

Fortunately this idea was shelved at around midnight with us all buying beef burger and chips for the hotel room. Why I am not sure, nothing could have soaked up the alcohol, as I lied on the single bed and tried my first bite. Martin had the other single, and our hosts the secondary room off ours fit no doubt for a family. We said nothing and there was soon silence; simply both shot to pieces and without an appetite to match.

Sunday 24 June

I woke this morning wondering where I was and then realised what had happened, when we were picked up, and wished we had drunk one stubby less! I was still on the bed and fully clothed with Martin tucked up under the covers. My hamburger was looking the worse for wear, with a single bite mark missing, there's nothing like cold burger for breakfast. Where do they put all that beer? This is criminal, black coffee, and then I thought of Arthur, perhaps he wasn't so loopy after all; things can only get better…

Through out these pages this was my only such discretion into the murky world of too much of a good thing! I had to report it just to confirm such lightheaded matters sometimes exist, even without two beans to rub together…

We now left Mackay, and continued on our route north towards Bowen further on up the coast, where the lads from PNG dropped us off in the high street, having said we could stay onboard until Cairns if we liked. But then we thought of the missed places on route, and that it was highly unlikely, I could make another session with them, which even Martin had found a bit "heavy going."

Bowen it has too be said is no beauty and far from it that should be, with its deserted streets; the dusty surroundings, and a drought affected harbour. This in effect decided us that north Queensland's earliest settlement, established in 1861, was not for us and especially as tomato picking doesn't even start until next month.

The beaches are supposed to be spectacular near here, but then strangely we have seen many of those in the past few weeks to satisfy our needs.

"Bowen can be our reserve option," Martin remarked, as we soon set our sights on another trek further north with a fresh lift. We could have been there much earlier, but I didn't mind, my brain was only too grateful for small mercy that it would be clear in the morning.

We arrived in Townsville as the sun was at its hottest and immediately noticed the vast improvement to most of the places we have seen on route, with a little added character thrown in for good measure. It's much cleaner, fresh and spaced out in a more natural environment, but still not full of inspiration. This is the state's third largest city, which serves as a port for the agricultural and mining production of the mammoth inland region.

Townsville was founded in 1864, by John Melton and Robert Towns who realised a settlement further north was becoming increasingly important to local stockmen. The real problem with Bowen was the distance that they had to travel, when the Burdekin River invariably flooded. Now with Townsville established, they had their own market close at hand. The prosperous goldfields also accelerated its future development

130 km inland at Charters Towers, from between 1872 and 1916; at its peak it reached an outlying population of 30,000, coupled with the Ravenswood's gold discovery in 1868. All of which was of benefit to the local environment with the passing trade and the supply of provisions through the local harbour and by road.

During the afternoon we left our rucksacks at the police station and climbed a steep mountainous range of 290 metres above Townsville, towards the Castle Hill lookout point. I could now see the flood plains and Rosie Creek meandering towards us from far into the distance. We must also approach from here when we visit Ayers Rock.

Martin has never mentioned much about that, and yes we still have to do it. How can we claim to have experienced Australia, and surely not? Perhaps that is for later on when we have more money; things are getting bare. But I still have a money order to pick up in New Zealand when the time comes, which might mean changing my plans, and heading for the Rock afterwards. It's a long way out into the distance and half way across a vast continent, without too much to see, rather like an endless sea of Outback that leaves Townsville with plenty of scope for its future development.

Monday 25 June

We were in no hurry this morning, having camped in the bush, and walked back into town for a little sightseeing, and to make our plans. I had rather hoped this might act as a launching pad for better things. But one glance at the job centre left us in no doubt this was not going to be our window of opportunity. There was nothing to keep us here now, after writing a few postcards, and then making our way towards the highway, for the continuation of our trek towards Cairns.

It was here that we met a Canadian who had been standing besides the road for eight hours together with another hitchhiker from Germany, which left us in doubt of ever leaving, and struck up the thoughts of splitting up again.

"No problem, we will start to walk up the road and out of sight. It might help you both, there is no point in all of us standing here," I replied.

But how wrong could I be, when two minutes later, with us still walking a rustic coach in dire need of fresh paint, shuddered to a halt on the gravel in front of us.

"Jump on, there is plenty of room," Chris the driver, in his twenties said.

"Thanks very much, where are you going?"

"Cairns, I have driven this machine through the heart of the Outback, and right through the centre for the owners who want it renovated," he replied.

"I wondered about that when I saw the number plate, with the home of the America's Cup on it," I remarked.

"Yes good that, it's usually the state of excitement, but someone decided on a change, everybody has mentioned it coming across," he said.

What luck, as we again met our two friends, who were soon joined by a Frenchman, and an Australian, which bolstered our international gathering to seven young people representing five countries from three different continents.

It was all going too well, when 130 km south of Cairns the wreck-mobile finally swaggered to a halt after a journey full of stops and starts due to airbrake problems. We all hoped the vehicle might hold together; so near and yet so far, but as soon as we got onboard the problems started to escalate again and then finally we came to a halt to move no more.

"That's it, I thought we might just make it," Chris remarked.

In this instance, oil was spurting out of the engine, and effectively has taken us off the road indefinitely, all done and dusted.

At least we had a place to sleep, and some uncomfortable coach seats to sleep on for the night, with the candle of adventure still burning bright. There was also a local pub only two hundred metres away for us to frequent; things could have been a lot worse, as we all piled out and bought Chris a drink, it was the least we could do.

Tuesday 26 June

Our breakdown truck arrived fairly early but to no avail, the coach would have to be towed on towards its destination, and meant that we all had to start hitchhiking. It is illegal for anybody to sit in a vehicle while being towed along.

Martin and myself began to walk, rather than decide who would begin hitching, and who might watch and wait their turn. In the event we probably made the right decision when after a ten minutes walk we found ourselves riding in a slow 1960s open topped farmyard van, typically Outback like and with our packs resting in the back.

There had been no sign of our friends passing by, which probably meant we arrived ahead of the others in the capital of the far north, now both very humid and full of tropical vegetation. Cairns originally developed as a post for inland gold, and in turn tin mining, but now sugar cane is its major industry. The biggest surprise came when we walked towards the beachfront only to notice the presence of mudflats instead of Queensland's usually sandy coastline.

We hung around, as you do, and began to walk about and take in the atmosphere. At such times people invariably find themselves in the park, and we were no different to that. It was here that I met my first middle-aged Aboriginal, who started swearing at us for no other apparent reason than a cry for help.

"You European racialists you're responsible for my plight," he bemoaned.

Martin remained silent, in hoping like myself, that he would leave us be. This is not our problem, we're only guests here ourselves.

"Why, don't you do something about it and stand up for yourself," I replied

The Aboriginal seemed somewhat taken aback by this attitude and assumed we didn't care. Nobody had ever given him the encouragement he needed to breed confidence.

"Why what can I do?" he said.

"Work together, back your Aboriginal leaders, then they've got to listen," I replied, with those negative thoughts visibly subsiding from his outgoing mannerisms.

The Australians do invariably agree on one point though, that Queensland is approaching a 'police state,' where hitchhiking is supposedly illegal. I have been worried about 'thumbing' towards Cook Town, as apparently we are just as likely to be fined $50 or put in jail for three days, such is the pessimism that people pass on by word of mouth.

In Mareeba adverse publicity has come about where a sergeant, with a good record of catching drug peddlers has recently been transferred. Now the moral of his ways depicts that he refuses to go and wants to know why. Television and newspapers have lapped up his command performance of paid interviews, which has hardly impressed his superiors, and especially the comments concerning the alleged corrupt practices that have been going on recently. Some people say the fuss is all about money and his devotion to the limelight, while for others, the jury is firmly out on what is really behind these headlines.

We now left our newfound friend, who smiled and I felt refreshed, it might do some good, and who knows. We presently met a fellow young pauper who invited us along for, "a free meal at the Salvation Army, everybody's welcome," he said, and was obviously in a hurry himself.

Had our dreams of adventure really come to this?

"What do you think?" I said.

"We haven't eaten yet today," Martin replied.

"Alright then, it might be interesting," I agreed, and soon questioned such wisdom when an apple whizzed past my ear in the canteen.

"Friendly bunch," I remarked, glancing about me, and just about the only hikers in the place, among the locals down on their luck.

Our friend though appeared to be in a good mood.

"I found a child's bicycle at 2am, that's the best time for finding things when nobody can claim them," he said.

"Why's that?"

"The ten dollars I sold it for will come in handy," he remarked.

I couldn't think and didn't really care, why are we here?

"Have you a job?"

"No, I was sacked from my porter's job after inventing my credentials at The Hilton, you know the mugs believed me," he said.

"So what happened?"

"Oh, my alarm clock failed on my first day," he replied, unconcerned with soup and a main meal to keep him happy.

For us it was soon time to leave and we would not be back. Martin did not feel too easy, and perhaps he was right, as he preempted my own decision; I would soon follow, out into the fresh evening air and agree the idea is best left alone from now on.

"However hungry we might get," he said.

"That's maybe, but never forget a gift horse, it might be all we can afford soon," I replied, and somewhat uneasy at such thoughts.

Saturday 30 June

Glancing through my guidebook, our next logical move, work wise, might be to search out the Atherton Tablelands, inland from Cairns. These are actually three plateaux's of varying height. They were named after John Atherton, who cut a route through the dense forest in 1877 to make the tin deposits at Herberton a viable possibility; the land rises from the coast, and then glides gently towards the Great Dividing Range. It has a rare combination of warm temperatures at altitude, the tropical temperatures, heavy rainfall, and some rich volcanic soil that combines to make it one of the richest dairy producing areas in the tropics.

This was not, it has to be admitted, our most successful of missions. In what is strangely cold by recent standards, and especially at night with all our jumpers on. A rise in height can be deceptive. The real problem has been our timeless attitude, or time and nothing much achieved that should be.

We began our search at Mareeba, the centre of the tobacco, and rice growing harvest. The CES could not be of any help, indeed we wondered why they were here, in giving us relevant information, or even seemed to know anything about their local area. At least in Atherton they made some enquires for us. However, the farmers only needed experienced people in the sugar cane industry; the tobacco crop does not get underway until September. Martin seemed quite relieved at this, and can it really have been that bad? We even tried the potato board, but again local farmers only had the odd day available.

Hitchhiking around here was an easy exercise due to everybody's rather laidback attitude to life. We then headed for the area's main attraction, the Tineroo Fall Dam, which has in turn created Lake Tineroo. This is a kind of boating haven, where the waters are fed via a channel system in order to irrigate the crops in the Mareeba/Dimbulah area. Unfortunately that just about sums it up, very little happened and there is nothing much to report.

We might have stayed longer in these parts had it not been for the freezing nights huddled in our sleeping bags near the picturesque Milla Milla Falls. Our last night was even spent in a graveyard, or should I say an overgrown field containing seven headstones, all dated between 1932 and 1935, after which people either stopped dying in these parts, or merely 'moved' on to better things.

Sunday 1 July

Hitchhiking was almost impossible at times, as we struggled in today's heavy winds, so much so that Martin appeared to almost give up momentarily on the highway outside Innisfail, and preferred to read while I too sat down, a little deflated on the rucksack. My thumb was outstretched more in hope than the expectancy of attracting a passing motorist, but this is also Sunday.

Eventually we obtained a lift from a young Australian who seemed interested in talking about England, where he once lived. As a travelling salesman who clocks up 75,000 km a year he decided to drive us into Cairns, 40 km out of his way, and illustrated the distances nicely.

"No worries, it's only a hop skip and jump by Australian standards," he remarked.

Monday 2 July

At the post office I received £200 from England, which is my rebate on the original Australia-New Zealand air ticket, bought in order to obtain our working visas. The exchange rate is at a disappointing low due to the four month's old miners' strike in England; it has caused the world's money markets to show a lack of confidence in the pound. In all I received $305.17 which could not have arrived with better timing as our finances have now plummeted to a combined $15.

Tuesday 3 July

Our prohibited campsite on the esplanade has ceased to be an alternative, due to a city counsellor instructing us of our law breaking activities, first thing in the morning, as we completed our packing for the day. Still we could not complain it was only a matter of time before this became apparent, my only surprise had been how we got away with it for so long. It's something we decided to continue until the yellow card was shown, or we moved on, before the police made it red.

We then started walking towards the shops, when a girl appeared at a window of her colonial styled house, with wooden steps going up to the one storied living space. There were three students present and they seemed keen to chat, having seen us for the past two nights, and decided to introduce themselves over coffee, and toast. It was here in turn we met a friend of theirs who hired us to load up his van with cartons of beer and kegs, for $15 each, coupled with a look around the Cairns Castlemaine Distillery, and time well spent. We will always remember the following radio advert, as will any Australian for that matter:

'I can feel a XXXX coming on.
Got the taste for it, just can't wait for it.
I can feel a XXXX coming on!'

Our good fortune appeared to be continuing when I found a five-cent coin, and an empty purse. We then watched a small roll of rope fall off the back of a post office van, which soon disappeared into the dusty horizon, and left us wondering what to do with it. The main depot was close by, and with the day still young we decided to drop it in to enquire if there was a reward. However they did not seem too interested in handing out some small change for the safe return of their property.

In the evening we found Anita, an Aboriginal woman in her thirties, who was full of her matrimonial problems, when we met her on our previous visit. Anita and her friend had insisted upon buying us drinks, in a local bar, while they drank their sorrows away in self-misery. Again we chatted, but this time it was our turn to repay our debt of buying.

"Hey guys, let's go and do something exciting," she enthused, with her glass held in the air, and a mischievous look on her face.

Heaven forgive me, she's on the pull! The dance floor would never have seen anything like us in hiking boots, and freaking out with a disenchanted Aboriginal woman, it was time to leave.

I now bought another drink to prepare our departure, and wished her well in sorting out these problems. There is no future in the glass, but at least it eased the pain for the time being, and helped me feel a bit better about not being able to do anything.

When we made our apologies. Anita's eyes were full of tears

in a similar way that they were before we arrived. You can tell when the sadness has been this deep for sometime, or ever since she could recall.

"If only we could have helped," I said outside.

"We did, just by listening," Marty replied, as we walked into the dark.

Wednesday 4 July

The early morning hike into town took the best part of an hour, which at least warmed us up, after another cold sleepless night on hard ground. We therefore left our rucksacks at the youth hostel on the seafront and paid $5.50 each for a warm night's sleep, now nicely ahead of us.

Cairns has inevitably begun to grow on me, with its tropical gardens, the surrounding hills and a friendly atmosphere created beneath a warm haze. I liked the place and thought that at last we have found somewhere nice to live along this stretch of highway, which has been inevitably dry and arid through out.

We also needed variation, and for this we reached the station just in time to catch the tourist train, along the Kuranda railway line. These old styled carriages enabled us to stand outside at the ends to view the rugged scenes, and its beautiful valleys below, coupled with the Barron Falls. Kuranda is 34 km away, and fifteen tunnels long. The line was completed in 1888 at great expense and engineering know-how, situated on top of the Macalister Range.

From here we could have hitchhiked along the Kennedy Highway to Mareeba, and is perhaps where we missed a trick or two on our original trek out of Cairns.

In commenting on the small town of Kuranda, the view is worthwhile, and the Sunday market is supposed to be a hive of activity, but this is really just a place to buy your souvenirs, to enjoy a beer in the sun, and then reflect on the descent.

Nothing else of interest enlightened our lives and we met nobody to record, but that simply does not matter, not on this journey at any rate, until we again boarded the train and looked out of the windows, where everything remained fine, and very fine indeed…

9. The Great Barrier Reef

I would like to demonstrate my know-how of sea life, but knowledge could hardly describe the coral and my understanding; with a distance map that stretches for 2,000 km, along the Queensland coast from Gladstone towards PNG. This makes it the world's most extensive reef structure developed from living organs anywhere.

Coral is a primitive animal, and forms its hard surface by excreting lime. The hard skeleton is left to build up the reef after the coral itself has died. This is a process, which is continued when the new coral begins to form on its dead predecessors.

It is all quite interesting and something that should not be avoided. How can anybody claim to have 'seen' Australia without swimming in the Barrier Reef? As with other vegetation, coral has many pre-conditions, when for a start the water has to be non-salty, clear for sunlight, and even then it will only grow up to 30 metres in depth, together with a water temperature of 17.5°C. Hence the muddy water flow of the PNG Fly River and the low temperatures south of Gladstone, which stop the reef system from developing further.

Thursday 5 July

The islands can be divided into two types; those like Magnetic Island, off Townsville, are the tops of flooded mountains and have vegetation similar to the adjoining land; alternatively Green Island, 27 km off Cairns, was formed when coral took it above the waterline. The sand was created by water action to form beaches, while other vegetation eventually obtained its stranglehold on the island's barren open spaces.

It was Green Island that we found ourselves approaching this morning in the most appealing of winter's delight. Can this really be winter, and surely not, not a scorcher, but nicely pleasant for our purposes of getting to grip with the colourful coral below the water. Small in size, the islands sandy beaches and shallow waters enabled us to walk barefoot on the reef.

Today we have set our sights on an even closer inspection, as we changed into wetsuits, fitted our flippers, those goggles and finally struggled to put an oxygen tank on our backs.

At first I just swam around on top of the warm water in order to adapt to breathing through the mouthpiece. John, 'The Yank' our instructor, blond haired in his mid twenties, seemed to think I knew what I was doing! He apparently echoed such onboard as he watched me struggle to balance the lop-sided cylinder, and with it my swimming into a metal buoy, or to be accurate the only object in sight; it has left a small graze on my forehead.

Martin had echoed some nervous reservations about this, but to his credit was determined to rid himself of his underwater inhibitions, and a similar fear I have of parachuting. John kept in close contact with him in order to generate confidence, which left me examining the beautiful coral with its odd shapes and sizes.

My initial problems were soon put behind me when he let the air out of the life jacket, and let's just say I was soon away with the ferries. You see the Barrier Reef does these things to you in the most spectacular of manners. The radiant colours are quite spellbinding, and a sight nobody could ever tire of. Surely this tropical paradise is indeed nature's first wonder of the world, and could anything possibly match such a peaceful air of underwater tranquillity?

The most striking inhabitants are the coral polyps, while the skeletons are usually white. Complementing these are clams, which are embedded in the coral and individually have a different fleshy area. Starfish, sea urchins and tropical fish, also add to the sparkle in their own mystical ways.

On the other hand there are invariably the party poopers to be avoided; that surprisingly 'do not' include sharks, unless I am silly enough to keep swimming out to sea. Divers though have to keep an eye open for the scorpion fish. These are quite often colourful to warn off enemies, stonefish on the bottom for my feet, and the stinging jellyfish, along some of the coastal waters at certain times of the seasonal variations.

A minor controversy seems to be brewing up, due to John's insistence that his daytrips are perfectly safe under his own tuition. The official courses argue that more training needs to be undertaken before rookies like us are left to our own devices.

I would admittedly like to have obtained my diver's certificate, but at $120 over three days we could hardly afford such luxuries. It was only John's cut-price route to the coral that has given us our lifeline, although a less competent swimmer might admittedly struggle. He arrived here two years ago from America, liked the atmosphere and realised he could make a living in the all round summer conditions, rather than back home where the trade is all tied up with red tape.

"It was much easier for me to start up here," he said, who seemed pretty content, with no such signs of wanting to return home. "There is nowhere I would rather be than here doing something I love, and besides the water is so much fresher than off California."

Life could be much worse, doing a six-hour day in the sun and being paid for your efforts, which amounts to a little patience, and swimming on the Barrier Reef; it's no wonder he wants to remain providing he can stay ahead of the regulations, which seem destined to be tightened in the foreseeable future, due to his rivals' external pressure and a need for enhanced safety measures.

Friday 6 July

We were hitching on the outskirts of Cairns when an elderly couple stopped to pick us up; they seemed keen to chat, and especially when we said we were from England, and myself from the southeast in particular.

"We saw the Union Jack, and thought what harm can they do," Dorothy remarked, from the passenger seat.

"Yes that's what persuaded us to stop," Sid said.

"You can stay with us the night, if you like, and then we can drop you off on the highway in the morning. It would be so nice to have visitors from the old country," she presently said.

We now found ourselves in a plush new compartment, somewhat isolated of shops and the community. This was just right if you want peace and quiet and a mild winter, but what price in the summer for the ventilation? The view from our bedroom window at Yorkys Knob, north of Cairns, is simply spellbinding. In front lay a flat plain of tropical vegetation bordered by long sandy beaches and clear salty water coupled with a sunny breeze. In the distance the mountainous background acts as its rightful natural overlord.

"You know we've been out here over thirty years," Sid said.

"We have never been back," Dorothy added.

"Don't you ever want to?" I said.

"Perhaps, we have nostalgic memories of our time there when the gas lights were still in their element, but what smog there was at the time. They had no choice of banning the fires in London. You could hardly see anything in the winter mornings," he replied.

"I don't think it would be the same anymore, we lost contact with our friends, who might be dead for all we know," Dorothy said.

"Besides it might be a disappointment, seeing everybody again, and how they have changed. Sometimes it is best to stick with the memories," I said.

"Yes there is something in what you say there, it's just that your presence has stirred our memories," Sid said, silently thoughtful of a life long ago.

Saturday 7 July

Our hosts drove us up to the small town of Mossman this morning, along the beautiful Cook Highway, built in 1933; it runs poetically parallel with the Coral Sea at various stages. Mossman signals the end of north Queensland's sugar cane industry, and almost the road's end.

During World War II the United States offered to build a route free of charge connecting Cape York with southern Queensland, in return for permission to install strategic defence bases along the shores. However the Australians disliked any ideas of foreign forces being permanently housed in their country, together with the mistrust of becoming her allies more permanent satellite state, which is fair enough. There is nothing like your own independence that we all cherish and are loath to surrender, even in such insecure times. It is not difficult to see their logic, and in time the road is about to take another leap forward.

Our hosts dropped us off along a dusty road, besides the Daintree River where the road ends in branching off the main highway, and we are on our own. This is where the ferry connects the two sides, and a little divide between peace and harmony. I could hardly complain about the $1.20 crossing fee, as swimming would only have attracted the waiting crocodiles that doze in the water beneath some shaded vegetation.

"Big brutes aren't they," Martin remarked.

"Fancy a swim?"

"No just a beer," he replied.

"Have you got one…oh good man!"

The road through the tropical rain forest is fairly rough and in an unsealed state. It is exceedingly dusty, whenever a motorised vehicle passed us by. We now walked for about 10 km, up and down steep hills, making fairly good progress, until a rickety old campervan completed our projected 41 km journey across shallow fjords and past numerous campers having pitched for the night. There was no sign of any commercial life, beyond an information place early on, until we reached a site besides some rich sandy beaches beneath a paradise of tropical vegetation.

"Not bad this travel game, choose a palm tree to camp under," I remarked.

"We can put both tents up here, how about in the corner with the bushes behind us?" Martin said.

"Sounds good to me, it's a pity we do not have a hammock to sleep in," I replied; a winter spent in such a way would be sheer bliss, without ever wearing socks in the shade.

Sunday 8 July

It was all very quiet when I began my stretches in the shadows and asked the boy if he was up, only to find a deserted tent. He had already slipped off for provisions and breakfast. I then followed suit in guessing where he was and found the only colonial styled shop around here nicely under the palms. In all Australia, this was to be the nicest place we could imagine, and with the camping free! It's as if the place has been left to organize itself, for the benefit of the free spirited intent on making the effort.

I now made small talk with a young man outside who told me that we could live on a commune, twenty kilometres north of here, for $20 a week, however it was not clear if this is where he came from or not. The shop is typical Queensland, and constructed of wood, single storied, setback from the road, or the ideal place for my rocking chair in the evenings.

The Highways Commission wants to push through a road towards Bloomfield, which can be linked up with Cooktown. The town has never had a sealed entrance to it before, but apparently the alternative routes are too expensive for Queensland's sparse population to afford.

"The road will kill off some tropical vegetation, and especially where it meets the Barrier Reef. The developers are already buying up the cheap plots of land like vultures in anticipation of rich pickings," our friend said.

Further down the coast, near Yorkys Knob, our elderly hosts had shown us a plot of sand dunes covered with undergrowth.

"I sold this for three-quarters of a million dollars, only to be offered double that one week later," Sid said.

"So what happened?"

"Simple really, the bottom fell out of the market, and our developers had to cut their losses. The expense of building houses where nobody could afford to live made the whole venture impracticable," he replied.

Australia does not have any capital gains tax at present, which has been beneficial to the residents of the Yorkys Knob and the Port Douglas areas. Most people here feel the government will win their fight in the end, although it might take time with the added expense of fighting a committed but small array of activists who are well organised and appear to be gathering support for their cause.

"We intend to blockade the road if workmen move in, we can make it difficult which would advertise our cause. You see what happened in Tasmania, people like us really can make a difference," he remarked.

"It would certainly be a shame to disturb this little piece of paradise," I said.

"Even the federal road building minister has a financial stake in these parts," he replied.

"All of which means there's only going to be one result?"

"That's maybe, but we have chains and tunnels all encompassed into our defence plan," he said.

The problem here is a feeling of isolation in the extreme, when gathering a worthwhile protest group together, for what will be only a road and not the wanton destruction of an area of outstanding beauty. But I can see their point of view. A way of life invariably changes with communications. Build a three-lane motorway through the heart of Africa and see the effects to a life cast back in centuries of time. Outside people would arrive and the community that is being protected might change forever.

"You certainly aim to make your point," I replied, in slight admiration.

At least they are trying to do something, even if it would appear a forlorn gesture. It's mighty difficult these days to stand in the way of progress, however people might not like it in an ever-evolving world.

This was not one of our most efficient pieces of planning though in deciding to hack our way through Cape Tribulation. Our idea was to go on further up the coast towards Cooktown, and over the Broomfield River. It all seemed rather easy, sitting there on the sandy beach, with the shop close by. This was one of those over enthusiastic ideas that perhaps might have been better left behind for another time, when the communications have improved and the disputes have sorted themselves out.

Captain Cook named Cape Tribulation for the very good reasons that Sorrow Mountain just behind the Cape is named; this I can now acknowledge. For a start we betrayed the old adjective, of always staying together, or I did that should be in trying to blast my way through the dense vegetation. Then tried a right-handed route, only for Martin to disappear into the undergrowth and beyond. There was nothing for it but to keep going and hope I could find a way through, which seemed to be pushing me further out into the sea and my bearings.

'This is thick stuff,' and unlike England, the most dangerous element might be a twisted ankle in a rabbit hole, or a wild boar in Kent. But not here, there are snakes and lizards, and what about a spider's biological home. This is certainly no place to be at night, in the darkness of the twigs moving, silently crawling towards me, creeping and slithering under the leaves.

'I've got to get out before dark! This is no good, and no good at all. I'm scratched and hot, the sweat is almost uncomfortable on my back, as I tried heading inland, and still could not see the top, and the chance to head down the other side; it's no use this is just too dense without a cutter. I'm going to have to abandon this idea and head back to the beach, and then think again. That water down there looks mighty inviting, with the waves nicely right for sitting on the sand and letting it roll all over my body.'

Soon the sun began to disappear over the horizon, only for an orange glow to appear at sunset and right then on the beach everything remained as one.

Monday 9 July

I rose early and still found no sign of Marty, who could not be too far away, and wondered what he might do. In some respects we should have kept together, but then we would both meet up on the beach, instead of different sides. I soon made my way towards the shop, where I would remain until midday or then leave a message. As it happened he turned up at 10.30am, fresh looking and well rested, having fortunately read my mind.

"It's a long way up there, you can get through inland a bit, but it's going to be a long hike. Do you really want to continue?" he said.

"No not really, that was enough for me, this time around. Besides we still have to get back," I replied. The road towards Cooktown is apparently only a dirt track and beyond that four-wheel drive territory only, or trial's bike terrain on the way to the northern summit of Cape York.

In 1770 the Endeavour ran aground on the Barrier Reef 341 km north of Cairns. It's fair to note that Captain Cook must have been a worried man, as he looked out across the Endeavour River and the reef, in its threatening presence. He put ashore at Cooktown, and so 'established' the first British Australian settlement.

To get off the reef their only option had been to lighten their load with the heaviest of items like cannon, and shot being thrown overboard, which were recently recovered by divers. The Endeavour itself was repaired on the banks of the river. Here there is a lookout where Cook may have stood, viewed the scenery and wondered how they might find their way back?

In a way his biggest concern was further out to sea, and what might happen if they became grounded in a storm. The seas can get mighty rough and inhospitable at times and especially in unchartered waters; at Cooktown the good Captain was a man with a problem on his mind, the seafaring safety of his men was his greatest concern.

A hundred years on and there were thirty thousand gold prospectors along the nearby Palmer River. By 1874 it was second only to Brisbane in population, with the Chinese of more than two thousand complicating the issues of this lawless time, and the racial overture that it inevitably brought with it. Cook could probably never have imagined such a time when he arrived, and he became such an important part of this little piece of paradise.

Today Cooktown is more laid back; the prospectors have all gone away, similar to our band of pear pickers who all congregated around the orchards until there was no more fruit to pick, and a living to be made. Now those huts are empty and gaining dust for another six months or so, until the people begin to arrive in the readiness of a fresh harvest, with the goldfields now all a thing of the past.

How we were going to obtain a lift I could not tell, without any passing traffic was unclear, but beggars cannot be choosey, and if we had to hike all the way back to the river then so be it, a day would suffice; but the faster the better and what luck that should be.

We started out with a fresh impetus, and sometimes having to take our walking boots off to wade bare foot across various shallow streams, without a 'croc' in sight it has to be said. There's nothing like wet socks, to make life uncomfortable with an aroma to match. After an hour's sweltering walk we managed to hitch a lift, to Cairns, in the back of an open topped truck with the wind wonderfully cooling our minds.

"This is the life," Martin remarked, on the open highway.

"Not bad; early evening, we should do it before nightfall," I replied, and smiled.

It had been another memorable adventure.

Thursday 12 July

The previous evening had been spent camping at Mission Beach, an 8 km stretch of sandy coastline looking out towards the mountainous mound of Dunk Island. In another instance we might have caught a ferry across to the small mass 5 km in size. Dunk was the subject of *The Confessions of a Beachcomber*, by E.J Banfield, who lived there between 1897 and 1923; in what must have been an idyllic lifestyle cast adrift of the world we know today. It would have been nice to sit and read his book on the beach, as he once did, in the place he knew so well and to search out his descriptions, of the rainforest and bird life. But we now had more pressing matters time wise, and have to continue south.

Fortunately Bruce picked us up, having again noted my patch, and thought that being from Cornwall he ought to stop for a bit of nostalgia. He has been here for two years now, and travels around the country in his capacity, as an agriculture consultant selling tractors or simply just acting as a go between with their various showroom outlets. He had his hotel pre-booked, but said we could camp here in the evening and to be ready in the morning when he could take us further on, providing we did not mind a short wait in Tully.

"No problem," Martin remarked.

We now waited in a rainstorm, and true to form, while Bruce had some business matters to attend to. Tully is reportedly the wettest place in Australia, with an average sprinkling of 440 cm a year. Sugar cane is again the dominant crop, but it is rumoured that banana picking is due to start in this locality soon. However, the nearest CES office is further north at Innisfail, which meant we were unable to check out this information.

Unfortunately the post office in Townsville did not yield any of our letters from Brisbane, which had not been posted as promised. Our situation was to go on for a further twelve frustrating days. I even phoned through, only to be told 'They've been posted,' which let's say wasn't exactly true, when the postmarks were eventually inspected. People are overstretched in their own busy lives, and our concerns were not theirs. We have decided to continue to use the post offices in future, as they keep letters for a month, and in turn will also forward them to us or eventually return any letters to the sender. At least the matter will now be more in our own hands.

Friday 13 July

Magnetic Island is one of the cheapest islands for travellers to enjoy in Queensland, with two camping sites and two youth hostels. Captain Cook named it in 1770, when he possibly imagined this block of mountainous land resulted in his compass performing cartwheels.

The island is barren looking without nourishment, on first sight, faded green in vegetation and is made up predominantly of granite. It is 11 km long at its furthest points, surrounded by 40 km of coastline, and 8 km across the Cleveland Bay from Townsville.

Our visit has been planned to coincide with Ian, whose letter has finally been received. I was still feeling slightly guilty about this, but knew deep down things have turned out fine. He in turn seemed in pretty good fettle. However, his dates have been brought forward, which meant our paths would cross ironically for one night only, Friday the Thirteenth.

"How have you found it?" I said.

"Great, I spent a lot of time watching cricket," he replied.

"Still dotting every ball on the scorecard!"

"Of course," he remarked, and the quite the essential Englishman abroad, with blue jeans and a knotted handkerchief shielding his head from the sun.

"Same old image then!"

"I'm going home soon, my sixty day bus pass will take me back to Melbourne in three weeks, next stop Ayers Rock," he replied.

"No work then?"

"Nothing in Melbourne or Adelaide," he said, somewhat half-heartedly.

"It's time to go home, Ian, you've done it. I'm proud of you. The locals have a saying something like, Good on ya cobber," I replied, as we celebrated in the shade of nightfall and swapped anecdotes; in the morning he would soon be gone and far away.

Sunday 22 July

I awoke to see the first fall of rain, and hoped that Martin had remembered to pick up my bag and camera. But when he and Rod returned they said they had not seen it. After a thorough search of the beach I found it, where I had stopped to put my trainers on, before Sheila and myself had climbed the footpath out of Rocky Beach last night, after celebrating Rod's birthday. Was it only last night that eight of us huddled under a blanket together, while he blew out the candles, to the echo of 'happy birthday,' as our final finale?

Magnetic Island has been like this ever since Ian left. It's a shame; this has been our social highlight down under, at the youth hostel. No sooner have some left, than another group arrives. There was Astrid from Germany, and Stephanie of Switzerland, with her tanned bikini to recall, and then Catherine and Tanya, sun bathing on some elevated rocks. Only for me to climb up to say hello and in turn find them topless, before we then went for a swim. Yes I am going to miss my time here in seclusion, with plenty of wild terrain to explore, and badminton partners.

Then there are the nights out pulling faces to *Thriller,* while Rod's crazy dancing style will be remembered by all concerned. He flies back to England shortly, and to think his return flight has only cost him £110 due to his father being an airline pilot; I could do with one of those! A cut-price air ticket might have left us with some room for manoeuvre. Still everybody seems to be in the same 'boat' as to speak, and purely grateful for our affordable environment.

Martin, and myself had our final swim, packed the rucksacks, then cooked a meal, and hiked off towards Picnic Bay where we intended sleeping on the sand before catching the ferry in the morning.

Unfortunately the rain, and prior to that another social gathering crept around a fire to keep me awake. In which case I merely walked out of the darkness to join them, when for some reason Martin had left me to my own devices.

Magnetic Island has proved a most memorable experience with an array of hikers invariably present to pass on their tales and information. Everybody has seemed so friendly and relaxed; the island brings out the best in all of us, without any pressure and no stress, or to us, where people can remain themselves. So much so that it is a shame to ever leave, but then we could not stay indefinitely, or could we…

Wednesday 25 July

My enthusiasm for hitchhiking to Ayers Rock has waned considerably due to the distance, time and our low finances. We seem to have achieved most of our objectives along the way, but still that elusive job has fallen out of our grasp. Timing in life is everything and to this point it has to be admitted we have fallen short. Everybody we have spoken to informs us we are indeed entitled to social security money because we hold a working visa, in exchange for the Australians in England, or as one person said: "It's only fair."

I have never been keen on this idea on moral grounds, but we are likely to pay our tax dues in the future, when others following us will likewise take advantage of these opportunities. We now unanimously decided to make further enquiries in Brisbane, some seventeen hours away.

The heavy tropical rains never relinquished on this most potent of days, when the water level slowly eroded our one piece of shelter, and for once in an official camping site, which slowly became immersed amidst an earthly quagmire. I soon began to have visions of *Radio Caroline* sinking in the North Sea, and would have little choice but to scuttle our pitched tent and hang our soggy belongings in a covered way to dry.

Whatever happens we are going to get drenched if we decide to move, at which we elected to stay put and wait until tomorrow for dryer conditions. We even contemplated catching a coach, but at $77 each by Greyhound we soon realised the futility of such ideas.

Some of the roads, including the main highway towards Alice Springs need forward drive vehicles, according to radio reports. How far inland this persists is unclear. I can put together another game plan in Brisbane; although it looks more than likely this will have to be a solo effort from now on.

During the evening a young girl invited us back to her mother's caravan for shelter and some video viewing; ten minutes on and we were left alone.

Nobody seemed too concerned about us stealing anything, when the inhabitants all went out for an evening's recreation. A neighbour appeared somewhat later and offered us a beer, and then he also left, but we never did see the owners again. They simply put a video on, which "has not been released in America as yet," and disappeared to where I'm not sure. We finally switched off the television set and the lights, bar one, for their benefit when they finally returned.

Friday 27 July

Yesterday's grey clouds, which brought with them twenty-four hours of tropical rainfall, was replaced this morning with a radiant blue sky. Fortunately we only have to walk out onto the highway close by to start our journey, with our sign 'Brisbane Please,' or about 1570 km. Distance never seems to faze us now. Invariably we reach our destination, and more often than not in quick time.

This was to be one of those days, when Greg a travelling salesman seemed intent on reaching Brisbane early Saturday morning, and wanted the company to keep him mentally awake. He also appeared quite relieved when Martin offered to do some of the donkeywork driving through these eternally distant highways. However I had to decline his offer, as my international driving license is still clogged up in the British bureaucratic system. None of the motorists I have hitched with have been stopped, which might just lead to one of those sod's law situations.

On this occasion, true to form, a small kangaroo presently jumped out in front of us, giving Martin no time to react in the dark or even swerve. The only blessing was the severe dent beneath the bumper meant it never suffered, having unfortunately been blinded in the car headlights.

Our only stopover on route was to be at Australia's sugar capital of Mackay. The surrounding area is responsible for a third of the country's output. It was here we changed hire cars, and sat in a café for about two hours contemplating the journey ahead. For me it would be the backseat and sleep interrupted by some none-stop music to keep either driver awake.

John Mackay was a settler who began farming the fertile Pioneer Valley in the 1860s. The town, situated on the Pioneer River, is now also a coal exporter, mainly to Japan. But its most memorable attraction remains the burning of the sugar cane. This is planted in November, only for the land to become covered in a blanket of dusky green leaves, rising above head height, during its seven months of growth.

Before cutting begins the fields are fired to burn out the leaves and to maximize its sugar content. Five minutes south, we pulled up on the grass verge, with smoke drifting across the highway, to watch this most picturesque of agricultural methods, also designed for clearing the crops of its resident snake population. The flames illuminated the dark backdrop, with just the hint of a star to be seen through the naked flames.

Monday 30 July

When you have got money anything is possible in life, but if the kitty is dry there is nothing much left we could do except to find a job or sign on. In the circumstances we opted for both, in an effort to obtain some kind of an income to get us through our remaining weeks.

It was during this time that we encamped ourselves in a student pad, where exam fever has laid everybody low. By the time we decided to leave we had become paranoid of every little noise, of switching on the radio or slamming a door, and even the creaking floorboards. It's nice to pass with flying colours, but the fear of failure is often the motivating factor, when we are judged by exam technique. The reality is that some children can kick a football and others could practice all day, every day, and still would not have a clue; so it is in life with most things.

It was soon time to move on as neither of us were too keen on stirring the memories of our recent revision and learning something that at any other time we could have looked up in a book, without a moment of stress.

The sands of time though are slowly decreasing. Martin has decided to bring forward his departure time to August 24th. We therefore decided to relax and enjoy our company and the menagerie of friends we have met on Magnetic Island, who nearly all seem to be in Brisbane.

For my part, I have rebooked my flights with a departure date of September 9th and return on January 8th in preparation for another pear picking season. I am also amazed to note here, on August 11th, I recorded we are now living off my account until the social pay up, or that Martin receives some money from England to pay me back!

Our time in Brisbane was one of distraction, and knowing that the end was fast approaching. Things will work out fine; it's more a case of having to make do by myself from now on. Tasmania was a good dress rehearsal for the future, which will have to be clasped with both hands.

At nearby Indoopily we again made our approaches to the social security people, and this time found more luck. I'd almost given up on this angle, but Martin persuaded me to amble along, and besides we had nothing else scheduled for the said morning. Here a rather beleaguered girl made some phone calls to Perth and Melbourne, who said they would send on our particulars, together with those from the immigration department.

It has been a strange experience, and self-inflicted, but finally when it really mattered our persistence paid off, with the news on August 8th that we would get our entitlement of $78 a week, which in effect lasted for two weeks and a total of $156 each. Put it another way the Australian economy has had its pears picked, the hops dried, a garden renovated and originally received an advance payment of four hundred pounds for the privilege!

10. Immigration

William Edward Humphrey was born on December 11th 1861, and the third of seven children born to Stephen Humphrey, also born in my Sussex village and his wife, Amy (née Crowe). Although no direct link can be found with William it is a fair bet that our two families might have been originally related, as my great grandparents were born around this time. Village inter-marriages were normal in those days, when the horse and cart transport dominated most community lives.

On February 5th 1883 William and Mary Ann (née West), his recently acquired bride, sailed from Plymouth, England, aboard The Duke of Devonshire as free passengers. This concession was fully granted by the government to immigrants and their families of particular categories; it was duly reviewed from time to time in Queensland.

As state conditions changed, so too did the stipulations, but these included at various times female domestic servants and married couples without children. The applicants were required to pay the sum of one pound, and a similar amount for each member of their family counted as a statute adult. To be eligible they had to be unable to pay their own passage; must not have resided previously in any Australian colony and intended to live in the state of Queensland.

When we were pear picking a cheerful craggy-faced Irishman told me how in 1974 he was offered a free ticket, departing from England, with its only stipulation being that he had to commit himself to stay for two years.

"What happens if I don't like it, then I'm really high and dry, which is why I paid my own fare," he remarked.

Australia has now reached its optimum population levels as far as the 'Everybody is welcome' criteria is concerned. Indeed with Britain entering the European Economic Community in 1972, and in turn blocking out many prosperous markets, the unemployment levels approaching 300,000, and memories still lingering about the Governor General interfering with internal matters. It all means that British immigrants are no longer welcomed in their droves, when this vacuum has been filled.

According to the magazine *Australian Outlook,* any future success of the economy will greatly depend on large scale migration with up to 120,000 migrants being accepted annually without causing problems in the labour market, as population figures expand from sixteen to twenty five million over the next seventy years. It is felt that they will contribute to the growth of demand for goods and services. The country would also have to look towards Asia and the Pacific for many of these people, in spite of the widespread concern for the imported culture mix.

Australian attitudes towards a change in the environment, whether natural or man-made, have now become very protective, with an opposite reaction to those early pioneer views of 'If it moves shoot it, if it stands still chop it down.'

Standard requirements for all migrants include good character and health, together with the following criteria:

1. The Applicant's prospects in Australia are assessed through a points system under the present criteria: employability, skills, age and education. This points system applies to skilled Labour migrants, sponsored adult children, brothers and sisters.
2. A general assessment is made of the Applicant's prospects of settling successfully in Australia.

From these two assessments a general picture of the applicant's suitability for migration emerges. A decision is taken whether migration would be favourable to both the individual and Australia.

I'm not planning to become an Australian citizen myself, although one thought of January back home and I might be persuaded! To my knowledge, the only alternative means of becoming an Aussie either means finding a wife, buying your passport on the black market, discovering a long lost grandparent, or waiting for the annual ten year amnesty which is invariably mentioned, when people can apparently give themselves up in return for citizenship.

However this is all a far cry from William and Mary on the high seas.

Generally most voyages of these early immigrants had notorious hallmarks, featuring cramped accommodation, wet bunks and a shortage of both food and freshwater. There were weeks, running into months, spent at sea with little to occupy their minds on these long voyages from England and around the Cape of Good Hope to Moreton Bay, where my namesakes first stepped ashore, all that time ago.

I can only hope that they fared better than myself on the ocean waves, amid the prevailing gale force winds, when passengers were battened down below hatches for days on end, in sweltering humid conditions of almost total darkness and inadequate ventilation.

It is estimated that up to five hundred immigrants cooked their meals. Then ate and slept in these atrocious conditions. Sanitary arrangements were very primitive, with little or no effort being made to make their living quarters hygienic. We can only imagine the stench that arose from such crowded steerage decks when the hatches were finally lifted in calmer waters. The children, and those weaker than normal would have suffered so much and invariably had measles or scarlet fever, while typhoid was also rife throughout.

It is believed that William had a market garden in Brisbane for a short time, before floods forced him to move to Westbrook and then onto Burenda, near Charlevieille. Tragedy though stuck when their eldest son, William Edward, died from sunstroke on November 28th 1889, aged three years old. On March 24th 1896, William applied to select land in the Wellcamp area. The date of license to occupy was January 4th 1897, at a purchase price of £587 13s 11d, for their 156 acres. This is where they resided for another forty-three years before seeing out their final days in Toowoomba.

As I remarked timing will always remain an integral ingredient in all our lives and this was to prove true, when some months later I received a letter from an aunt who informed me: 'That we now have a distant cousin living somewhere near Toowoomba.' However an unfortunate piece of planning means that I have never been able to meet Jenny who is a direct descendant of William and Mary's daughter Mavis.

In 1981 Jenny decided to trace her family tree, which indeed takes me back to a local newspaper, *The Kent and Sussex Courier,* article in 1984, entitled: *Calling the Humphrey's of 'a Sussex village.'* This was an intriguing headline, which has led to the exchange of some correspondence with Jenny since then.

Her book: *The Humphrey Family of Australia* makes both interesting and relevant reading. My ancestral namesakes have also marked their time down under; two male and one female convicts even came to Australia on the very first fleet, bearing the Humphrey name (sometimes spelt Humphries).

According to Jenny's research, some colourful characters were soon on their way to these new horizons, of which I have picked out the following three examples of interest.

Edward Humphrey was tried at the Old Bailey for stealing

after he pretended to be a dustman and a servant let him into the house. For this he was sentenced to seven years transportation.

Henry Humphrey in turn received a similar sentence for stealing at Exeter in 1786.

Mary Humphries, 26, who sailed aboard the Lady Penrhyn in 1783, was better known as 'Hell Fire Moll,' when she was tried for highway robbery and sentenced to 14 years deportation.

11. Twice Goodbye

Sunday 12 August

Over the past six months Martin has invariably mentioned his desire to be somewhere within sight of a television set during the Olympic Games, and especially for the athletics, which has admittedly now rubbed off on me. This time they are held in Los Angeles; the Soviet Bloc countries have withdrawn for political reasons in tit for tat retaliation because America pulled out of the Moscow Olympics in 1980, after sighting the Soviet aggression in Afghanistan, for their withdrawal.

On August 9th at Brisbane post office, we sent the following faxed message to Britain's 1,500 metres quartet. We could just sense Sebastian Coe's eventual golden defence and Steve Cram's gallant silver were about to become reality.

"How long will it take?" I said.

"It has just reached Los Angeles," the postmaster replied, having taken out our Intel postage message and handed it back to us much to our surprise.

"That's the way of the future," he remarked.

Dear, Seb, Steve and Steve:

Good luck in the heats/final. We both wish you Steve (Ovett) a quick recovery after your illness in the 800 metres final. We will be watching and cheering you on from Australia, where we are travelling around at present.

Congratulations Seb on your well deserved silver medal.

Now lads win that gold medal for Britain!

Two Poms from Down Under

We therefore sat in front of the television, with our beer cans, before the race final on Sunday and hoped for a British triumph. It did not matter to us who won. What we really wanted was a race to remember and of course a victory if at all possible from one of our runners. The anticipation was tense and when there is a chance to win the pressure is all the more gripping than when it is make the numbers up time.

Our three were all world class and current champions in their own right. When the cameras turned to Steve Ovett, shortly before he would be forced to pull out during the race with heat exhaustion, he said: "I would like to thank everybody who has phoned and sent telegrams of support, and especially as half of them came from Australia!"

Saturday 18 August

Eight months and eleven days since flying out of Heathrow Airport, Martin bade me farewell Sydney bound. Time has flown by with so many experiences to look back on, and draw upon during our lifetime. In all, our only disagreement flared up over my desire to keep pear picking one day, while his thoughts were none too surprisingly on his mail from England.

There were times, I am sure my laid-back approach to life must have annoyed him. However I could not hope for a better travelling companion to hack around with during this time. The key was to agree from the outset that we would continue together, until our ideas and vision took us in different directions. Or a kind of elastic attitude with no commitments that immediately squashed any friction between us before the seeds of resentment were ever sown.

No doubt our mutual respect we have always maintained had much to do with this. We merely just acknowledged our respective strengths and got on with it. Human beings I once read are estimated to produce an eighty four percent negative thought ratio. Certainly we had our fair share, but at no time did either of us lose sight of our original objective to experience Australia, and to this I think Martin will leave here feeling pleased with the outcome.

In this respect leaving Perth, somewhat sorrowfully was an important first step. Mainly life could have turned into a lazy luxurious affair, especially if we had found some part-time work. This in turn might have resulted in us merely scampering around Australia on a month's coach trip, and all very nice, but not part of our original idea. The time was right for him to go home, we are all made different. Martin's apprehensive thoughts about his future once surfaced while we lounged on one of Queensland's white sandy beaches, when he echoed his concerns about: "What am I going to do after this is over?"

"Don't worry about it, these are our best years. Post academic, pre-stability, besides we've got over forty years of active work ahead of us!" I replied.

Standing back and looking at society from a distance has got to be an advantage, compared with the thousands of pounds people spend on education.

"Surely our experience here will put us in good stead for the future," I remarked.

If only to act as fulfilment and not having the regrets of what life is like beyond our own environment. No there would be no regrets for me, but Martin would go off in search of stability, the ladder of life, and a family. For myself though, I knew, would be staying on the outside looking in for some time yet.

There is just too much left to see for that to happen!

Monday 20 August

I now found myself finally cast adrift in Australia when potentially five became one. 'Oh what' we could have done with money and a real gang of us for the camaraderie and nights out! The security and those greyhound buses, without sleep, 'no not for me,' it would not have been quite the same, not at this stage anyway. That is what has put the edge on my time here.

I still have friends, and a place to stay with plans afoot, but first to my night out in Brisbane and a club somewhere in this city, with a dance floor. The girls entertained themselves, while I leant against the bar, and chatted to Hayden who wanted three to become four. I told him they are mine; 'what you can't have both of them! Sisters, sorry both taken, but that's not fair. I know life never is.'

"Now what was that you said about a horse?"

"Oh it's only money. I'm 23 and have already made two fortunes in daddy's gold mining business. Mind you, I also lost them somehow," he said. "Have a drink."

"It's alright, I have to go soon," I replied.

"Money breeds money, after all how many people could afford to lose $2,000 on a horse race," he remarked, and Martin's kind of talk, take off a few dollars. They could drink and discuss how to win! I don't think Marty ever did back a winner with his $5 bets.

"How's that?" I said.

"Well, I would have made a fortune, especially as the beast obligingly won," he remarked.

"So you won?"

"Well no not exactly, you see too many people knew about it. I mean you could see they were different horses," he said, through the bottom of his glass.

"Here have a drink, it's my shout," I replied, and wanted to know what it was I missed out on, with the disco lights flashing all around.

"You see the horse," he said.

"Yes the horse, what about the horse?"

"The horse, it was a ringer an un-fancied loser, anybody could see that, but the risk was worth it," he replied.

"A friend of mine is still in the country; he left last week for Sydney and enjoys Randwick, knowing him it was his first winner!" I replied.

"So which one is his?"

"How do you mean?"

"The two girls."

"As I said hands off, they are both mine."

"You're kidding, aren't you?"

Of course and right then that was most important. I had their trust and this is how things were to stay with a long journey ahead of us. What I didn't need was a tangent to lead the mind astray.

"How did you know about Saturday's substitution?"

"Oh it was generally known around the racecourse, if you were in the know. Unfortunately too many people latched onto the grapevine," he replied.

Somebody is for the high jump when the shock waves stop reverberating around the racing world. The flat racing community is now under the microscope with various trainers, owners and jockeys being investigated by the police and officials alike.

"Are you sure you don't want to come back to my place, it's only a short drive away," Hayden remarked.

"Thanks but I've got to get them home."

"But you can…."

"Bye," I replied.

Wednesday 22 August

I have admittedly become frustrated that my travels have seen few new horizons over the past month, even though we have had an eventful, and at times exciting succession of days doing precisely nothing! In a way I can look back on our stay here and claim to have lived in a second Australian city, but it is time to pull my socks up, and that must begin right here and now. The original idea had been to begin the day after Martin left. But then one of my 'sisters' asked if she could tag along, having said to the other, "do you think he will mind, try to find out…he won't mind," and nor did I. Apart from the calendar, which meant waiting around for the best part of a week and using up that vital piece of shading at hand.

"Sure why not, but it will be tough going at times, and we might have to sleep rough," I replied.

We were standing in the kitchen of a mutual friend who had lent us the use of her living room as a base to enjoy our lives with banter. In life the saying goes that all good things have to come to an end, and when there were once four, only two remained. Amy has been here for a number of weeks living in Sydney and then her sister spilt up with a boyfriend and needed a break, which another sister paid for I gather, in bonding these two together. In what Amy said had been a drift apart for no apparent real reason, or whatever.

Anyway the trip had done the trick, the two were now the very best of friends and laughed as one, of which I can take pleasure from. It's always nice to help bring people together, and this was one of those times. And of course it has been fun. Hopefully we can all look back in years to come and say the same, as we are now destined to splinter off in different directions.

It was one of those days which seemed to take an age, the three of us all slept late, and then drifted about the house in an unreal haze, in the knowledge that things were about to change, or reverse the crossroads that we have all met at. Sheila is flying home to California in order to complete her final university year, first thing in the morning. This explains our lethargic attitude this morning. There is no transport out to the airport, which connects with her flight, first thing in the morning. We did some shopping and waited around, played a few hands of cards, and still it was only the mid-afternoon.

In the back of your mind you know this is it, and yet the day dragged on and on, until the moment arrived for the taxi to arrive in the evening, and the three of us piled in with Sheila's rucksack in the boot. This is the kind of tale that we all experience from time to time on the road, and then people are gone far and wide. We soon arrived at the airport, and checked the flights, before calculating we still had eight hours at least of which an hour was spent in a bar; then from mid-night to five, we sat in the covered way of a bowling green and played cards to fill in our time.

There was nothing else and the watch ticked by slowly, and very slowly that is, as we finally walked back to the airport and handed over Sheila's rucksack. It was an unreal feeling; airports are like that, as the moment of an embrace finally arrived, and the 'write to say how things turned out' were said. I then stood back to let them have their final moments together; we waved through the crowds and then again on the balcony, as the plane slowly glided into the air.

When only two remained.

12. Ayers Rock

I left early on to collect my remaining post from Waverly Road, but unfortunately the household had all gone to work earlier than anticipated. In desperation, as time was a rapidly diminishing commodity, I unlatched a half open window to let myself in. It was a bit of a liberty, but leaving Brisbane today has become of the utmost importance in our quest to reach Ayers Rock. I then found my second cheque on Adrienne's dressing table and left an apologetic note for taking such a liberty. This would be my last such payment as there will not be time for any further interview appearances.

The house remained still as I glanced around at some fond memories, of social events and the friends we made here. Outside the garden remains as we left it. The wooden rails are bound together to make an elevated lawn, now without life. I wanted to stay and simply watch the grass grow, but time has to move on. I now made sure the window was fastened; even tighter than when I arrived, and slipped out into the street once more, where people walk as individuals, or with a baby in its pram.

The afternoon was spent trying to cash Amy's US$300 bank draft, but unfortunately the powers that be were unable to do anything for us until it had been cleared in the United States. Panic stations loomed until we managed to persuade a schoolteacher friend of hers to cash it into his own account, and thankfully to wait for it to be cleared sometime next week.

Eventually we caught a late train at Roma Station to Bold Hill, where the highway welcomed our outstretched thumbs. In some ways things have now changed for the better. Amy is far

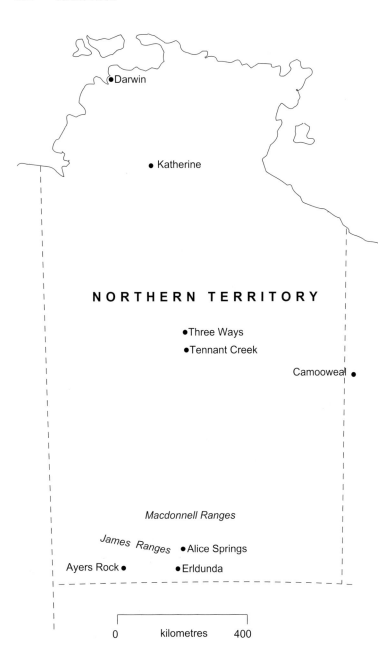

NORTHERN TERRITORY

●Three Ways
●Tennant Creek

Camooweal ●

Macdonnell Ranges

James Ranges ● Alice Springs

Ayers Rock ● ● Erldunda

●Darwin

● Katherine

0 kilometres 400

more appealing to look at, with her wavy light curls. But with it also comes a fresh kind of responsibility. There could be none of this splitting up, or taking our chances and finding ourselves stranded. Although with no large city ahead, bar Adelaide, this should not be a problem. Besides I promised Sheila that I would look after little sister, and escort her safely back to Sydney. Then it might have been far easier to take the direct bus south towards New South Wales!

Our only lift, amid a fading light, came from a friendly girl who originates from Haywards Heath, in West Sussex, where she is going back to live in January, who seemed keen to chat about our local area.

"Why go back into the winter?" I said.

"I know everybody says that, it's just that I have a job waiting," she replied.

We now found ourselves in a small township called Kallangur, and somewhat unsure of what to do next. When in doubt we decided on its one and only public bar in order to take stock of things so far. Here we met Colin and Gary, two of the locals who frequently spend their time in such places.

Talking to them was difficult at times, but they were naturally friendly and harmless enough, as we put off our decision of where to stay, and enjoyed the company. A bit of bonding between us might also prove useful, with this being our first night on the road together, and the parameters now somewhat different.

"No worries, I'll ask the landlord if you can sleep in the campervan at the back, instead of walking about in the dark," Colin remarked, which in turn persuaded me to buy him another stubby of fosters and continued the conversation. The night was young, and we now had time on our hands. In an hour Gary left the three of us in the bar, with the landlord. He then provided us with a bite to eat on the house, which we thanked him for, but no other customers appeared.

The time soon came to leave when we asked for the way.

"Through the back door, I'll show you," Colin replied.

What he didn't mention was that he would also be sleeping in the campervan with us, and three in a bed on a double mattress fitted into the back. No doubt numerous other individuals have slept off their hangovers here, but rarely will Australia, California and England have been represented together!

Colin also seemed intent on informing us at every such interval that the near freezing temperatures were keeping him awake; I slept in the middle and shielded Amy from his wandering hands.

"You didn't say you would be sleeping in here as well," I remarked, with an iron bar sticking into my back for comfort.

"I thought you wouldn't mind," he replied.

"It's fine," Amy said, in the dark.

The adventure was already igniting her imagination, when we could say:

"Do you remember that night in the campervan!"

Friday 24 August

The dew was still sparkling on the fresh grass when the three of us woke early on. It has been another strange night huddled with a complete stranger, who seemed to be in an oblivious state of mind and was now wearing Amy's jumper!

Eventually we managed to get a cup of coffee from his sister nearby, who in turn used her CB radio to obtain another lift for us with a travelling sales Rep, towards Nambour and a further string of short lifts. This ultimately led us to Ian, at the old gold mining town of Gympie, who in turn asked us to "Come back to my place for a meal, and then I'll drop you both in Marlborough."

In some respects I was not sure. We really needed to press on, but at least he offered to keep the clock ticking over, even though his farm turned out to be well off the beaten track; a small railway junction possessing a pub for the local framing fraternity was its closest description of life.

"That's a pretty unpleasant bite mark you've got on your neck," I remarked.

"Oh, I had a blue with my sister about selling the house, she's pretty violent you know, everybody's scared of her," he replied, and obviously a girl worth avoiding.

Ian's elderly mother then served us stew for dinner, after which we sat out in the garden, or should I describe a field without boundaries where green grassland and valleys surrounded the stilted house.

'This is the life,' sitting on the veranda, and dreaming of my rocking chair, or the perfect setting on the most pleasant of days. Why would they ever want to move? This is the place to be, albeit a bit isolated and somewhat removed from society. Few people are likely to come a calling, but then 'who' cares with a good balcony and a railing to put my feet up on. The radio could hum its tune and the icebox would remain fully stocked. What else could I ever want, with the mellow tones of the twittering birds, singing to their hearts content?

After Ian had dropped us off on the highway, in the mid afternoon sunshine, it was not long before Mark, a truck driver picked us up, and began to assume we needed a place to stay for the night; when it became apparent we were simply going with the grain and needed distance rather than sleep. In the light of this he offered us the share of his hotel room, a hot shower and coffee in the morning. Although the breakfast was out, as nobody must know we were in residence.

Saturday 25 August

The morning started with a lift back towards Rockhampton where Mark, had trouble obtaining diesel, when his company credit card became invalid for some reason. This meant he was short of finance to see us through to our next stop, which begs the question of what would he have done without us!

Amy now lent him $50 until we reached Mackay and was the least we could do for him, when he finally dropped us off, on the highway. It was here that Steve picked us up, and who had planned to stopover in Bowen for a rest stop, but like us urgently needed to press on towards Townsville, to start his new job. We agreed I would keep the conversation brewing, in order to stop him nodding off to sleep at the wheel.

"He's good at talking!" Amy chirped from the backseat, as these night owls glided along the sparsely lit roads.

Sunday 26 August

After spending the night in my usual Townsville campsite beneath some palm trees. We walked out towards the Mount Isa crossroads where I found a discarded Alice spin sign gathering dust, with the letters gs mysteriously missing from its tail end. There is only one route to follow in the Outback, "But it might act as a cricket bat for hitting stones," I remarked.

Reaching Charters Tower, another arid soulless environment, proved easy enough via a middle aged Portuguese man living locally. It was here I noticed a young Japanese 'student' pedalling his way around Australia; lumbered down with panniers and a spare tyre.

"A bit of a lonely life," I said, in non-oriental phrases; his English likewise seemed redundant and we just smiled. An individual can cycle for hours without seeing a soul, when the heat of summer is likely to prove unbearable, and what about meeting people. For now though I could understand the wisdom of his endeavours, to lead such an intrepid existence; it's something I might harp back to in the future, when my hitchhiking days have run their course.

On the outskirts of town John, about thirty, presently eased to a halt.

"Don't worry about my driving. I normally keep the pedal hard down on these roads," he remarked.

"That's alright," I said, and decided that Amy ought to sit in the back.

The decision each time was to be mine, when somebody stopped. I would say hello, and be ready with the excuse, or a change of plan for the driver's benefit. If I turned around and asked a leading question it was her job to follow my chain of thought and to agree in principle. We could always talk about it afterwards; at the time we felt one judgment was better than two, unless she had any reservations of her own, in which case she could change our plans with an excuse, and tell me when the car was in the distance. What we didn't want was a situation of self-doubt between us if any such occurrence came about.

John's mind seemed to be elsewhere, and distant of focus.

"I only left Mount Isa yesterday for Cairns," he said, which made a round trip of 2,500 km in twenty-four hours. Why I wasn't sure, it's not my business. Amy remained quiet, and just let the driver 'concentrate' on his steering wheel. None of us spoke much, as an odd atmosphere continued through the miles of monotonous straight lines. His mind was obviously in turmoil.

It was nice to finally stop at a service station, and for us get some fresh air with the three of us just staring at each other in moody silence, and none of us really knowing what to say. What was on your mind, how can we help if you will not say?

"My wife has left me," John remarked, quite abruptly and much to my surprise. "She is living with another man in Cairns, since last week. She just up and left with this guy who she knows from when she goes home to see her family."

"I'm sorry it might be best to let her go, the hurt will pass," I said.

"That's different, you don't understand, my wife left her three children. What woman would ever do that?" he replied, obviously bitter at his plight, and yet desperately hoping the wife he so loved would have returned with him.

"The children asked me when mummy would be back, I just couldn't say," he said, opening up his hand to show us their wedding ring, and the final nail of any relationship, when time just stood still. Amy remained silent, with her bubbly nature also somewhat subdued.

The mind can play awful tricks when one is alone, and especially along these Outback roads, which tend to go on and on, through hours of nothing but straight highway shielded by scrubland. It must be a welcome exercise to move over for oncoming traffic, or the odd road works detour. John seemed glad I could feel, of somebody to converse with; his life must have felt like a kind of living hell. One of lonely rejection and hurt, as the realization of his domestic problems gradually sink in.

"It's the children you've got to think of now John, they need their father more than ever," I remarked.

Sunset over the Australian continent is a magnificent sight of splendour and once seen unforgettably missed. The bright yellow ball in the sky just above our horizon made motoring seem impossible, in which case we stopped until the sun had disappeared from view. In front we were left with a yellow semi-circle bordering a blue background, as a star-studded sky soon developed and the colours slowly began to change into a rich orange glow, before darkness installed its firm grip on this wild and beautiful terrain.

Driving at night poses many hazards apart from human error, punctures, and a lack of fuel. The highway is covered with animal corpses ranging from kangaroos, sheep, cows, and even wild horses. On numerous occasions John turned his wheel or braked hard to avoid potential disasters, with the animals caught in our lights, and ready to cross the highway, or just looking on.

Obviously this remains an extremely dangerous situation. Queensland does not possess a large enough working population to be able to foot the bill for fencing off thousands of kilometres of road. As the situation stands, both human's and wildlife alike remain at risk.

By the time we arrived in Mount Isa, a journey of 750 km, at 10pm, John had drifted back into his own oblivious world. I tried shaking his hand as a parting gesture, but no words seemed appropriate. He simply stared right through me in a hopeless daze, and light years away from the present.

In the darkness we then trudged into a camping ground, but nothing stirred. The reception was closed, in which case it seemed in order to take a look around as everything was lit up. My knees and face appeared dusty, so we considered a night's paid accommodation might be a worthwhile expenditure, but it was not to be. Suddenly through the shadows a figure approached us, and obviously a warden, of about forty.

"Excuse me," I began.

"Get out of here, your type aren't welcome in Mount Isa," he replied.

"I'm sorry, we're only inspecting your facilities," I tried to say, but this was pointless. He was drunk.

Inevitably I was bound to find myself in the wrong place, at the wrong time. But that's not to say I enjoyed the threats of police action and being docked.

"Now get out of here," our assailant gestured.

Inside I felt angry. What right has he got of treating us like this?

My assailant wanted to make me look small in front of Amy, in a kind of power play, and which admittedly he almost achieved, without a sound of retaliation. This was no time for a fight, and besides we had to stay focused on the task in hand. When behind us an over zealous individual continued his rants to the sounds of "Piss off you bastards, now get out of here, and don't come back!"

Monday 27 August

Mount Isa is a mining centre, which came into being in the 1920s, and is situated between the coast and Three Ways in Northern Territory. It is the only place of any real importance on this stretch of Australian Outback, and nothing to write home about. The town is rather gloomy set against a huge mountain of waste including copper, lead and zinc; or is it really the world's largest city as claimed on a nearby signpost?

In any case beauty is in the eyes of the beholder, and people actually live here, no doubt for financial reasons. It has to also be acknowledged that a lonely housewife might easily become disenchanted and lust for a more tropical lifestyle in Cairns, rather than stuck in the middle of nothing. We only saw the town in the dark, and then from the road first thing, but it is hard to describe such a large piece of waste hanging over your shoulders like an uninvited shadow, with nowhere to turn and friends in sight.

With 'our' popularity being at an all time low, and last night's assailant close by we decided our best bet might be to start walking. I could have had a word in daylight, and taken the high ground with a stare into his eyes, to see exactly how he felt with a little bit of his own medicine. But that seemed petty and would achieve nothing apart from a few brownie points, almost instantly forgotten.

Motorists often like to help people seen to be making an effort rather than just slumped on their packs. It's only natural to help out, with a sneaky feeling of admiration for that get up and go attitude. There are some pretty clever people out there who can relate to their own hard earned efforts, and know what it is like to follow their goals. It was for this reason we started to hike out of town and why a local vet stopped for us within five hundred metres of town and took us 188 km towards Camooweal, a small dusty wooden settlement predominant for its truck driver's stopover, and a restaurant. The vet dropped us off here, and we thanked him for his help, when Amy walked in ahead of me and in turn called me over to her latest find, a stuffed crocodile on the wall.

"George!" she exclaimed.

Somehow I had managed to invent a tale about my pet crocodile George, that left Sydney three days ago and who is racing us to Ayers Rock. It all may sound rather absurd, but it's a story, which has been added to at regular intervals and has sounded more ridiculous with each new chapter or free moment along the way.

Amy thought she had outdone me at last.

Below 'George' there is a pay phone connected to the wall, and not wanting to be beaten at my own game I picked up the receiver, and pretended to talk into it, as Amy took her triumphant photograph.

"It's alright, Sid, George's son, will be here in two days, he left Sydney on Saturday!" I remarked.

Crocodiles are better as they are, out of touching distance or mind! There are two kinds in the 'Top end' of Northern Territories, and try asking them which they are! The freshwater is known as Crocodylus johnstoni, or 'Bashful.' They live in freshwater, and grow to three metres in length; they eat seafood and small mammals, while living exclusively in freshwater rivers and billabongs. Their distinguishing features are the narrow snouts, and some neat rows of spiky teeth. Rumour has it, they are comparatively friendly, and 'might' only nip, but then this is only a rumour…

It is the saltwater, Crocodylus Porosus, we all have to avoid who live in both salty, and freshwater. At up to six metres long and weighing 1000 kg, they remain master of their domain and have no serious competition as predators, when even the 'freshie' is fair game, not to mention human beings. Our Crocodile at Camooweal appears to be a 'freshie' to our uneducated eyes.

"Poor old George he would not have hurt a fly, and now look at him," Amy remarked.

"Yes, he's been stuffed!"

"He was too young to die," she said, as we both bowed our heads in respect and remembered him with great esteem.

Outside, we decided to hang around town, hit a few stones, and hope one of the cars might stop for us on the outskirts with a meal ticket insight should we fail. There was no shortage of pull up space as eventually Paul, a Czechoslovakian photographer, gave us a lift towards Three Ways. He then planed to go north towards Darwin, while we head south.

The road although sealed began to deteriorate somewhat as we crossed the border. This only added to my problems, with Amy sitting on my lap for the next five hours, of a constant dead leg, and the occasional movement to alleviate the blood supply. However it also gave us the chance to meet up with another background from across the iron curtain.

"You are the first non 'Australian' to pick us up, how long have you been here?"

"I last saw my wife and three children at Christmas," he replied.

"Don't you miss them?"

"But of course, it's just they didn't give me much choice in the matter. Being a photographer, the magazine wanted some pictures of this part of the world. I'm the only one available with something to lose, or who is guaranteed to go back," he said.

His country is captive amongst the Eastern Bloc countries, which shield the Russian power base from western influence. Neither Amy, nor myself could relate to this kind of influence, especially as the three of us at first glance might have appeared to be from similar backgrounds.

"I hate the communists. What with their repressive regime, and captive in my own country; yet I can do nothing apart from take photographs," he said, in frustration.

"I'm sorry," I replied, it's all any of us can say.

Tuesday 28 August

Three Ways has nothing to report. It has a roadhouse, and a huge dusty area for truckers to pull off the highway to cover us in dust. In logistics my guidebook states: 'Mount Isa is 643 km, Darwin 988 km, and Alice 537 km,' which is good enough for me to take their word! A hitchhiker appears to have a one in two chance of being stranded here, and a passing motorist quite confident that the driver continued in the opposite direction, such is the plight of being left here. Fortune was to favour us as we walked across the huge expanse of gravel, dwarfed by the juggernauts, and headed for the far corner to give people time to look and see us; when a local worker took us a short way into Tennants Creek, 26 km, and the only place equivalent of a town going south. To the north Katherine is its equivalent in linking Darwin.

The story is that a wagon full of settlers broke down here and they drank the beer onboard. They then decided to stay as things began to look much brighter for all concerned! It was also the scene of a small gold rush nearby, which helped its establishment. But who else would want to live in the middle of nowhere? There is simply nothing here, and we wanted to keep going. I was none too hopeful of a lift either, what with two other people trying to hitchhike further along the highway. Our chances were enhanced though, as we were the first ones a motorist might spot.

Sure enough after a considerable wait, and countless hands of cards, Fritz, on his way home to holiday with his sister, picked us up. He seemed both pleasant and at ease with life, he also gave us an ideal opportunity for Amy to sit in the front seat and to enjoy some comfort after spending more time in the back than seemed reasonably fair; I dozed behind, as the countryside resembled an all too familiar piece of barren terrain, lacking vegetation or evident animal life.

It also gave Amy the chance to converse on her own terms, rather than fitting in with my tune and perceptions of the moment. Fritz it has to be said surprised me when he said his occupation was a slaughter man; however this is how we finally arrived in Alice Springs, along a route similar in barren vegetation that is remembered for some foolish efforts of the pioneer age.

It is hardly surprising that the disorganised Robert O'Hara Burk and William John Willis should perish in 1860, after they left Melbourne, at Coopers Creek, Queensland, in an attempt to make the first south-northwards Australian crossing. Their impatience of Victoria state's £6,000 sponsored trip was to cost them their lives, when they decided to press on before all of the back up supplies was in place.

Burk's order was for the depot force to remain at Coopers for at least three months. Instead they returned five months later only to die under a scorched sun, having previously reached the Flinders Estuary, and within distance of their elusive goal. One other man died of exhaustion, while another survived the ordeal by making himself useful to a native tribe.

Fritz dropped us off shortly before dusk, much to my relief at not having to search in the dark, and worry about disturbing a hibernating snake or spiders for that matter. Neither of us was flushed with dollars, which meant forsaking the hotel room, and the shower in the morning, never mind the swimming pool; the luxurious lifestyle will have to wait for another time, Amy would have to do with the outdoor lifestyle; hidden away from view and admiring the stars!

Wednesday 29 August

Alice Springs is a pleasant enough place, literally situated in the centre of a 'continent' surrounded by a combination of mountain ranges and barren wasteland. The view from the hilltop ANZAC war memorial gives it an appearance of a small watered green patch dotted with streets and houses, surrounded by a dusty bowl. Certainly there can be no complaints about lack of scope for future growth and improvements.

These are the winter months, which are still warm at 20ºC. During the summer thermometer readings often exceed 40ºC day in day out. When the great heat breaks, the cyclone floods can turn gorges into raging torrents with the plain becoming a marsh almost overnight.

In Alice everybody seemed to be going through the daily routine of life in an orderly fashion. Nothing of any interest seemed to be on the horizon, in which case we spent $10 on food and wrote our journals for want of nothing else to do. This was to be a rest day and a time to explore, before kicking on in the morning first thing.

It was a small café with just the occasional customer, all quiet and pleasant for any traveller to chill out, and contemplate our next move towards the Rock. People pass through here all day, everyday, and will continue to do so. There was no point in moving on before sunup, as where would we stay, and besides we both needed time to relax, after the efforts of reaching centre point Australia.

I felt inertia in my veins, and suddenly had no immediate enthusiasm for constant movement. Unfortunately though we were in the wrong place at the wrong time, when the proprietor took objection to us loitering and again told us to go with the use of another four-letter word, I shall not repeat.

What is it about people out here? Only last night our camp warden had also been rather abrasive due to our late arrival, which when you travel half way across a continent by hitchhiking can be difficult to predict.

"They must learn their manners from a wallaby," I remarked, and designed to make our assailant conscious of his own shortcomings.

There is only so much abuse an individual can take; three times was once too many for me and this time it was daylight!

Thursday 30 August

Sorry this is one I have to tell.

"Come on, Amy let's go swimming at the beach this morning."

"Gee Baz, that's a swell idea," she replied, when packing her rucksack, and I was standing around kicking my bare feet in the sandpit.

"Actually I'm thinking we could do that before breakfast, and then continue our journey."

"That sounds great," she remarked.

"There's only one problem."

"What's that?" she said, wondering what I might say.

"We're in the centre of Australia!"

One day and two nights is enough time spent in Alice Springs we concluded. Apart from some museums, the old Telegraph Station, and an outdated disused jail, there was little left to explore. We therefore had breakfast, and began walking out of town when Barry, a lorry driver took us 200 km along the Stuart Highway to Erldundah, from where the Lassiter Highway runs 243 km, through scorched flat Outback terrain towards Ayers Rock. It was named after an old prospector who claimed, in 1931, that he found a giant nugget of gold, 'somewhere' in this oasis of nothingness. However on his return journey he failed to retrace his steps.

This has resulted in various explorations being undertaken for Lassiter's gold. But so far his tale has remained part of the undiscovered Outback, where man still has to set foot. It was here I experienced my most memorable, if not zaniest lift 'ever,' and all because a young Australian approached a car full of Aboriginals parked up, and enquired if they could take an extra pair of passengers.

Five minutes later we were squashed on the backseat with three drunken individuals. I'd wondered at the wisdom of such a snap decision, but realised the Australian had only been trying to help us and didn't want to offend his good nature. Half an hour further on we stopped at a garage, only for Jacob the driver to point towards me.

"Here, you drive," he said, in a slurred voice.

"Perhaps that's not such a bad idea; stay close to me, this could be interesting!" I said, looking towards Amy.

Peter, was the only other to speak English, who sat to my left, with Amy in between. He certainly had his merits when he constantly smiled and echoed the words, "Mad Max. Come on Mad Max!" Behind me his four friends instantly joined in with the chorus. I liked these guys, 'they're alright.'

In mid journey Jacob insisted Amy buy them a carton (12) of Fosters lager. Unfortunately the hotel proprietor refused to serve her as he rightly sensed that our merry friends have had their 'daily' quota of beer. However, on their insistence, I dropped them off and went back alone. Amy would be perfectly safe, as the atmosphere was one of total merriment. This might at least distract them altogether it often seemed, from handing out a constant barrage of incomprehensive driving instructions, with a slurred voice.

My other main concern was driving into the sun, with this yellow ball slowly beginning to set in the west. Time and time again I had to brake when cattle 'shadows' suddenly appeared out of the blinding haze.

"Amy, can I borrow your sunglasses?" I said.

Normally most people would have stopped, but the explanations seemed impossible. There was also the added problem that if I stalled the rustic Avenger automatic, it could not be started again without the use of jump leads.

"You OK?"

"Sure, how about you?" she said.

"Spinning, I just hope there are no highway patrolmen about," I replied, in total concentration, and intent on not taking my eyes off the road. Try explaining this one!

Amy just smiled, in loving the adventure of our trip out west, towards Yulara, the Aboriginal name for Ayers Rock, now still forty mad cap minutes away.

The gang was still full of merriment when we eventually arrived at a massive 'mirage like' shopping complex, 15 km west of our target, where western life has congregated in these parts. Our Aboriginal friends had a further 30 km to travel yet as Jacob now took over the wheel, and the others all sang their virtuosos of "Mad Max, bye Mad Max," with their slurred voices.

The car then revved up, as our friends smiled out of the windows; we all laughed and swapped jokes before Jacob pulled off into the distance, with their legs and arms waving out of the windows, and us raising our hands at them into the dusk with pure amazement. It had been priceless, and what great sports; drunk admittedly, but still people to be missed.

"I don't think we shall ever see anything quite like it again!"

"They sure liked you," Amy remarked.

"Crazy, just plain crazy," I replied.

Yulara has come into being as a direct result of a growing tourist influx approaching an estimated 100,000 people a year, compared to the grand estimated total of 22 visitors, between 1931 and 1946, thought to have actually climbed it. Local hoteliers and the large well known companies, like The Sheraton, have all moved into this impressive $110 million complex, which accommodates 5,000 luxurious rooms; but can such a gamble pay off when people stay for perhaps only two nights at a time; it is all getting a bit too touristy and many will not experience the Outback in quite the same way as it has been in the past.

The Aboriginal

The Aboriginals appeared friendly enough, but naive in their communications, on any intellectual level; all around Australia the same picture is duplicated. My visions of drunken black men lying around the parks in Cairns and Townsville remain fresh of mind. Their temperamental language and infighting amongst themselves also hardly gives outsiders a good impression of Australia's native people.

Certainly they are a 'simple' race by 'modern' western standards. But their knowledge of Outback survival was far greater than ours, and an art, which has slowly been eroded while many struggle for recognition in this alien world.

A number of 'Australians on route' still brand the Aboriginal as a rather 'ugly or a dirty race,' but has there been enough effort to understand them? Their origins lay back thousands of years together with their beliefs and survival skills, which had been passed down through each generation. It is still only one hundred and fifty years since a new form of human life began to impose itself, and slowly at first, upon them. Naturally adapting to this culture change has been difficult. Many of their lands were taken and in Tasmania, a once proud race was literally wiped out by the 'white man,' and now instead of 'conforming' they often live in the wilderness of despair.

The authorities though seem uninterested in clamping down on this drunkenness for their own good. Then perhaps Aboriginal education standards might improve. Certainly this would have to be forced upon them at first, for the good of all concerned.

Many Aboriginal have admittedly adjusted well, excluding those few who still persist in the traditional ways in Western Australia, and Northern Territories. Some concessions have also been made. However there is still a long way to go, before the governmental post of Aboriginal Affairs can hold its head up with renewed pride, as if to say: 'We are now equal blood brothers representing our country as one light.'

Friday 31 August

Ayers Rock was 'discovered' by William Gross in 1873. He in turn immortalized an otherwise little remembered South Australian Premier Henry Ayers by naming it after him, and an idea which early British colonists had been very fond of. The Rock, as it is affectionately known, is the world's largest monolith, resembling some kind of giant pebble, sandy brown in colour and half embedded in the earth's crust. Nobody though can be entirely sure how such an isolated, solid and immovable object was formed; Tony was right, there could be no other conclusion to my travels here, without such an experience.

Riveted into the rock face can be found a number of name plates, mounted in tribute to the unfortunate souls who have either had heart attacks on this strenuous climb to the summit, or merely slipped to an untimely death. This hardly acts as encouragement, but it does warn climbers of the possible risks involved through over-exertion. Handrails are also needed for the first five hundred metres to cling hold of, as there are no manmade steps, in order to protect the rock from erosion. The 1,600-metre climb wends itself through dips and a gradual rise and follows a white dotted line for safety reasons, before we finally reached the summit of so many fulfilled ambitions.

Looking out across the vast 'ocean' from the top, one can easily imagine the difficulties, which the early settlers had to cope with. Dehydration from an overhead sun and the obvious lack of water were just two factors to discourage adventurers in the days before macadamised roads, and the motorcars became part of 20th Century Australia.

It would also have been a wise man that marked his journey, and became proficient with a compass. The nearest colony out here before Burk and O'Hara must have been Adelaide, 1,600 km away. West of Ayers Rock, 27 km away, The Olgas, a collection of twenty-eight giant domes can be seen in the distance. They merely act as a welcome backdrop to tourist photographs, which inevitably cry out for some imaginative scenery.

In 1980 the world's press focused their attention on this barren scrubland, when Mrs Lindsay Chamberlain claimed that a dingo ran off with her young baby, ten-week-old Aziria. Her husband, Michael, a Seventh Day Adventist Minister, claimed he and his wife heard a 'short sharp cry' from Aziria before seeing a dingo leave her tent with 'something in its mouth.' Lindsay then ran into the tent, only to find her baby gone. Both had chased the dingo, but her husband admitted almost immediately that 'all hope of finding Aziria were gone,' after they failed to keep in touch.

Some claimed Mrs Chamberlain must have murdered the child. The crown prosecution alleged she had cut her baby's throat while sitting on the front seat of the family's car. This in turn resulted in her being jailed for life, somewhat controversially, two years later. About a hundred people, including Aboriginal trackers and tourists had searched the surrounding areas, but to no avail; the Northern Territory police killed two subsequent dingoes and two wild dogs during their search.

On February 20th 1981 the court's original decision had been that a dingo had indeed taken the baby, and that an unknown person helped to dispose of the child. But nobody will ever know the absolute truth of this matter. Certainly dingoes have 'never' been known to eat a human being. The Australians seem genuinely divided upon where the truth actually lies, as I write.

(Lindsey Chamberlain was eventually released in February 1986, after a baby's matinee jacket, identified as belonging to Aziria, was found with other matter near to The Rock. This in turn prompted forensic scientists to challenge the original assessment. In June 1987 she was pardoned and her conviction was finally squashed on September 15th 1988.)

At sunset the Rock's colour changes to red, orange or strangely even grey, depending on the angle at which the naked eye is witnessing it; an illusion brought about by light reflection. We now sat and watched Ayers Rock slowly dim into a darkened black outline, with the stars soon twinkling above. It's quiet and peaceful just sitting on the rucksacks, taking in our Outback surroundings, and thinking nice thoughts. Neither of us had much to say, as we remained silent in solitude, or simply aware of the surrounding environment, and those dingoes in the night.

Saturday 1 September

Uppermost in my mind is that we might have to catch a bus soon, and with our money supply now down to about a combined $500, all of which means cutting our spending to a minimum of outlay. It also follows that paying to pitch a tent in such an oasis of nothing only to freeze at night, would seem somewhat illogical. Instead of undressing it is a matter of three pairs of socks, trousers, five jumpers with a hood tucked up in my sleeping bag, and lying on a rock hard ground beneath leafless bushes, just merely willing for the sun to raise its radiant smile!

Sunday 2 September

We spent our second, almost redundant day sitting beside a gravel kerb watching each solitary vehicle pass by at ten-minute intervals, near the junction where Jacob picked us up. Statistics tell me Sydney, and my flight to New Zealand is one week, or approximately 3,200 km away.

The Stuart Highway is named after John Stuart who departed from Adelaide in 1860 chasing a £2,000 reward for the first south to north crossing. Mount Stuart is indeed Australia's geographical centre, which he reached shortly before his enforced abandonment of the expedition. A second attempt in 1861 again failed, but Stuart was obviously a determined individual who learnt from his own setbacks, for in 1862 he managed to reach the north coast, near Darwin. The highway apparently follows a similar path to this epic adventurer's journey.

As mid afternoon approached, it became apparent that we might become stranded here indefinitely. Sunday is obviously the quietest day for commercial traffic, and impatience was beginning to settle in on my part. Amy now agreed that hitchhiking north towards Alice might prove our wisest move.

"It's our best chance," she remarked, as we began to walk back towards the 'miss, and you blink' town of Erldunda. But nobody seemed interested in noticing our outstretched thumbs, not that many vehicles came our way. Amy's pleasant looks and light flowing hair had been invaluable so far on our journey; all of which gave me confidence to approach an elderly farmer, who seemed to be doing some running repairs under the bonnet of his pick-up truck, just up from where we stood. He could only say no, or he was not going our way.

"Would you mind if we jumped in the back, as our finances are down to 7 cents ready cash?" I asked, with one of my sheepish looks.

"Sure hop in," he replied.

Alice Springs at 8pm appeared a dark and deserted place, where even the fish and chip shop is closed; at least we are no longer stranded in no man's land. The 'gods' have given us a sporting chance now. After drawing some money out of my almost redundant cash point account, we ate in the local Kentucky Fried Chicken restaurant, and discussed our next plan of attack. Things might have been better, but whatever we have achieved our objective.

"If I buy us two coach tickets to South Australia, we'd be almost half-way to Sydney with five days to spare," I suggested, after some lengthy deliberations. The only problem was that it would almost clear me out, and what a way to travel! Amy was happy to go along with this, but it also puts me in debt once more.

"Then I could pay you back and lend you some money if needed, for the next few days," she replied, in also proffering the safety option first strategy.

"My contacts will tide me over until I can cash another money order."

Monday 3 September

The sandpit behind the youth hostel provided us with an unusually comfortable night's sleep, for once on this trip. Perhaps it was the ruts, which keep the warmth in, as my thoughts began to move ahead. I now felt fulfilled that my time here had been spent so productively. There would be no thoughts of what it's like sitting on top of Ayers Rock. We have 'been there done that' as the Australians are fond of saying, and could now move on with our lives.

I then looked at Amy, as enthusiastic as ever, with her tanned American looks. We have been good for each other. The parting of the ways will soon arrive, and something I would have to take in my stride as ever, smile and enthuse with another departure looming.

Presently an Aboriginal woman appeared over the horizon, as we emptied our sleeping bags of sand. She seemed pleasant and at ease with herself. I guess she is pleased to know that Ayers Rock and the Uluru National Park is to be handed over to the Mutijulu Aboriginal Community in 1985. Six families will lease the land back to the Commonwealth to be run as a National Park. This may not solve all of the problems, but November's announcement has begun the goodwill mission, which most genuine Australians, hope will lead to a more balanced society.

"My family were all killed in Typhoon Tracy on Christmas Day 1974," she remarked, and somewhat solemnly, in remembrance of her husband.

The storm struck Darwin on the north coast at 2am, which flattened everything in its path, as the eye of the cyclone arrived in an hour. It distributed a trail of destruction, and made half of its estimated 48,000 people homeless. The winds are reported to have reached 179 km an hour before the gauge on the weather tower blew up, together with Darwin's power supplies. HMAS Arrow, the naval patrol boat, even capsized and sank in the harbour, before life again returned to 'normal' by 5.30am.

"You were lucky, I hear it was pretty bad," I remarked.

"Yes I still remember when we buried my family, but I have remarried a white man now, who takes good care of me," she replied.

"I'm glad for you," I said, with a slight smile, when she slowly turned and trudged off home for breakfast at first light.

Darwin has been restored with a reinforced structure since then. It was the crew of HMS Beagle who sailed into its harbour in 1839, and named it Port Darwin. A number of them had accompanied Charles Darwin (1809-82), who developed the theory that man and apes have common ancestors, made famous in his book *On the Origins of Species,* to the Galapago Islands in 1835. They then went on to Sydney's Blue Mountain region by which he described their 'desolate, and untidy appearance.' Darwin was not too impressed on what he saw, when he remarked of Australia that, "Nothing but rather sharp necessity should compel me to emigrate!"

Darwin remains 1500 km north of here. It would have been nice to make this journey. But with time at a premium I will have to rely on other traveller's comments, and quite often the most reliable source of information, or that I am not missing anything too significant. My student card also obtained a $21 discount on our coach trip to Adelaide, in bringing it down to a more respectable $74 each with Ansett Pioneer.

We therefore boarded the coach, and settled into our seats of disjointed arms and shoulders intermingled in the cramped conditions, which was to last for twenty-two hours; it seemed to pass by fairly quickly as sun turned into rain, the tarmac to dirt, and finally life became sleep.

Eventually we were able to stretch our limbs, in what was to prove our only such stopover at Coober Pedy, or the 'white fellow's hole in the ground.' This is a place where opals are mined nearby, and at which point local rivalries and trust invariably come into dispute, according to our driver, who told us over the coach intercom "Not to stray out amongst the opal fields at night, otherwise you might find yourself in for a shock from the locals concerned about claim jumpers." He also warned us of buying dud merchandise and recommended some trustworthy opal outlets to buy from.

Temperatures here are so acutely adverse, that they range from a summer high of 45°C towards freezing point in the winter. Most people have dug rooms into the rocky ground to live in, where temperatures can be maintained at about 22°C all year around, including a small church, with its inbuilt charm.

The main drawback is the constant lack of water that makes overland travel, into the wilderness, so inhospitable and dangerous to all but the most efficient of navigators, and map-readers. Knowing your direction is easy enough by the sun, but it is the distance factor, and water, that can prove so dangerous, that must never be underestimated.

The opals, discovered in 1911, are a very valuable commodity to the local community, which seemed scarcely populated when looking around the red dirt expanse of a coach park, otherwise known as town centre; however they are not drinkable, able to water the garden, or even wash the car, such are the problems the residents face in their isolation. Artesian water from the Great Australian Basin beneath the earth's crust is ironically available, but this is full of salt; visitors are invariably allowed showers for only one minute, such is the freshwaters scarcity in these parts.

It doesn't take long to look around, sit in the church and watch our fellow passengers buy the occasional opal for their troubles; before long we were standing around waiting for our allotted time to depart. There's something about these long journeys; restlessness occurs when I'm away from my seat, as progress is not being made. Nobody wants to be cooped up, but standing around people watching is time wasted when we could be moving south, and with it a renewed optimism. We had no problems as such now, and would sleep through the night, with Amy besides the window, ready to wake me at daylight for the final leg of our journey east, from where my trip from Perth originally left off.

Tuesday 4 September

We arrived in Adelaide early, and very early on that is, with the city still in a state of insomnia. Amy has not seen South Australia's premier city as yet, which meant doing the sight seeing routine to remind me of when Martin and myself were here. We didn't seem to get far in eight months, or did we. It has all been accomplished to fuel the memory, rather than on a conveyer belt, set at fast foot forward.

The trees are now naked of their leaves, lend us the stale feel of winter when few people appeared in the park, or around the cathedral, bar an occasional jogger and a 'homeless' dog rummaging in the undergrowth. Adelaide would soon begin to stir to the rumbled sound of motorised transport, in alerting us that we still have a journey to complete.

After taking a train out to Pooraka, an outer suburb, we obtained our first lift in a fire engine, for 15 km. This was doubled by a van driver, and then an elderly couple for a further 150 km; who were intent on bickering at every twist of their steering wheel, and even in the bar which they frequented regularly, it appeared, by them being on first name terms with the barman. Rarely though have I been happier to say goodbye along the route, when even Amy's abundant enthusiasm seemed to have nose-dived towards some silent thoughts of her own, and mine that marriage with the wrong person might imprison the soul.

Two more lifts led us to sleeping in the garage of a small

bungalow, at Renmark, the state's last major town before the NSW border. The economy here is dependent on its vineyards, and fruit growing fraternity. We were the guests of a dark haired Vietnamese man, who has endured extreme hardship throughout his life, and now has real hope for the future.

Kar's story is one full of the world headlines many times over, and the kind we all hear about, but rarely meet. It also puts my own recent trials nicely into perspective when Amy asked how he found himself in Australia.

"It was a terrible wrench, leaving alone and chancing everything on a boat that might have sank. I was desperate, we were all desperate to escape; it was our only hope," he said.

"How long did it take?"

"I had to endure fourteen days on a boat, where many of my fellow countrymen died of dehydration, and then the storms, which lashed the decks where we were all sat outside; there was no room below. It was horrible to watch, the experience will haunt me forever; people either died or were swept overboard," Kar, about 35, remarked.

"I'm sorry, where did you end up?" I said.

"The Indonesian navy picked us up, and their government provided a refugee camp for us; even that was better than going back. I thought they might send us straight home, but when there is time there is hope," he replied.

"How long were you in the camp?"

"About six months until they decided what was to happen to us, they treated us well, but you never knew if today was our last; I couldn't bear it," he said, eighteen months on from the Australian government offering to take their quota.

"Pretty unbearable, so you are alone now?"

"No, not really. I have a fellow refugee nearby, and a wife and children still living under communist rule," Kar replied.

"Australia must seem light years away from your roots," Amy remarked.

"Letters are of little consolation," he said.

"Perhaps things might change, one day for you to return?"

"Oh no, I could never have lived there, even at the loss of my family. This is our only chance, for me to be able to help them," Kar said, with the conviction, now that he has a part-time job in a nearby supermarket stacking shelves.

"The social services and immigration people have been really good; they found me a job after setting me up here," he said.

His confidence is still thin, but his English has improved with time, to such an extent that we had no problems communicating; again his first three months were difficult, but with tuition he has crossed this bridge and can now move forward.

"I hope to be able to send money home shortly, it's a shame I do not have much in the fridge for us to eat," he remarked.

"That's fine, it's been a privilege meeting you," I said.

I couldn't think, neither of us could relate such thoughts, being from the free world and able to choose our own path. Now here we were under the shelter of a refugee who seemed so humble in his outlook; his wife had apparently told him to try for freedom and hugged him at the door fully knowing that she might never see her husband again. Parents make many sacrifices for their children, but this was the ultimate of its kind; to risk life and limb in the search of the unknown, or where it might lead you, fully aware that if you failed the consequences on your return might be an imprisonment in your own homeland.

Wednesday 5 September

We didn't have the best of starts this morning after Kar dropped us off on the highway outside Renmark; indeed time spent in a truckers' café might best describe the morning, until a kindly soul gave us a lift in his huge articulated lorry bound for Sydney. It would have been nice though to see the passing Outback as we drove through the dark and stared into the night sky.

"There is nothing to miss except for desert and long stretches of highway until we reach Wagga Wagga," Don, 50, remarked, before we joined the Hume Highway at Yass in the battle of the roaring giants.

Here was one of nature's more cheerful knights of the road, who was just grateful for a life that has only recently recovered from cancer.

"Who knows how long I've got, it's my daughter's wedding on Saturday, that's why I'm in a hurry. She will never forgive me if this truck breaks down!" he remarked.

"Thanks for picking us up, we were struggling a bit," I said.

"I did think twice, the last hitchhiker I gave a lift stole my wallet, while I stopped at a service station," he replied.

"Did you ever catch him?"

"No. I'd like to tear the so and so apart, but life's not full of dud apples. Most people are genuine enough. It wouldn't have been so bad if I hadn't bought him a meal myself and then ended up borrowing $50 in Sydney to get home," Don said.

I naturally felt embarrassed at such liberties; we should all be able to help each other in return for some interesting verse.

"Perhaps he went to Queensland; they will soon sort him out," I remarked.

"Don't they like hitchhikers?" he said.

"You could say that!"

Nature seems to stand still in the whispering Outback; but reality was soon to bring us into the present with a most dramatic thud. The newspaper headlines are full of 'Bloody Sunday's' motorbike gang massacre in the Sydney suburb of Milpera. The

Bandidoes and Commancheros, two sworn enemies, decided to settle their fermented differences with an exchange of violent shotgun cartridges, at an agreed point.

How it can all come down to this is anybody's guess, and how a man can walk the streets in the knowledge he might be shot at is incomprehensible, and for what? To say the other gang members are dead, in a kind of suicide pact, which would inevitably put the survivors behind bars with their inbuilt negatives. Has it really evolved to this in modern day Australia?

Seven people have needlessly died, including an innocent fourteen-year-old girl selling flowers on a street corner. The horror says it all; a desperate form of hatred has descended upon these shores in the most dramatic of circumstances, and brought with it a sober feeling to all that have read about it. Eventually nine gang members would be found guilty of murder, and a further twenty-one of manslaughter.

Sunday 9 September

We arrived back in Sydney with time to spare, and a place to stay with a contact of Amy's from her previous time here; another female student named Toni, who seemed quite nice and said to call back in January "if you need a place to stay," which as ever was useful to know. Sydney is not a place I can just amble into, and catch a train to at the last moment towards the airport. Rather I need to be here the day before, and it was certainly worth keeping in mind.

In the meantime we had an unexpected piece of calendar shading to experience the lights of Sydney from the outside, to stand on the steps of the Opera House and remember our life together. I did mention the yacht, but not the seasickness! Amy seemed impressed. The next time I might just keep going and sail around the world, but then she didn't believe that and neither did I. The bridge is wonderful, when the memories live on. Amy will remain part of this wherever life takes us.

When I walked into the airport, it is fair to say I assumed that nothing else could possibly go wrong, every crisis had been met and somehow dealt with in the time ordered manner, without ever having to bend a rule, or break the law intentionally. But of course there was to be one final twist in the tail.

I had anticipated that booking my luggage in would be a mere formality, when unfortunately the lady on duty noticed I did not have a re-entry visa. My air ticket was scheduled to fly me back into Sydney on January 6th 1985, and the travel agents had not mentioned anything of the sort, or even on the ticket vouchers warning non-nationals. It's ironic, that here I was trying to leave the country, which was not possible, until I had obtained my re-entry visa.

"This may be a formality to you, but we cannot allow anybody out of Australia who plans to return," an immigration official remarked.

He therefore gave me an emergency stamp for December 9th, which had already been cleared by official channels in Brisbane, to help me on my way, and that it was no longer his problem. Coincidentally I met a fellow Brit in Auckland, who had also overlooked this same stipulation. Unfortunately he was flying out on the very day of his visa's expiry date, which resulted in him having to buy another air ticket at a later date. I also might not have got my money back, or at least a discount, and probably not at this late hour. All I needed was to be refused another Australian visa, and the problems would again mount up.

"So this is it," I remarked.

"The end of the line," Amy said.

"It's gone all so quick, write me in Auckland when things

have settled down," I replied; now it was when two became one and my turn to say goodbye.

Martin seems to have been gone for months and Sheila, was she ever here, or that there were once two sisters. It's all been so incredible we have been through a great adventure together, and something that would remain forever deep in our Outback thoughts. She smiled and we embraced in celebration, and I made my way gently past the customs officials. I now turned and waved enthusiastically, as people do at airports and thought of when we might meet again, one day soon.

13. Publishing a Book!

When I sat down, with my typesetter, to asses the original layout of *A Hitch Down Under*, it has to be admitted the initial results left me a little disappointed; I had planned to include hitchhiking around New Zealand, and two short, but eventful stays in The Philippines and Hong Kong. However the number of words included would have meant a book inflated in size and one that moved away from my original objective.

When it also came to designing a cover I found myself constantly drawn to an image of Australia and soon realised that I was about to do an injustice to such a fine country and the people who welcomed me over the next four months as a kind of kindred spirit.

I therefore decided to cut this out, which would leave me nicely placed with a follow up that answers some to the questions left out here; of what happened to Martin, why Amy left Australia before I returned and what of India, our first port of call on route to Perth; I can also stay focused on New Zealand and sleeping in a park near Dunedin, only to wake up with a hedgehog under my chin at 3am!

I shall now return to Australia and January 1985, refreshed and once more in search of the harvest, my saving grace, and a country that now seemed like a home from home.

It was be good to be back.

14. Australian Encore

Australia remains very much the same as I remember it, sunny and heating up daily. Bob Hawke's Labor Government has retained power, although Andrew Peacock's Liberal Party fared much better than expected in the parliamentary elections on December 3rd. I am only sorry that I was not here to register my surprisingly qualified vote. Apparently, if you have been resident for six months in Australia with a fixed abode of at least one month, you can apply for voting rights. Technically that includes me with my working visa having still been valid. However, it is also noted that citizens failing to register their vote face a $20 fine.

I arrived back in Sydney with a week to spare, and a roof over my head in the suburb of Stratfield with Toni, who was as busy as ever and said to come and go as "you please." She is a friend of a friend really, although in this existence friendships tend to blur into each other's lives, as they invariably overlap. It was useful, for what else would I do; simply hang around waiting for the pears to ripen once again. I just hope the harvest is better this year.

At one stage I even a wandered around by the Opera House and remembered my stay here with Amy and taking photographs of each other to record our time together. Across the water the Luna Park amusement arcade remained still, now cast in the shadows of the Harbour Bridge, and what of Martin, as we sailed close by. The memories of which remain fresh in mind and context. Yes it has been a fulfilling time, keeping my head above water. I've been extremely fortunate, and especially as Toni and her boyfriend invited me to a party at the small coastal town of

Altimer, 70 km south, which would send me nicely on my way back towards Sheparton, and in time for this year's harvest.

This was to be one of those times when the hitchhiker came to stay and floated around not really knowing anybody, and felt a bit at odds with his environment.

As the night wore on it only confirmed those song lines about finding myself in the kitchen at parties, because this is usually the only lighted area to see who I might talk to, or get to know for that matter. But no, this was not one of those nights to stimulate the mind and being slowly thinned to the stragglers intent on seeing the night out.

The floor space appeared rather cramped, in which case I gathered my sleeping bag and then made my way down the hillside towards a sandy beach area in anticipation of hitchhiking at first light. Nothing stirred bar the waves gently gliding in and out, with a light breeze. There was nobody about, no movement, and no nothing in the early hours. No beach parties, or gatherings of people. They are all asleep now ready for a bright new dawn.

Sunday 13 January

7am: I awoke to the sound of children roaming free with their surfboards and the sight of bikini clad girls stretched out nearby. Their tans are light brown in colour and soon began to clear my dazed mind. But nobody even looked my way though, or really cared, as I slept surrounded by these beauties of the bay. I then gathered my sleeping bag and felt more part of the scene, yet still nobody noticed as if this was the norm around here and so found myself walking up to the house.

It's now Sunday morning and the party has died its final flame. My hosts do sleep, as I tip toed around the collapsed bodies in search of my belongings. Who they all are is a mystery? My original friends are nowhere to be seen. I had arrived almost unnoticed, then made a coffee, and left undetected, with the hitchhiker now simply gone on his way.

During the evening I started my aimless hike out of town in the growing dim of Sunday's light, until that is I reached the suburb of Unanderra. Here a short train ride took me to Albion Park, where I camped in a nearby playing fields, together with my stomach pains which were slowly evolving into an uncomfortable night... Wollongong, 80 km south of Sydney is a heavy industrial city, which includes Australia's biggest steel works at Port Kemba. Despite this ugly sounding slant, I was quite surprised to find it clean, spacious and supporting some idyllic looking surf beaches.

Monday 14 January

After yesterday spent here in an unmolested state of inertia, I decided to make more of an effort this morning in this my flight south, in what would prove to be some exceptionally hot conditions at 39°C.

By the time I reached the town of Moss Vale, just off the Hume Highway, I was beginning to feel the bugs had overheated my thermostat. For while petrol flowed into the tank, curdled milk was being flushed down the sewage pipes. Incredibly this would be my only such day's illness of note, on this entire trip, and why I am not really sure. A couple of beers would not make any difference, and sleeping on the beach had been the kind of thing I might have thought about as a kid, tucked up in bed and dreaming of such moments, with the key being a balanced diet of fruit and dairy produce.

My day ended in the capital, unplanned, and where my lift

was destined for with any further physical activity redundant of effort and in a severely weakened state. I had my spot in Canberra, which was better than being stuck out on the highway, and if still ill tomorrow I would at least have somewhere central to recover from.

My lift dropped me close to an idyllic lakefront devoid of vegetation, which was good, without strength and feeling light headed. Nobody was about, nor would they be, as I fell on the ground, and then rolled over onto my knees and grabbed my sleeping bag, without fear or a care for the world. I was slightly lower than the road and reasoned that nobody would notice, providing I stayed low, and didn't advertise myself. There was no chance of that though as a deep sleep soon followed.

Tuesday 15 January

It was a revitalised individual who appeared this morning along the roadside, having been disturbed by the bells of a passing cyclist at first light, and back to the fitness of the past year. Fortunately I easily obtained a lift towards the small town of Yass, in three separate journeys, on what is another scorcher of a day, and the hottest of the hot, even for these surrounds of late.

Everywhere the riverbeds are drying up what little moisture is left; it meant I could only find the odd patch of water to cool off in this climate, between lifts, and standing on gravel. One spark and the vegetation would just go, with a slight breeze to help it along; once green valleys are now hay coloured and in desperate need of nourishment. I would also like to know, what that bloodsucking black worm like creature was? It grabbed hold of my leg in a shallow watery pool; when I was bathing my feet of their sweaty discomfort, and held on to inflict blood!

Sydney is now 296 km north of here, and the roadside café I

spent sheltering from the blazing heat that can be cut like a knife, such is the intense humidity. Hitchhiking was certainly on the back burner for much of the afternoon.

"Where are you going?" Keith asked, as I began to walk across the forecourt at 5pm, when having decided to chance my luck.

"Shepparton, I'm going to do some pear picking," I replied.

"Hop in, I can take you to Benalla," he said.

The journey through New South Wales and into Victoria was a pleasant one, as we conversed on the route and stopped off for a quick drink at a roadhouse designed for truckers.

"I reckon those boys will have their jobs cut out," Keith said, at the sight of a small fleet of fire engines.

Tonight as forked lightning shot overhead and the atmosphere tasted of smoke, three such fire fighters were shortly to lose their lives in an attempt to safeguard the well-being of others, and demonstrating the constant risks incurred. In four month's time, the rains will descend from above to transform its vegetation, but for now we have to abide with an almost total fire ban.

"I'm staying with my sister in Wangaratta tonight, if you want to sleep in the back, I can take you on further in the morning," Keith remarked; darkness was upon us, and as ever I was beginning to wonder what was in store, with a bit of luck I might be invited in for breakfast!

"Sure why not, another first," I replied, and shortly found myself curled up on some sacks in the back of his removal van, parked outside her house.

Thursday 17 January

The huts and surrounding area all appeared very quiet, and just as I remembered. I had no aspirations of advertising myself to the authorities though. It would be just my luck to be asked for my visa, now that it has run out. Rather I made my way directly to the huts that were so familiar to me, from what seems to be a lifetime ago, and to think it is 1985! I'm still broke, but have grown richer in fulfilment and experience since last year's end of harvest.

Nothing stirred on first sight, but then the faint noise of a local radio station began to reach my ears, as I approached the kitchen steps, and thought of the dust bowl inside. The weather report is always interesting, from Whiskers, with a hovering sound of a propeller in the background broadcast each morning.

Last year 'they' were all 'here' waiting for the crops to ripen. Where might Terry be, did he come back this year and certainly not here though, but perhaps to the original grower we worked for? I now felt relaxed and in anticipation of some company as I opened the paint-less wooden door and found myself looking down on a lonesome figure sitting at the table, simply browsing through some old magazines left over from last year's pear picking season.

Sunday 3 March

Stewart, a young bespectacled Kiwi had been here for two weeks picking apricots, and waiting for the pears to ripen. He plans to use the money as a launch pad to travel the world, and see what it has in store. As he said, Napier is not exactly the "centre of the universe."

"I'd almost given up hope of having any company," he said, as we spent an hour swapping stories of our past. He was in my position now, as when we landed in Perth; in a year's time he will also be a different person, perhaps not outwardly, but certainly inside.

The farm has changed owners recently, which meant walking 7 km to ask for a job. I had a choice of half the district in which to look, but chose the devil I knew, and can always move on if necessary. Stewart seems to be a pretty happy go lucky sort of person, which is reassuring, because life has decreed that we are stuck here together and will just have to get on with it, be civil, and make the most of the situation.

Fortunately the rucksack could be left behind for once, after buying a week's provisions. I now had a grand total of 30 cents to my name with no funds left in England, and naturally began to 'regret' the demise of my old paper round money, as a child, gleamed as ever with the skin stuck to the frozen handlebars in winter, and some other efforts that have now evaporated over the past few years of insecurity. It's what 'you' wanted to do, and I did not want to follow the grain, my remaining NZ$70 had in effect left me with a mere A$39.

Our living accommodation is very good, with thirteen beds between two! We even have a fully fitted kitchen, a black and white television, which some pleasant soul was throwing out and thought we might like, a shower and an ancient washing machine to freshen things up.

Each morning we are picked up by Geoff, the foreman, and taken to work, where the days seem to pass by uneventfully until heat exhaustion invariably strangles us late in the afternoon. This is our biggest problem, and especially at night, when sleeping at times has been impossible due to the humidity and mosquitoes.

The evenings are the best time here; soaked in sweat we take a short walk towards the local canal and jump in for our cold swims to escape the 40ºC temperatures. I often dream of this moment in the heat of day and then the moment arrives to a sudden shock, and what bliss! It is quite safe we are told.

"Nobody has been lost yet!" Geoff had remarked.

It was during this time that Ziv, an Israeli traveller, arrived and looked on from above.

"Just jump in," I shouted, as he promptly joined us by diving from the above metal pipe railed bridge, to say hello. This though put a stop to our using Stew's rather basic bicycle for our homeward journeys along the dusty gravel lanes, as three riding 'The Pommy Express' would make life an even more painful impossibility than riding back saddle along these bumpy lanes has proved so far!

"It was the cheapest available, I only needed it for some short journeys, then it can be left behind afterwards," he said.

We have certainly had our laughs and mishaps here.

Firstly I locked myself in the toilets, which meant unscrewing the lock to make good my escape, while unfortunately one of the chickens neatly nicknamed the Marx Brothers was eaten by the farmer's dog! In fact, all our menagerie of animals have also been 'baptized.' There's Fred and Ginger our tap dancing calves, Bugsy, no introductions needed; the Osmonds, seem to resemble a never-ending supply of innocent white doves, and finally Geoff's puppy who ate my raw beef burger, left out on the kitchen table, when we were at work! We know this because he left his paw prints, and was actually seen in possession of the said object.

"Oh I wondered where he got that, it was all dirty, and you could not tell it for the dust. He buried it first and then went back," Geoff said.

Money wise, it has been quite productive, but there have been a number of scares. One day on the radio it was announced that six illegal workers from France, the UK, America and Poland had been caught working on neighbouring farms around the Shepparton area. 'The suspects are now being transported to Melbourne, where they will face extradition,' a newscaster solemnly read. Nobody had ever asked for my working visa originally, so why start worrying now?

"I've got little choice," Ziv remarked, in an uneasy tone.

"We're just have to keep our fingers crossed," I replied.

Our post could now stay put, while the social life would be shelved or a perceived social life that should be; the reality is that tired and parched at the weeks end Saturday mornings were our only such diversification from the orchards, and had to be met with a flat bat now; don't talk and advertise who we are or why we only stay a short time, never enter the pubs, and leave without a word; even then I looked around to make sure nobody was watching in which direction we headed. The gravel roads are isolated, so there was no chance of an escape, bar hiding in the scorched undergrowth.

In the main we only saw the occasional Ute pass us by, and nothing official. They could catch us any time unawares, but that is the risk; in all I will have been here for less than a year, that my original visa declared.

A Message from the Sun

During one of our enforced days away from our beloved orchard, Stewart and myself sat down in front of a tape recorder to send some goodwill messages home. Sandwiched between two sides of banter, came the following edited lines, which might be of interest and lend an insight into life on the road, as we stepped back for a few moments of reflection. It also captures the flavour of the moment and the enthusiasm of being young, without the problems of everyday life.

Barry: 'I think people from our western societies owe it to themselves to take these travel opportunities while they're young.'

Stewart: 'Have you visited Napier High Street; marvellous!'

Barry: 'Merely flying from one side of the world to the other broadens the mind. Suddenly it's a much smaller place than I realised.'

Stewart: 'Yes, it's in your reach if you want to try it.'

Barry: 'I think it's a case of disciplining objectives to get the money together in the first place.'

Stewart: 'And see something different to your own environment.'

Barry: 'I have had to take some risks, but then I don't rate working as a sin! It's really been a case of getting the best out of each difficult situation.

'Since leaving England I have met people who have been literally everywhere imaginable. One chap even worked as a chef in Saudi Arabia, and then travelled through Iran and Afghanistan. He thought it was safe enough, but I'm not sure. Israel looks decidedly dicey, but Ziv assures me it's safe for hikers, providing you stay clear of the border regions'.

'We hear so many bad things worldwide that one wonders what the future might bring. Indeed, I hear England appears to be taking quite a battering with IRA bombs, snowbound weather, accidents galore, together with a violent crime reported every five minutes.'

Stewart: 'The best thing is to find out for yourself, Britain can't be that bad!'

Barry: 'It all depends on your gullibility. There is a lot of good happening back home, but unfortunately this doesn't sell newspapers.'

Stewart: 'There are parts of India that appear safer to avoid, with lots of pirates and guerrillas making a living out of poor souls like ourselves.'

Barry: 'India seems such a poor country, that it is no wonder these people turn to such activities, or that so many crave for a British Passport, and think they have a better chance overseas.'

Stewart: 'Yes, it's no more dangerous than Napier High Street!'

Barry: 'That might be correct, but only if you keep your feet on the ground.'

Stewart: 'Or even advertise you're a tourist!'

Barry: 'That's very difficult, especially in the Third World, where our fair complexions stand out to waiting pickpockets. Indeed, my money seems to disintegrate on just surviving.'

Stewart: 'Yes, I get tired and irritable at times, and ask myself why am I doing this? But then there's nothing like a long night's sleep, and an early morning dip to renew my enthusiasm.'

Barry: 'People seem to be very helpful if you are the kind of person to give it a go. Be friendly and open, but not pushy in asking questions. I think then you have a good chance of being offered an obliging hand.'

Stewart: 'Everybody has different attitudes and experiences to draw upon.'

Barry: 'I think you do change.'

Stewart: 'Oh yes, its got to broaden your outlook, life's never been this good.'

Barry: 'I've got little choice at present, travelling alone. It would have been nice if those friends back home had shared my adventures. But it is better in many ways, because a real effort has had to be made to meet people, while together it's easy to remain immersed within a small confined group, and in turn fail to obtain an insight into the country's inhabitants.

'The only problem for example, is that nobody I know has

been to Tasmania, bar Jarv, to share my memories with. I'm sure when I see Martin we'll enjoy our moments of reflection.'

Stewart: 'Well, as soon as you get home, you'll be able to sit by a raging fire and reminisce.'

Barry: 'You're right, it's important to think of my family and friends back home. I hope that they take an interest.'

Stewart: 'Well, it's too bad if they don't, because you're too far away to know better!'

Barry: 'Side one was a pretty nutty collection of pranks, and at times stupidity, but that's how life has often been. Everybody along the route has been generally smiling and so easy going.'

Stewart: 'Yes, we've had such wonderful fun up those pear trees!'

Barry: 'We have?'

Stewart: 'Originally we crawled out of bed at 5.30am, and preceded with our daily pear picking session at first light, only you discovered that Deputy Dawg is on television at 6.30am!'

Barry: 'I also think it's important to use your contacts. People who have 'really' travelled know the name of the game, and quite often have welcomed me with 'open arms,' or have even directed me towards a close friend, family or an ex-hitchhiker.'

Stewart: 'We can't repay those people, but indirectly it's our duty now to help fellow travellers back home in an effort to spread goodwill. It's really wonderful here; we have three diverse people from different geographical and religious backgrounds.'

Barry: 'I appreciate this freedom, but then it's not a very secure lifestyle. Paul was going to come with us, and now fifteen months later it's congratulations on your engagement. I'd like to be there, but it's really in the lap of the gods!'

Stewart: 'So Baz, what does the future hold?'

Barry: 'My crystal ball dictates that I put some of my hard

earned lessons to good use, and venture forth. A traveller's tale can be put together over a lifetime's experience, when this has really been a trial by error effort.

'After all how can you get it right at the first time of asking, if you haven't attempted anything like this before?'

Monday 4 March

I left the orchard shortly after breakfast on the back of Neil's motorbike, clinging on to keep my balance, as he decided to drop me on the Benalla Road for Sydney. The young farmer, from near Gin Gin in Queensland, turned up with his friend and neighbour Wayne two weeks on, to give us a final total of five all told living here.

After last year's grand army it has certainly been different, in the camaraderie stakes. Some of my friends might have been here somewhere, and perhaps I should have ventured into Sheparton one Saturday morning to see some fresh faces, or the old brigade, if that is they are about?

Neil is down here to earn some money to supplement the farm, with his brother looking after the everyday jobs, due to it being a quiet time for them and agriculture going through something of a lull. We then had a chat on the open road, and said to stay in touch.

"I might see you in England one of these days," he said, with a spark of imagination fuelled by his three foreign travel companions.

He then rode off, which left me stranded adrift with another 'family' now in the past. It's been fun I thought, and started hitchhiking. This would be my last such journey and a 'most' memorable one, but for all the wrong reasons.

It all started normal enough with good time being made

towards the Victorian border town of Wodonga. It is possible here to see in the New Year, and then cross over the River Murray to her sister town of Albury in New South Wales, where celebrations can indeed start again, due to its one-hour time difference, although there is talk of this changing shortly into the future.

Perhaps I should have listened to a car full of 'Portuguese' sounding locals, who warned me of the perils of hitchhiking out of this town. Unfortunately our language barriers lacked detail, in what might follow. They only meant their warnings in good intention; nothing has happened much so far and this is the end of the road. One more journey, and it will be time to draw a line under a hitch down under and then move onto fresh pastures.

Once I got out of the car and waved goodbye to mama in the back I noticed some local toilet facilities, and naturally felt the call of nature. But as ever had a glance around me to check that nobody was about, before venturing in. It was daylight and seemed deserted, at which point I was slightly surprised, 'while relieving myself,' that a scruffy individual should appear close by; and naturally tried to ignore his insinuations, in this alien environment, as he tried to chat me up!

Is that the word people might use in such circumstances?

Certainly he had me at a delicate moment of the proceedings, facing the urinal and clasping myself, as you do in such situations. I am only trying to set the scene here, and so glanced over my shoulder to see an empty space behind me. Little did I know that this was the local pick up joint, and the place was being watched by the community 'that way' inclined. This is what my Portuguese mama was trying to explain no doubt, when the penny dropped, and the man became more descriptive two urinals to my right.

"Sorry it's not my scene," I replied.

"But how do you know if you haven't tried it?"

"There's nothing wrong with a pretty girl," I said.

"You ought to try it!"

"Have you heard of Aids?"

"Oh you can't catch it if you only play," he said.

By now my 'relief' was complete, and our conversation had nowhere else to go. When another scraggy looking individual entered the rather basic facility, with a non-threatening mannerism admittedly, but simply not the kind of place to hang around any longer than absolutely necessary.

It is fair to say that when I entered the sunlight again the air had a whole new freshness about it, as I tried to dispel my negative thoughts, or visions that should be, and began my walk towards the nearby traffic lights in letting down my guard momentarily. I then heard a toot of a horn, and noted a parked car in front of me, and did not think much of it when the driver offered to give me a lift towards the edge of town, which was a tidy hike judging by my previous visit here.

In hindsight I remember seeing his trouser button undone, but was unconcerned, due to my immediate experience and his rounded stomach. The driver, dark haired and thirty something was likeable enough, coupled with gentle mannerisms. But my mind would soon flash back to those early student days, when a gay scholar used to calmly sit with the girls and discuss their respective boyfriends together. He also seemed pleasant enough with everybody; indeed, I felt quite sorry for him when he left, supposedly because of a broken heart, much the same as many students experience at one stage or another.

The driver though appeared somewhat more interested than most in asking me questions about my travels rather than swapping anecdotes. He often made an effort to turn his head towards me slowly, rather than to concentrate on the road ahead.

How long he steered with only one hand on the wheel, I'm not sure. I didn't notice in the traffic and only then thought it odd when he kept looking over my way instead of an occasional glance, and found myself following the line of his arm down to his hand, suddenly aware of his unzipped flies. The man was in masturbation for my benefit, which lets just say only takes a glance! One look is all I needed, with thoughts of, 'oh my god, this is what you hear about,' and now I'm in the position anybody would dread.

"How far are you going?" I remarked, with a hopeful whim that perhaps he might notice my hint, and quite determined that I was neither going to look at him straight in the eye, or even towards his left hand.

"Oh, just around the next corner," he replied calmly, making his intentions fairly obvious through persistent 'finger work.' Though I desperately wanted to avoid a confrontation and especially as his weight advantage would prove decisive.

When people with split personalities get the bit between their teeth, just about anything is possible, which meant my priority was to remain calm at all costs. My pack was on the backseat, while jumping out at 60 km seemed somewhat drastic. I then remembered those people who had disappeared without trace and realised it might have been like this at first, before things turned nasty, but this was no time to panic.

It's an odd feeling being put on the spot; staring out of the window and into the undergrowth, with a stranger constantly prodding you for information, and staying on your guard with one hand on the door handle.

"Where did you say you were heading to, Sydney was it?" he said, looking for some encouragement.

Certainly I didn't care where I ended up, as long as my assailant left me alone, he probably had a flat somewhere. But I must confess to my unease at the situation, on edge and quite apprehensive; it would only be natural.

"I'm going to see my girlfriend, it's been two weeks since I last saw her," I babbled out, together with a description to lend relevance, more in desperate hopefulness rather than with an air of conviction. The tension was by now slowly becoming electric with two strangers shadow boxing in broad daylight. One was intent on keeping at arms' length, and the other finally resigned to driving his car slowly to a halt, 20 km from town.

Hope was now mine that he would give me time to get my pack out of the back, although this was helped by the deliberate leaving of the passenger door wide open, and the occasional car passing by. It's fair to say being cast adrift on a minor road, this might have posed a whole different set of circumstances, as I grabbed my pack and stood on some gravel shoulder, now looking at him through the passenger window.

"I'm sorry for back there. I thought you might be up for it," he remarked.

"Not my scene," I replied, holding out my hand in a kind of face saving gesture.

Why I'm not sure, it simply seemed the right thing to do.

Hitchhiking

The establishment might frown upon thumbing a lift with their reservations highlighted here. But it's certainly the cheapest mode of transportation available, and more interesting and a relatively easy way to build up contacts in obtaining information about the given country's 'pros and cons' for future reference.

In my experience I have found it an efficient way of reaching my objectives, but there have been a number of long waits, 5 km hikes out of town, and numerous occasions when I have had to seek the nearest place of shelter to avoid the elements, or otherwise darkness has curtailed my progress. Luck has to play some part; you also learn to bend things to your own advantage.

Martin, and myself, hitched many lifts together in fairly good time, but it was a definite advantage to have Amy along for the trip through the Northern Territories long desolate highways. Some drivers did echo their reservations about picking up two guys, which I could fully appreciate. Solitary hikers, like single drivers, can find themselves in a vulnerable position if things turn nasty. Incidents seem few and far between, but unfortunately we only hear of the unpleasant happenings rather than the good, which people bestow on their fellow human beings every day.

Two female's hitching together, are probably safe enough down under, even if there are reservations concerning this statement. But a solitary girl making her own way should be warned. A few years back in Queensland two of these hardy souls ended up in the mortuary, instead of their intended destination, while other hitchhikers have also disappeared without a trace.

Motorists usually have to make snap decisions. Long unkempt hair and a leather jacket is hardly going to act as a magnetic attraction, while the slick cool dude in fancy regalia, or a briefcase and suit, can also be equally off-putting. In between these two is a clean tidy individual, with a friendly smiling face. A pleasant personality also makes a lonely individual's time more rewarding.

It is also useful to display a polite hand held sign with your destination, accompanied by the world PLEASE. Good manners cost nothing, but can indeed go a very long way. If that fails, hold it upside down, or write TOKYO! All I'm really trying to do is being noticed, and then it's just a matter of time, providing motorists have a pull up area.

I have always given up hitching at night for a number of reasons; firstly, motorists cannot see me standing on the kerb, which technically can be a very hazardous occupation. It takes a long time for humans to grow strong, but life can be extinguished in one moment's hesitation due to other people's lost concentration.

In the dark it is also more difficult to assess a drivers credentials. Being able to say 'no thanks' is equally important if he appears drunk, just as one short hitch to no man's land might leave you stranded; lifts can prove difficult, due to a motorist's suspicions of why is he stranded out here? It's not unheard of for hitchhikers to make such a nuisance of themselves that their irritated drivers have promptly ejected them.

Even if a lift is accepted, there is still the renewed problem of finding a sleeping spot in the dark. Sometimes this is unavoidable, but again, especially in large cities, it can place an honest traveller in a potentially dangerous situation. In other words, try to spot the problems before they evolve. I have been fortunate in my walkabout, when others still bear the scars; being seen from afar by as many people as possible is always your safest bet, as nobody likes being caught with plenty of witnesses about to say: 'I saw her get into a red car, with a man of about thirty five; yes I'm sure, I was just collecting the children from school, and she had distinctive ginger hair.' It's amazing what people notice, and for that reason alone you want it to remain that way. Be seen is my top tip.

Most of my lifts tended to ask how I liked their country, and how I've been treated along the way. No matter what, my golden rule has always been to reply favourably, as that's how people want their land to be perceived abroad. It's pointless projecting a negative aura. Most people naturally prefer their own environment they grew up in, and know well. Then how might I feel if a foreigner started to moan about my Sussex heartland, while I sheltered him or her for the night? Goodwill and polite manners may cost nothing, but they tend to travel a very long way.

Down Under

I invariably wondered how it might feel at the road's end, and after almost fifteen months here, of which I have tried to paint a picture of my life and some of the people who were momentarily part of it. Many have not been mentioned as we all met at a crossroads of life and are now getting on with their lives. Some will no doubt be seen again in England and others may not, it's only natural. To all I must feel gratitude in helping me to this finishing line.

There is a fulfilled feeling within together with an insecure route home ahead, and one that might prove to be a mistake from the outset, but try I shall. There is a line about to be drawn under my time here, one that suggests my goals have all been achieved and to some extent far more than could have been envisaged at Heathrow Airport; the memories of which will be cherished from the point of departure as the plane takes off, this time heading north towards Asia and an idea too far.

Bibliography

The research for *A Hitch Down Under* was completed many years ago and is the way I wanted it to stay, rather than more updated and elaborate. In the event some of the references may have been left out, or perhaps a line or two was duplicated on the historical side; on factual subjects it is difficult to write a fresh angle, although the bulk remains the original material of my own journals. I would be only too pleased to acknowledge any mistakes, as keeping within the bounds of camaraderie remains uppermost in these lines. *BSH*

Australia – A Travel Survival Kit. Tony Wheeler: Lonely Planets 1983

Work your Way around the World: Vocation Work. Susan Griffith

Australian Journey. Paul McGuire: Heinemann 1939

Australia. Robin Mead: BT Batsford, London

The Long Way Home. Helen Vintner

Humphrey Families in Australia. Jenny Gersekowski Cranbrook Press (Toowoomba) Pty Ltd 1985

Taking Off. Robert L Liebman

Complete Illustrated History of Australian Cricket. Jack Pollard: Pelham Books

Chronicle of Australia. Ply Ltd 1993

Kings Queens and Bastards. David Hillman: Sutton Publishing 1998

Postscript

During our time in Queensland it was plainly obvious that all was not well with the way the state was governed under the leadership of Sir Joh Bjelke-Petersen, (KCMG in 1984) the leader of the National Party, who held a narrow majority, after years of a coalition with the Liberal Party; their members had slowly changed allegiance to hand the National Party outright power. He was Premier from 1968 to 1987 and won six consecutive elections, having been made the Minister for Housing in 1963, after entering the Queensland legislative in 1947.

In 1971 he declared a state of emergency so that the South African Springboks could play rugby in Brisbane despite widespread anti-apartheid demonstrations. This in turn gained support from the rural community who elected his then Country Party in 1972, with about twenty per cent of the vote, such was the way of things in Queensland that rural votes counted disproportionately to those in the cities. Needless to say Bjelke-Petersen was a skilled manipulator who consistently hung onto power and even changed his party's name to gain more widespread support.

His key to success had been the encouragement to businesses, tax cuts and anti-union legislation, which mainly arrived from England "like a disease" and ground the country towards a standstill.

"Glad to get rid of them, a bloody nuisance," was the common theme of many people we spoke to, for which I once had to disown and say they were "nothing to do with me!"

"We all need unions, but they went too far," one man said,

and it was not a coincidence that the Conservatives were at present in the process of following Australia's lead in curbing the unions in England, even though it was causing riots and a change of life, in particular to the coal mine communities. "But nothing can survive on subsidies alone to the detriment of the tax paying community, we all have to pay our own way," has been the common theme.

The rug though was pulled from under the carpet in the mid 1980s when an Australian Broadcasting Corporation television programme confirmed what most Australians kept saying that there was widespread corruption in Queensland in both the National Party Government and the police force in general.

An independent inquiry chaired by Tony Fitzgerald finally led to the police commissioner, Terence Lewis, being jailed for fourteen years and four ministers being found guilty of corruption, a fifth died before his trial, and were also imprisoned for their sins. Bjelke-Petersen was finally deposed as National Party leader in November 1987, aged 76, and he resigned as Premier on December 1st. The inquiries findings led to a criminal prosecution (reportedly the 213th person to be charged) against him for perjury, but he escaped on a hung jury that could not decide his fate; the Crown prosecutors though eventually decided not to retry him due to his advanced years and a reccurring health problem.

A Hitch Down Under is an independently written account and one that has gone through a learning process. I hope you enjoyed the contents, and have learnt from my mistakes, or even been inspired in parts; then there is still *A Hitch Down Under II*, the New Zealand leg to be negotiated. It's only a short chapter, but adds a comparison together with The Philippines and Hong Kong. The trick now is to improve in the written sense and project a fresh impetus, this time for *My Golden Max: a Cycle Ride Across America,* negotiated in 1986, for the most memorable of conclusions to any traveller's tale.